MONASTIC WISDOM SERIES: NUMBER EIGHT

Edited by Patrick Hart, ocso

A Monastic Vision for the 21st Century

Where Do We Go from Here?

D0728210

MONASTIC WISDOM SERIES

Patrick Hart, ocso, General Editor

Advisory Board

Michael Casey, ocso	Terrence Kardong, osb
Lawrence S. Cunningham	Kathleen Norris
Bonnie Thurston	Miriam Pollard, ocso

MW1 Cassian and the Fathers:
    Initiation into the Monastic Tradition
        Thomas Merton, ocso
MW2 Secret of the Heart: Spiritual Being
        Jean-Marie Howe, ocso
MW3 Inside the Psalms: Reflections for Novices
        Maureen F. McCabe, ocso
MW4 Thomas Merton: Prophet of Renewal
        John Eudes Bamberger, ocso
MW5 Centered on Christ: A Guide to Monastic Profession
        Augustine Roberts, ocso
MW6 Passing from Self to God: A Cistercian Retreat
        Robert Thomas, ocso
MW7 Dom Gabriel Sortias:
    An Amazing Abbot in Turbulent Times
        Guy Oury, osb

MONASTIC WISDOM SERIES: NUMBER EIGHT

A Monastic Vision for the 21st Century

Where Do We Go from Here?

Edited by

Patrick Hart, ocso

Introduction by
Dom Bernardo Olivera, ocso

CISTERCIAN PUBLICATIONS
Kalamazoo, Michigan

Cistercian Publications

Editorial Offices
The Institute of Cistercian Studies
Western Michigan University
Kalamazoo, Michigan 49008-5415
cistpub@wmich.edu

The work of Cistercian Publications is made possible in part by support from Western Michigan University to The Institute of Cistercian Studies.

Library of Congress Cataloging-in-Publication Data

A monastic vision for the 21st century : where do we go from here? / edited by Patrick Hart ; introduction by Bernardo Olivera.
    p. cm. — (Monastic wisdom series ; no. 8)
    Includes bibliographical references.
    ISBN-13: 978-0-87907-057-1 (alk. paper)
    ISBN-10: 0-87907-057-9 (alk. paper)
    1. Monastic and religious life. I. Hart, Patrick. II. Title: Monastic vision for the twenty-first century. III. Series.

BX2435.M587   2006
255—dc22

                     2006010971

Printed in the United States of America

In grateful memory of Thomas Merton,

whose prophetic vision embraced

monasticism in all its expressions.

TABLE OF CONTENTS

Foreword   ix
    Patrick Hart, ocso

Introduction   xiii
    Dom Bernardo Olivera, ocso

"Soli Deo Placere Desiderans"   1
    Bonnie Thurston

Thoughts on Monasticism's Possible Futures   23
    Michael Casey, ocso

The Secret Ingredient   43
    Kathleen Norris

Thoughts on the Future of Western Monasticism   57
    Terrence Kardong, osb

Monasticism as a Schola:
Some Reflections from the Ivory Tower   73
    Lawrence S. Cunningham

Old Vision for a New Age   89
    Joan Chittister, osb

Monasticism: A Poetic Perspective   105
    Robert Morneau, D.D.

Fragments for a Vision of Cistercian Life
in the 21st Century   119
    John Eudes Bamberger, ocso

Enclosure: The Heart of the Matter   145
    Gail Fitzpatrick, ocso

To What Holiness?
Monasticism and the Church Today   165
    Francis Kline, ocso

The Fruits of Monasticism:
A View from Washington   185
    Daniel P. Coughlin

North Woods Abbey: On Lake Gogebic   199
    Mary Margaret Funk, osb

Epilogue: *Lectio* on the Easter Proclamation   225
    Miriam Pollard, ocso

Notes on Contributors   231

FOREWORD
Where Do We Go from Here?

by Patrick Hart, ocso

At the first meeting of the new board of directors of Cistercian Publications following the "alliance" with Liturgical Press in January of 2005 at Mepkin Abbey near Charleston, South Carolina, the suggestion was made by the participants that we should seriously consider publishing a volume of essays on the future of monasticism. I was asked to contact not only monks and nuns of the monastic tradition, but also laypersons who have had a very real and deep experience of monasticism through their retreats over the years.

My question was expressed this way: what can the church and the world expect from monasticism in the 21st century and how do you see it ideally incarnated for the future? I asked a dozen persons to contribute to this volume which we felt would be of interest not only to monks and nuns but those legions who faithfully make retreats in our guest and retreat houses all over the world. Then, too, witness the extraordinary popularity of Taize, and more recently Bose in northern Italy where the same kind of phenomenon unfolds before our eyes.

As anyone who has ever edited a volume of this kind will realize, each participant approached the subject from a very personal perspective. As far as I know none of the authors contacted one another to compare notes as the work progressed. So we ended up with a wide range of approaches to the topic, all quite different from one another in their vision of what would be the essence of an authentic monasticism for the years ahead.

Opening the volume is Bonnie Thurston's clarion call from her anchorage outside of Wheeling, West Virginia, which sets the tone for what follows. I'm happy she includes in her very personal essay two poems, which balance the prose poem of Sr. Miriam Pollard's in the Epilogue. They form bookends for the stimulating and at times provocative presentations by both monks and nuns of the Benedictine and Cistercian persuasions, mixed in with laypersons who have a great love for the monastic life and desire nothing so much as to see it continue to flourish in the years to come with God's help.

Of course, we all know that there is nothing in the Scriptures which assures us that monasticism as we have known it in the West will continue to the Parousia. We pray each day, and many times a day, that the reign of God will be established in our midst, although each particular form of monastic life may be altered in various ways.

When I was younger in the monastic way I had dreams of a kind of monasticism in the Christian West that would be open to young men and women who after completing their college work, and before deciding on a life situation, would retire to a monastery for several years as part of their growth process, much like Hindu and Zen Buddhist monks of the Far East have done for centuries. Most of these men and women would return to "the world" following their monastic training, which hopefully would deepen their Christian commitment, and would prepare them for the awesome responsibilities of raising a family in a secular culture with its emphasis on doing and having rather than on being. It was my hope that three or four years in a monastic setting would deepen the person's commitment to Christian principles and develop moral values that would remain with these young men and women for the rest of their lives. I also hoped that some of these who after some years in the monastic milieu would decide to make it their life's vocation and enter the monastic way as a permanent commitment.

The dozen authors have in the following pages explored some of these possibilities with forthrightness which might prove challenging. Fr. Michael Casey and Sr. Joan Chittister in particular offer new ways of incarnating the monastic charism which some may find provocative. Monks and nuns who have been well seasoned in the monastic way, reflecting on their many years of fidelity to the monasticism of the West as handed down to us, now look to the future with ideas and suggestions that will undoubtedly unsettle the satisfied, and satisfy the unsettled, to paraphrase Dorothy Day's dictum, "to disturb the comfortable and to comfort the disturbed."

Fr. Terrence Kardong's stimulating presentation is a masterpiece in its own right. He does not hesitate to quote Chesterton in his closing remarks about Christianity not having been tried, and suggests that we apply it to our efforts at monastic renewal during the past half century. Auxiliary Bishop Robert Morneau of Green Bay knows monasticism well having made retreats and preached them to monks as well as to diocesan priests throughout the world. He approaches the subject of the future of monasticism from a poetic perspective (mainly George Herbert) which is refreshing. Lawrence Cunningham of the University of Notre Dame is a professor of theology who knows and loves monasticism in all its expressions, and speaks from his particular "ivory tower" with great insight.

The essays by Fr. John Eudes Bamberger of Genesee Abbey, Sr. Gail Fitzpatrick of Mississippi Abbey, and Fr. Francis Kline of Mepkin Abbey articulate a solid monastic vision built on a tradition that goes back to its origins, although with an openness to the Spirit's work in our own times. They present the future of monasticism as one in continuity with the past and present, but still open to surprises of the Spirit.

Fr. Daniel P. Coughlin, chaplain to the House of Representatives, writes of how his yearly retreats in monasteries, both Benedictine and Cistercian, have sustained him in his ministry over the years, both in his home diocese of Chicago, and more recently in Washington, DC. Kathleen Norris has had many experiences with monks over the years, especially at the Ecumenical Institute at Collegeville, where she lived with her husband, the poet, David Dwyer. Her writing in *Cloister Walk* and in her contribution to this volume expresses well her deep and abiding love for the monastic charism and how she was able to incarnate its values as a writer over the years.

Finally, closing this volume is Sr. Mary Margaret Funk's creative imagination at work as she foresees a visitation in 2030 by Irish Abbess Bridgit to her new foundation in northern Michigan. The visiting abbess ends up learning more about the new vision of monasticism from her dialogue with Abbess Gertrude and the novices who experience a great desire for the mystical life. It recalls Karl Rahner's well-known saying that "in the future Christians will be mystics or nothing at all."

A word of gratitude is in order to each of the contributors to this volume. May their insights encourage others to share their vision of the new monasticism for the 21st century and the centuries to follow.

INTRODUCTION

A Monastic Vision for the 21ˢᵗ Century

by Dom Bernardo Olivera, ocso

Institutions with a long history and a tradition built up over the centuries usually look more at the past than at the future. Based on what we can see, Christian monastic life as it exists today in western, North-Atlantic countries is no exception to this tendency. That is why a book that tries to steer the monastic vision into the future is one that stirs us up from lethargy, challenges us, encourages us, and even fills us with a new enthusiasm.

Human history shows a certain continuity in its ongoing processes. Sudden shifts are rare. This makes it easy to say that monastic life in tomorrow's world will be in continuity with the past even though open to new developments and exposed to the inevitable uncertainty of the future. In other words, it will be the same as now, but different, with the same basic motivation behind it, but in new historical forms which will always be contingent on the circumstances.

For better or for worse, I am quite shortsighted when it comes to periods of time. My shortsightedness makes me easily confuse the future with the projection of my own desires. When I am asked for a word about the future of monastic life, necessity rather than virtue makes me only able to talk about my longings and hopes, my desires and my dreams.

To put it briefly, my desires for the future of monasticism are reduced to longing for a monastic life deeply rooted in the Gospel of our Lord Jesus Christ for the glory of God the Father and the divinization of men, women, and the universe. Realism, common sense, and good humor oblige me today to talk about monastic re-evangelization. This gospel process implies three different realities which are intimately related one to another, namely, refounding, renewing, and reforming monastic life.

REFOUNDATION

Refounding refers to grounding our existence in the mystical experience of those who first founded the monastic way of life. There is a transforming encounter with the Absolute One. This encounter is the fruit of a dedicated search for the Living God. Search and encounter are lived in the purified passion which longs for his Presence.

It is worth repeating that the inner substance and purpose of this *quaerere Deum* is obviously the loving encounter with God. All monastic life is a way to this end, and this way is traveled every day, thanks to a certain number of meditations or *exercitia*. Among the exercises practiced yesterday, today, and always, the following should be listed: silent and continual prayer, liturgical prayer centered in the Eucharist, *lectio divina*, the asceticism of fasting, Vigils, work, voluntary poverty, and the different renunciations (chastity and obedience) leading to the heart's conversion and purification, with everything lived in a climate of solitude and silence.

Our cenobitic search for God is lived in a context of interpersonal and communal relationships. *Koinonia,* or life in the communion of love, is also essential to our monastic tradition. We search for and find God in community. Saint Benedict says it succinctly: "May he bring us all together to everlasting life!" (RB 72,12). We can add something more: each brother or sister is a "sanctuary" where we can meet God, since the Lord dwells in each of them.

To sum up, it is obvious to all seekers of God that the most important reality in their life is finding him. It is precisely that encounter which makes eminently worthwhile all the pains and crosses of their search. Monastic life loses all its meaning if mystical or contemplative union with God is taken away, since it is God himself who calls, purifies, embraces, and transforms the human person by means of the dazzling shadows of divine

Love. If monastic life in the future is not a living, updated edition of the *Song of Songs*, it will have very little to say to tomorrow's generations! Monastic foundations in the future have to be founded on the conviction that without mystery there is no mysticism and without mysticism there is no monasticism.

RENEWAL

Renewal refers to the fact of rooting the human heart in the New Covenant with its new commandment of loving God and one's neighbor as Christ has loved us. It is a single, yet double, precept which finds its unity in preferring nothing to the love of Christ, who is God made man for our salvation. The radical nature of this option for Christ is experienced in ardent and measureless love for one another.

Our monastic life today opens up to an unknown future. We are invited to follow Jesus by embracing the blessed radicalism of the Gospel. Our future will depend on our reply to this challenge. It is not a question of having a monopoly on the radical following of Christ, but of being faithful to our identity. The words of Jesus are challenging: *Be perfect as your heavenly Father is perfect* (Mt 5:49). The Master is telling us that our life does not consist of traditions, usages, permissions, and observances, but in the perfection of a love which identifies us with the Father who is in heaven. This requirement of love brings us to the very roots of Jesus' teaching, namely the kingdom of God as Father of every human person and the universal brotherhood or sisterhood that flows from this divine fatherhood. Radical nuns and monks are those who are *rooted and grounded in love* (Eph 3:17), *rooted in him and built up on him* (Col 2:7). If we believe—as I hope we do—that he loved us and gave himself up for us, there is only one option possible: to die in order to live in him and to serve everyone.

REFORM

Reform refers to the historical or institutional form that our monastic life assumes in order to become culturally or counter-culturally meaningful. History teaches us that the spiritual experience of any religious founder instinctively seeks forms of institutionalization so as to become meaningfully communicable. These institutional forms are always provisional, conditioned by times and places. Their relevance is determined by a double criterion, namely the ability to promote the spiritual experience of the founder and the possibility of bearing a meaningful witness to the Church and the world.

This is where we are today. We are invited to be creative in order to be faithful to tradition and to the Giver of all charisms in the Church. More specifically, crucial decisions will often have to be discerned and made. The object of our discernment and options could be:

- re-dimensioning our buildings according to the size of the present community;

- reordering our economic structure in relation to a globalizing world which shoves its poorer elements to one side. Yet this reordering must avoid getting caught up in this world to the detriment of the poor;

- readjusting our work so as to have it serve the spiritual purpose of our existence;

- inculturating our liturgies so that they express with greater feeling our worship of God in spirit and truth;

- simplifying the forms taken by authority, to make it serve the community and each person in particular both affectionately and effectively;

- examining the meaningfulness of many of our symbols, customs, and forms of expression;

- searching for new forms in which to live some traditional values, such as fasting, poverty, austerity, solitude, silence, and fraternal correction.

As monks and nuns we certainly have a long story to tell and, with God's help, we also have a story to create. There is a special place reserved in purgatory for those monks and nuns of all ages who sin by being slavishly faithful to tradition instead of daring to be creative so as to hand on an enriched tradition to others. There is also a corner prepared for those who reform without renewing or, still worse, without making sure of where they are starting from.

In the context of monastic re-evangelization, experience teaches us two things: that it is easier to raise up a dead monk than to convert a live one, and that it is harder to reason with a founding nun than to motivate an installed one. Dead or alive, retrogrades or pioneers, asleep or awake, we all dream of a more authentic future and, if many of us have the same dream at the same time, we can be sure that it will become a reality.

Perhaps in the past we have been too "prudent" and now we are too "farsighted." We need a little more passion and slightly less logic! Not, however, any type of passion, but God's own passion. It is this passion of divine love that made him become man, preach the revolution of the Kingdom of heaven, and finally undergo the supreme passion: dying on a cross out of love so that we also can learn to love.

"SOLI DEO PLACERE DESIDERANS"

by Bonnie Thurston

INTRODUCTION

The invitation of Jesus to His apostles when they return weary from the mission on which He sent them (Mark 6:7-13) contains the whole of the monastic project: "Come away by yourselves to a lonely place, and rest a while" (Mark 6:31). To "come away" is to separate one's self from everyday life, the larger whole, to be set aside for a special task, which is the theological meaning of "holy." It encompasses the renunciatory aspect of monasticism. "By yourselves" seems to suggest the solitude of an individuated life, one which resists the conformity and "mass produced-ness" of society. But as the pronoun in Greek is plural, it is, in fact, an invitation to alternative community, to relationship with all who choose to withdraw. "To a desert place" conjures up images of the geographical remoteness traditionally associated with great monastic (especially Cistercian) houses. But "desert" can be understood in contrast to "city." To be invited to the desert is an invitation to leave what passes for society, to leave the cultural norm for a holier alternative. The "desert" is the place where one meets self and God. "Rest" encompasses that greatest (and most neglected?) of monastic virtues, the end toward which the life is organized: leisure. To rest is not to be idle, but to avoid frenetic activity that prevents deep confrontation with who one truly is. To "rest" is to give up care and anxiety, to cast all one's cares on the One who cares ultimately for us. As Jacques Winandy,

1

former Abbot of Clervaux in Luxembourg, wrote, "To reform a monastery is to restore its rest."[1]

It is from this invitation of our Lord to come away and rest that monasticism arises. That invitation is the foundational idea behind the following remarks. Authors in this volume were asked to write essays describing the "monastic vision and how the monastic charism could be incarnated in the new millennium. Also, what could the church and the world expect from such an authentic monastic witness during the 21st century?" When I asked for clarification, it was suggested that I (who am not "technically" a vowed monastic but who has long acquaintance with monastic literature and has recently been living as a "semi-solitary") write about "how the monastic charism can be lived today, and what the church and the world expect from this kind of life." It says something at the outset when a well-known Cistercian asks a Protestant woman to write on the future of monasticism.

One of the first things that came to her mind is that the last 500 years and the Western church are not normative for two millennia of Christianity. As Enzo Bianchi, Prior of the Monastery of Bose, notes "monasticism *precedes the divisions in the church*"[2] (italics his). It includes, but does not begin with St. Basil of Caesarea and St. Benedict of Nursia. St. Benedict of Aniane (d. 821) persuaded Charlemagne to require all monasteries in the Empire to follow the Benedictine rule, and this had enormous consequence, but there have been many forms of religious life both before and after St. Benedict of Nursia. For example, from the mid-4th century the Egyptian church knew an urban monasticism in which *fuga mundi* ("flight from the world," "coming away" as per Jesus' invitation) was relative.

Again, while the suppression of the monasteries and hermitages in England in 1537–38, and the general Protestant resistance to monasticism, had great effects, they did not "stamp out" this form of Christian life. What pleases God will endure. Indeed,

---

[1] Jacques Winandy, "Benedictine Spirituality," p. 28. (Unfortunately I cannot give full citation as this material is from a chapter of a book sent to me without bibliographical reference.)

[2] Enzo Bianchi, "Monastic Life and the Ecumenical Dialogue," booklet printed by the Monastery of Bose (Magnano, Italy, 2001), of the text of a talk given on August 26, 1999, p. 9. Hereafter "Monastic Life."

there have been several forms of Protestant "monasticism" (for example the Bruderhoff and other sects of the radical reformation in Europe, the Shakers in America, or the Communaute de Grandchamp). The Augustinian, Martin Luther, was critical of monastic life, but later Kierkegaard understood it as "a reminder of the difference between following Christ and worldliness. Then, with Adolf von Harnack, Dietrich Bonhoeffer, and Karl Barth, the monastic *forma vitae* once again began to be accepted as legitimate and evangelical."[3] As recently as the 1980s some American Protestant intellectuals called for "some protestant form of monasticism to restore a lost dimension of spirituality."[4] I think it is precisely its spirituality that monasticism has to offer the church and the world, and as Thomas Merton noted in his essay "Basic Principles of Monastic Spirituality," "in its essentials—solitude, poverty, obedience, silence, humility, manual labour, prayer and contemplation—monastic spirituality does not change."[5]

What seems currently to be the diminishment of monastic life, manifested in a decreasing number of traditional (and this is crucial) vocations, may, in the great sweep of Christian history, prove to be anomalous. Certainly experimental and ecumenical monastic foundations like Taize in France and Bose in Italy are flourishing. It is my sense that monasticism is not in a period of decline, but of change. The two are very different. That brings me to my own life and its relationship to the question at hand. I suspect I was asked to contribute to this volume because after 27 years as an academic I resigned a professorship in New Testament to live a solitary life more or less in the "relaxed" mode of the hermits of the Celtic church before the Synod of Whitby or the English church of the 14th century, living the life but without formal vows (a matter which troubles my vowed hermit friends).

Where does monasticism go from here? What is the monastic vision for the 21st century? For me the "way forward" is in the hermitage. For monasticism generally, I suspect the way forward

[3] Bianchi, "Monastic Life," 4.
[4] James T. Baker, "Benedict's Children and Their Separated Brothers and Sisters," *The Christian Century* XCVII/39 (December 3, 1980) 1191.
[5] In Thomas Merton, *The Monastic Journey* (Kansas City: Sheed Andrews and McMeel, Inc., 1977) 36. Hereafter *Monastic Journey*.

is back to the roots, but roots freshly envisioned and newly articulated. In our age poverty, chastity, obedience, and stability have
the ring of iron on the anvil of life, harsh, and if not harsh, un-
attainable. So the question becomes "what is the spirituality or
life stance or Christian virtue that each of the traditional vows is
intended to encourage?"[6]

As a way of getting at the "attractions" of the monastic tradition, my essay begins with the story of my response to Jesus' invitation to "come away" and with my working out a rule of life.
The point is not self-revelation (horrors!), but a description of
how monasticism as I knew it helped shape my life. Essentially
what drew me to the monastic way was its hospitality, openheartedness, and detachment. Thus, the second, and more sub-
stantive, part of this essay describes these monastic gifts to church
and world. The reader might wish to progress directly to that
section.

AUTOBIOGRAPHICAL EXCURSUS

I have enormous hesitation about writing autobiographi-
cally. I am, in the words of a Jesuit psychologist friend, an "off-
the-scale introvert," a private person with a strong sense of "who
would care?" But if the issue is the evolution of monasticism, it
may be of some value to see how it has evolved in one person's
life. Perhaps it will provide encouragement—or be a cautionary
tale. For good or ill, a life has a teaching function, just as the
monastery has a teaching function by being what it is. Prior Enzo
Bianchi of Bose notes "we reveal the reality of the kingdom of
God through the way we live."[7] Or not.

I was raised by faithful parents in the Christian Church, was
"religious" as a child and observant my whole life. From high
school I followed an academic path because I was good at going

[6] I treat this issue in a small book published by Liturgical Press entitled *Religious Vows, the Sermon on the Mount, and Christian Living*. There I recast each vow
in terms of the spiritual virtue it hopes to develop.
[7] Enzo Bianchi, "What Spirituality Does Monastic Life Offer the Church?"
booklet printed by the Monastery of Bose (Magnano, Italy, 2001), of the text of a
talk given on February 20, 2000, p. 12. Hereafter "What Spirituality."

to school. I didn't know that being good at something doesn't necessarily mean you should give your heart to it. I did a B.A. in English and philosophy at a small church-related liberal arts college and an M.A. in English literature at a large public university. Like St. Benedict, as a young person I studied literature. In the course of Ph.D. work, because of the influence of a glorious parish church and a disturbing religious vision, my interest shifted from literature to the spiritual life. I wrote one of the early dissertations on Thomas Merton which introduced me to monasticism and to world religions which, along with scripture, I subsequently taught.

During the 1970s, the period of my graduate work, I frequented the Anglican convent of All Saints' Sisters of the Poor in Catonsville, Maryland. It is a great mystery that, although I did not have a vocation to that contemplative community, it shaped the rest of my life. A poem which I wrote on September 23, 1978, while not a literary masterpiece, introduces the themes that for me are the essence of monasticism: hospitality, stability, openness and community.

"All Saints Convent"

In an indifferent world,
Detached from the sands of time,
Your house stands on a rock
And gathers the faceless ones
Around a table
Where the undeserving
Are honored guests.

We come from darkness,
Bring our hungers and thirsts.
We join you, kneel at dawn
Under a single, amber light
No more strangers,
But sisters in the Silence
Who speaks us all.

Twenty years into an academic career, I experienced an insistent sense of dis-ease with my work (with which everybody else seemed happy). On retreat in 1995 the idea of life as a solitary arose. That year I left a Jesuit college to teach at a Presbyterian seminary, a place that was generous to me, but where I never felt at home. As Thomas Merton's friend, Robert Lax, quipped, "If you find you're part of a community that starts to hiss at you it's time to leave."[8] Increasingly I understood that what I have to offer in midlife is not best given in the academic context with its sharp divide between head and heart.

With the help of my spiritual and financial advisors I made practical plans to move toward something like a hermit's life. It is clear that I am an anchorite, not a cenobite; I probably need a warning label that says "does not play well with others"! Solitude assumes a basically ordered life, some degree of spiritual maturity, and accountability to spiritual authority. As Cassian noted, "If we retire to solitude or secret places, without our faults being first cured, their operation is but repressed, while the power of feeling them is not extinguished."[9] Quite. I wish I had known then that the setting up of a hermitage invites close attention of the powers of evil who play out their contest in the heart of the hermit.[10] I owned a modest home on 2½ acres of ground, had a small pension (I was widowed in 1990 after 10 years of marriage[11]), no debt, and few desires for "worldly goods." I figured (correctly) that I could supplement my income by giving retreats and talks and writing. I realized this was a trade-off, and I wouldn't be a "real" hermit, but it seemed necessary.

As the externals fell into place, I wrote a rule of life, in part because monasticism always invites persons to live ordered lives.[12] In Genesis, God moves over the face of chaos to create an

[8] Quoted in Peter France, *Hermits: The Insights of Solitude* (New York: St. Martin's Press, 1996) 202.

[9] Cassian, "Conference of Abbot John," Chapter 12 in Philip Schaff and Henry Wace (eds.), *Nicene and Post-Nicene Fathers* (New York: The Christian Literature Company, 1894) 494. (Material by Cassian edited by Edgar C. S. Gibson.)

[10] Mother Mary Clare, SLG, "Eremitical Revival in the Anglican Church in the 20th Century," in A. M. Allchin (ed.), *Solitude and Communion: Papers on the Hermit Life* (Fairacres, Oxford: S.L.G. Press, 1977/1983) 73. Hereafter *Solitude and Communion*.

[11] For how this fit into my monastic bent see my article "Monasticism and Marriage," *Contemplative Review* 7/1 (Winter, 1984).

[12] See Bonnie Thurston, "Rules of Life," *Spirituality* 9/47 (March/April, 2003) 73–76.

ordered universe. That is also the paradigm for the emergence
of the spiritual life. However monasticism evolves (and like every
other species, if it does not evolve, it will die), that evolution will
not abandon ordering principles for the life because as Esther de
Waal writes "a well-ordered life-style is more likely to encourage
holiness than a badly-organized one."[13]

In fact a "rule of life" is another monastic contribution to the
church and the world. In the current climate the notion of living
a structured life is countercultural and wildly unpopular. "Doing
your own thing" is dated '60s language, but very much in evidence in the way people live. Yet the call to a serious Christian
is to be obedient to a God who has given the beloved, chosen
people a structure within which to flourish. Realistically, everyone is constrained by something; "what?" is the crucial question.
To what will we be obedient? As readers of this essay know,
"obedience" comes from the Latin *obedire* which shares a root
with *audire* "to hear." And, yes, St. Benedict's rule begins *Obscu-
lata*, listen, "attend . . . with the ear of your heart."[14] At its best,
obedience to a rule of life inclines the whole person (the "heart")
toward "hearing" God. Choosing (in my case, writing) a rule of
life implies choice of that to which we will be obedient, to which
we will listen.

"Rule" reflects the Greek *kanon* (which can be translated
"limit, sphere, or rule") and the Latin *regula*, "trellis." A trellis
supports a plant's growth heavenward; it supports what can't
support itself. People don't do very well without a structure or
point of focus (as any undisciplined child or lawless society
illustrates). An explicit trellis for life gives the structure in which,
to paraphrase Thomas Merton, our freedom can "deploy itself
in joy."[15] This joy is the reason for Jesus' teachings: "These things
I have spoken to you, that my joy may be in you, and that your
joy may be full" ("matured" or "perfected" John 15:11). The reason

[13] Esther de Waal, *Seeking God: The Way of St. Benedict* (Collegeville: Liturgical Press, 1984) 116. Hereafter *Seeking God*.

[14] Quotations from the Rule are from Timothy Fry, osb (ed.), *The Rule of St. Benedict* (Collegeville: Liturgical Press, 1981) 157. Hereafter *Rule*.

[15] Thomas Merton, "Time and the Liturgy," in *Seasons of Celebration* (New York: Farrar, Straus, Giroux, 1950/1977) 46.

for submitting to a rule of life is to foster more complete love of God and to perfect joy. As recently martyred Br. Roger of Taize wrote "if you submit to a . . . rule, you can only do so on account of Christ and the Gospel. . . . So, far from groaning under the burden of a rule, rejoice . . ."[16]

I realize that I am "preaching to the choir," but in my own journey it was significant to study monastic rules and to write my own. It kept me grounded in the fact that, even for solitaries, monastic life is communal and that, especially for solitaries, it is crucial to regulate daily activity with regard to prayer, work, and rest. This is the practical value of a rule; it helps keep life properly oriented, ordered, balanced, and simplified. Order, balance, and simplicity hardly characterize life "in the world" today. (The essence of the rule I devised appears in an appendix to this essay.)

Having given you a glimpse of the monastic context in my own life, I now turn to what I take to be its basic life orientations and the values they offer the church and the world. I do so knowing the "newly converted" can be nauseatingly enthusiastic and with apologies to the real monastics who already know all this.

THE GIFTS OF MONASTICISM

The traditional "gifts" of monasticism are found in its basic vows: poverty, chastity, obedience, and stability, each of which is intended to grow the monastic toward greater balance and simplicity, to hone the personality to receive more completely Christ's gift of love. *Conversatio morum* and the practices of *Lectio Divina*, and liturgical and contemplative prayer are also significant aspects of the monastic charism. The practical questions are: What are the manifestations of these vows and charisms that draw souls to monasticism? How might they be articulated for the future? I suggest three monastic attitudes that attracted me, that have remained constant throughout the history of Christian monasticism, and that I think will endure: hospitality, open heartedness,

---

[16] Br. Roger of Taize, *Parable of Community* (London: Mowbray, 1984) 11.

and detachment. These three attitudes are intrinsically inter-related and are the fruit of monastic profession when it is well lived by the individual and the community.

Hospitality

Hospitality is simply the gracious reception of the guest (Latin *hospitalis*, "of a guest"), any guest. It is a response to Christ's statement, "I was hungry and you gave me food, I was thirsty and you gave me drink, I was a stranger and you welcomed me" (Matt 25:35). This word of the Lord is the basis of St. Benedict's chapter on the reception of guests which opens *"All* guests who present themselves are to be welcomed as Christ."[17] Similarly in the *Regula Orientalis* the porter is enjoined "to welcome *everyone* coming within the gates, giving them a respectful greeting with humility and reverence . . ."[18] (italics in both quotations mine). Interestingly, in all the resurrection appearance stories in the Gospels, the risen Christ always appears (rather like the angels to Abraham in Genesis 18 or the mysterious, heavenly beings to Jacob in Gen 32:22-32) as the "other," the stranger, the unrecognized one. In a world which increasingly fears, shuns, and demonizes the other, monastics stand ready to "take in" rather than "close off" others precisely because, as Mother Teresa of Calcutta noted, Christ often comes in "unfortunate disguises." In this context, it is useful to remember that the Latin connotation of "guest" is somewhat darker than the English word; *hostis* means "stranger" and "enemy." So monastic hospitality implies entertaining not only the known and invited beloved ones, but those unexpected arrivals with whom one might be at enmity.

In reading the literature of the 4th-century monastics I am struck by the absence of judgment or condemnation of guests who arrive. Generally they are received without judgment of the state in which they arrive. The "Second Rule of the Fathers" commands, "Let one offer to an arriving traveler nothing more than a humble reception and peace; let him not be otherwise

---

[17] *Rule* 255.
[18] Carmela Vircillo Franklin et al. Transl. *Early Monastic Rules* (Collegeville: Liturgical Press, 1982) 75.

concerned—where he came from, why he came . . ."[19] A major
distinction between a private house and monastic houses is that
the former characteristically invites chosen friends and the latter
accepts whomever shows up. When I first received monastic
hospitality, I was often staggered by the variety of people who sat
together at table. Now I find it not only delightful, but a powerful image of those who come "from east and west, and from north
and south, and sit at table in the kingdom of God" (Luke 13:29).
In this way, monasticism provides a living image of God's reign
and aspiration for human community.

And in a world of individualism, monastic hospitality is a
reminder of what Dietrich Bonhoeffer called "life together."

> The prisoner, the sick person, the Christian in exile sees in
> the companionship of a fellow Christian a physical sign of
> the gracious presence of the triune God. Visitor and visited
> in loneliness recognize in each other the Christ who is
> present in the body; they receive and meet each other as one
> meets the Lord, in reverence, humility, and joy. They receive
> each other's benedictions as the benediction of the Lord
> Jesus Christ.[20]

Whether we recognize it or not, we live together in a web of interdependence. Certainly this is true on the material and economic
and political levels. But it is also true at a deeper level. In *The Way
of Simplicity: The Cistercian Tradition* Esther de Waal notes, "having
nothing of one's own is to need others, and more than that, to
need God."[21] Interdependence is profoundly true on the spiritual
level where we live together in the community of mutual need.
In that community, as A. M. Allchin has written, we live not by
asserting self against others, but by finding self in and through
others.[22] This implies that somewhere we encounter the other.
Where shall we do this except in a community where all comers

---

[19] Franklin 35. And recall numerous of the stories of the desert fathers and mothers.

[20] Dietrich Bonhoeffer, *Life Together* (London: SCM Press, Ltd., 1958) 10.

[21] Esther de Waal, *The Way of Simplicity: The Cistercian Tradition* (Maryknoll: Orbis Books, 1998) 74. Hereafter *Way of Simplicity*.

[22] A. M. Allchin, "The Solitary Vocation. Some Theological Considerations," *Solitude and Communion* 4.

are taken in with respect and reverence and love? And where, in our world, does that community exist if not in the church? Rowan Williams has written, "The church is the community of those who live in God-like relation to one another." "The church is the community of those so overwhelmed by their indebtedness to God's free grace, that they live in a state of glad and grateful indebtedness to one another."[23] The monastery with its familial structure of Abba and Amma and brothers and sisters is the historic venue for this grand vision of life together.

I am suggesting that monasticism provides the balance to the rampant and (dare I say it?) repulsive individualism in American (if not Western) culture. At its best monastic hospitality images the openness of God who accepts all comers. And that hospitality encompasses not only the welcoming of the human guest, but of the divine guest and of unfamiliar thoughts and ideas. The gift of *ora*, of monastic worship, falls in the category of hospitality as it represents both the human longing for God to be present among us and the human response to God's invitation to communion. Worship and liturgy are acts of hospitality on both these levels. In worship and liturgy we host and receive the Host. As Merton noted, "Liturgy demands of us the sacrifice of what is merely individualistic and eccentric in our lives . . ."[24] By means of common worship we "pilgrims through this barren land" enter the household of God and are thus saved from ourselves. "There can be no doubt that it is through the liturgy that they [monks] enter into the intimate life of the Church, and make their own its thoughts, its sentiments, its interests."[25] This is true not only for monastics, but for all Christians.

Similarly, hospitality extends to ideas as well as persons. Scripture has been the preeminent "word" of monastic life, and it should remain so. But, historically monasteries were centers of learning, cauldrons in which new ideas stewed. This openness to new thinking, to unfamiliar ideas needs, once again, to be imaged for the larger society for we live in a period of history

---

[23] Rowan Williams, *Christian Imagination in Poetry and Polity* (Fairacres, Oxford: SLB Press, 2004) 8.

[24] Merton, *Monastic Journey* 29.

[25] Winandy 45.

when "different" or "unfamiliar" is equated with "dangerous" or "evil." The spiritual reading that monastic life encourages can be an example of the opening of the intellectual and inner or heart life to the ideas of others. We use the idiom "entertain ideas," but in what contexts do we do it? Such openness is vital in the Rule of Taize which says simply and powerfully, "Love your neighbour, whatever his religious or ideological point of view."[26] Especially in this era of bitter polemics and polarization, it is important to have an example of and a place where new and different ideas and thoughts can be welcomed, listened to, discussed, and understood if not always agreed with or ultimately accepted. The kind of hospitality of which I am speaking, the gracious and reverent welcome of the guest, human, divine, and ideological, can only occur in an atmosphere of openheartedness.

Openheartedness

The life orientation that allows one to be hospitable is openheartedness. Br. David Steindl-Rast, osb, has written movingly on the heart. "Whenever we speak of the heart, we mean the whole person. Only at heart are we whole. The heart stands for that center of our being where we are one with ourselves, one with all others, one with God."[27] Openheartedness allows us to be hospitable and generous, but it presumes that we have found, know, and live from our hearts. What precedes living from the vital heart center is often brokenheartedness. The shell around the heart must be broken for the life within to emerge. And when it does, it emerges into the center of the life of God and thus of all people. But the process of rending and healing is unavoidable and requires "heart hospitals," places where the sick at heart and the brokenhearted can be nursed to health. On the psychic level this can be done by psychiatrists and psychologists, but in what William Butler Yeats called "the deep heart's core," the spiritual center of personality, another physic is required, one monasticism

[26] Br. Roger 13.
[27] Br. David Steindl-Rast, osb, *Gratefulness, The Heart of Prayer* (New York: Paulist Press, 1984) 202. And see also his book *A Listening Heart* (New York: Crossroad, 1999).

has traditionally provided by means of its guest houses and spiritual directors.

Openhearted living requires the psychological health that comes from existential knowledge of one's self as profoundly loved. The ultimate expression of such love is God's openhearted gift of self on the cross. A few great saints and mystics received that love directly. Most of us first encounter it reflected in the love of another. Our task is not only to learn to reflect such love, but to learn how to receive it as gift even as our Lord received the gift of the anointing woman (Mark 14:3-9). That means we need to encounter unselfish lovers and generous communities of love. Ideally, the monastery is a place where people live from the heart, and thus monasticism can be the "place" and "means" of opening the heart center to the gift of love, accepting it, dispensing it. Many of us seek monastic hospitality precisely because it is loving, and we all need to be loved.

We live in a culture that has taken all too seriously the old, Wild West image of circling up the wagons. In a culture of "close up and protect," "open deeply and give away" is especially important. Certainly this is related to the more commonly known monastic ideal of detachment from "things," but, more profoundly, it has to do with self offering which is the fruit of openheartedness. Madison Avenue stands or falls on its ability to sell us things for self-preservation: bigger, "safer" cars or houses; cosmetics; drugs; gadgets. Often, ironically, called "time savers," we waste our time preserving these things and are, in fact, owned by our stuff. Esther de Waal reminds us that "Absorption in the world is the slavery to things . . ." and that "Christian freedom lies precisely in liberation from the oppressive power that they can exercise."[28] Our culture teaches us to "save ourselves," while our Lord teaches us to give ourselves away. "For whoever would save his life will lose it; and whoever loses his life for my sake and the gospel's will save it" (Mark 8:35). Monasteries should be places where neither self nor stuff is hoarded but freely given, and thus opened up to full and joyful life, and, consequently, "saved." The Greek word for "save" and "heal" is the same word.

---

[28] de Waal, *Seeking God* 102.

This attitude of openheartedness encompasses the traditional monastic vows of poverty and chastity because they are a move, not away from, but toward the poor and marginalized, and this movement is from a position of solidarity and freedom from possession. Living from a stance of openheartedness means living in *koinonia*, in common, in community with all the needy in the world whether or not we are physically living a cenobitic life. They are us. Evagrius said the monk is one who is separated from the world and united to all. Openheartedness is a return to a kind of interior mendicancy; it allows us to realize the universality of human need for "things" and for love, to experience our own need, and to respond without possessiveness to that need in others. Which is to say that those who aspire to be monastics must take up the begging bowls of the heart.

In this regard the Benedictine insistence on working with the hands *(labora)* retains its vital importance. Working with our own hands (or backs or minds or what ever part of ourselves that God calls us to offer, but especially with the body), opens the heart to those who work with the hands by necessity and who constantly live "on the edge." Those who have not experienced "tribulation, or distress, or persecution, or famine, or nakedness, or peril, or sword" (Rom 8:37) sometimes exhibit a shocking lack of compassion toward those who regularly suffer them. Hard work, hunger (fasting), experience of uncomfortable heat or cold, chastity, all the traditional asceticisms, are tools that chisel the barnacles from the heart.

But openheartedness is also a corrective for too severe asceticism. "Flight from the world" has sometimes been mistaken for flight from the good creation and the good body. This is bad theology and worse practice. In his book *A Listening Heart* Br. David Steindl-Rast, OSB, makes a plea for "sacred sensuousness" and "sensuous asceticism." "The path to God," he writes, "starts at the gates of perception."[29] "A listening heart recognizes in the throbbing of reality pulsating against all our senses the heartbeat of divine life at the core of all that is real."[30] According

---

[29] Steindl-Rast, *A Listening Heart* 27.
[30] Ibid., 45.

to Br. David, the body is made transparent for such experience by sensuous asceticism.

So the call of the openhearted life is also a call to openheartedness toward ourselves, including sister or brother flesh which is not evil, but impermanent. Mastery of this transitory body, not domination of it, is what I think St. Benedict had in mind when he said in the Prologue to The Rule that he hoped "to set down nothing harsh, nothing burdensome." But, he continued, "The good of all concerned . . . may prompt us to a little strictness in order to amend faults and to safeguard love."[31] Amending our faults and increasing our love are exercises for heart health. The danger of asceticism is vanity and pride, both of which close the heart. Its value is humility (humus, the common stuff of our common life) which connects us to others and further opens our hearts.

Silence is, as well, an aspect of openheartedness. Abbot Winandy wrote, "silence imposes a barrier that puts a stop to the sallies of a particularly refractory faculty."[32] Creating an atmosphere of silence around ourselves gives others who approach us space to live and breathe. Andre Louf says that silence "establishes a zone of peace and quiet around the one who is silent, where God can be irresistibly felt as present."[33] And it is also important because silence creates the environment for listening, and listening is an important kind of openness to others. Careful, nonjudgmental listening is the way the heart offers hospitality. To listen to ourselves, to other people, to new ideas, to the creation, to God is to practice another of the monastic skills that our noise-polluted world ignores to its peril.

Detachment

If hospitality requires openheartedness, then openheartedness requires detachment, that extraordinary ability to allow things and people to be as they are. It is important to understand that detachment is not indifference, not an absence of caring.

[31] *Rule* 165.
[32] Winandy 43.
[33] Quoted in de Waal, *Way of Simplicity* 79.

Etymologically, "detached" means "set apart" (and is thus related to the concept of holiness, that which is "set apart" for a sacred purpose), or "unconnected," and therefore possessing a certain freedom. We are speaking of passionate separateness not cold impartiality. A Carthusian writes in *They Speak By Silences*, "Too often people imagine that Christian detachment consists in loving nothing. This is terribly wrong. Never has there been a heart more loving than the heart of Jesus, and our hearts should be modelled [sic] on His."[34] Br. David Steindl-Rast concurs when he explains, ". . . detachment is not a withdrawal from love, but an expansion of love beyond desire."[35] Detachment is for the sake both of freedom and of love, that *disinterested* desire, and when possible work, for the good of another. Hospitality, openheartedness, and detachment all provide alternatives to the dominant, cultural mode. They are the way we demonstrate what St. Paul asserted, that "our commonwealth [or "citizenship"] is in heaven" (Phil 3:20). But it is detachment that gives monasticism its moral authority.

For most people the functional center of the universe is the self, the family, the workplace, perhaps the parish. Most people are so enmeshed in the surface aspects of life in the world and, in particular, in the "givens" of their particular circumstances and cultures that they either lose sight of, or never raise their eyes to see the larger human or cosmic picture. The translation of Psalm 17:14-15 in the *Episcopal Daily Office Book* (Year One) describes the issue with this petition: "Deliver me, O Lord, by your hand / from those whose portion is life in this world; / Whose bellies you fill with your treasure, / who are well supplied with children and leave their wealth to their little ones." The Psalmist continues, "But at my vindication I shall see your face; / when I awake, I shall be satisfied, beholding your likeness" (Ps 17:16).

Let us admit that there exists an almost universally unacknowledged slavery to custom, culture, and "fashion," to consumerism and "affluenza." Most of us in the world operate with

---

[34] n.a., *They Speak By Silences* (Kalamazoo, Michigan: Cistercian Publications, 1966) 24.
[35] Steindl-Rast, *A Listening Heart* 101.

a "my country (or family or church or political system or race or economic system or—particularly insidiously—taste) right or wrong" attitude. "Our part is to detach ourselves from all these attachments, big or little, which hold us bound . . . so that we can be free to be guided by God."[36] At its best, monasticism awakens one from these limitations to the awareness of God and God's perspective. In fact, in the last talk he gave, Thomas Merton defined the monk as "essentially someone who takes up a critical attitude toward the world and its structures."[37] Only those who have some measure of detachment and autonomy from "the way things are," from the false "authority" of "they say" and the commonly accepted "way" can step back and ask the important question, "*why* is it this way?" Only those who choose to live outside or at least lightly within the accepted temporal system and live instead in the light of eternity will have the perspective to raise such questions. Reflecting on Merton's contributions to monastic renewal, Archbishop Rembert G. Weakland highlighted his interpretation of *fuga mundi* "not as a selfish and individualistic withdrawal from the trials and troubles of the world around him but as a 'monastic distancing' of himself to help to bring about positive change in contemporary society."[38]

The pre-Constantinian Church and, at least in the first millennium of the church, its monastics were positioned to be the moral voice precisely because they were not aligned with the world's accepted and acceptable power structures. When the monasteries became part of the social and economic order their critical function was compromised. When monasticism aligned itself with the aims and servitudes of the feudal system (and the church's role in it!), it lost its way and desperately needed the subsequent reforms to invigorate the life. "The degeneration of monasticism," noted the late C. W. Previte-Orton, "was a recurrent theme of

[36] n.a., *Where Silence Is Praise* (Kalamazoo, Michigan: Cistercian Publications, 1997) 88.

[37] Naomi Burton et. al., (eds.), *The Asian Journal of Thomas Merton* (New York: New Directions, 1973) 329.

[38] Br. Patrick Hart (ed.), *Survival or Prophecy? The Letters of Thomas Merton and Jean Leclercq* (New York: Farrar, Straus and Giroux, 2002) xvi.

the later Middle Ages."[39] In my view this was precisely because monasticism lost the detachment that constitutes its moral authority.

But, as important as it is, detachment operates on a more profound level than the socio-political. Detachment is a fundamental spiritual attitude intrinsically related to reverence and chastity and even ecology. Detachment from things allows them to arise in their "this-ness," their created beauty and glory. It allows us to reverence things and persons simply because they exist and not because they fill some need in us. As such, it is a theological basis for ecology on every level and is closely related to the vow of chastity "understood in its widest sense as the refusal to possess, to manipulate, to exploit."[40] In this context, Enzo Bianchi reminds us that Augustine (who had some experience of these things!) taught that chastity is "well-ordered love *(amor ordinatus)* that does not subordinate greater things to lesser ones."[41] Chastity and reverence are closely related. As Lawrence Freeman, osb, notes, "A sense of reverence is born in a gasp of wonder."[42] We can only wonder at that which we do not possess, grasp at, or lust after. Things and persons are not "means to ends," (the root attitude of capitalism), but are to be respected, loved, wondered at, reverenced, allowed to exist in their own God-given right—and protected. Any other attitude exhibits an arrogant overreaching pride.

St. Paul wrote to the Corinthians of "having nothing, and yet possessing everything" (2 Cor 6:10). (*"Nihil habentes omnia possidentes"* is the motto of All Saints Sisters of the Poor where I first encountered lived monasticism.) It is that attitude to which monasticism aspires spiritually as well as economically or materially. Detachment allows one to live an unencumbered life. When we are unencumbered, we can move easily, a truth of both the external and internal life. Detachment is an attitude which fosters freedom, "freedom from" to be sure, but also "freedom

[39] C. W. Previte-Orton, *The Shorter Cambridge Medieval History* (Cambridge: Cambridge University Press, 1960) I: 506.

[40] de Waal, *Seeking God* 102.

[41] Enzo Bianchi, *Words of Spirituality* (London: SPCK, 2002) 76.

[42] Lawrence Freeman, osb, *Light Within* (New York: Crossroad, 1987) 94.

to," in this case to reverence and to love without restraint or possessiveness. Detachment allows one, in the happy phrase of Theresa Mancuso, "to live in the world without becoming worldly."[43] And the call to live *in* but not *of* the world is a call to the full aliveness which for St. Irenaeus defined the glory of God. The closed-heartedness and possessiveness that characterizes so many people are but unhappy symptoms of their lack of aliveness. There are a lot of zombies walking around in expensive shoes and designer jeans, a lot of people who are half dead and completely afraid of life. But when we profoundly understand that we don't make, own, or manipulate life, we are freed to love it fully and, importantly, to be able to let it go. Detachment gives us freedom to live *and* to die. Ironically, the great refusal to live abundantly is often rooted in an inability to accept death. A "love it and leave it" attitude about life is an enduring gift that monasticism can give the world. Finally, then, I think monasticism must evince the "abundant life" which our Lord said was his reason for coming among us (John 10:10b).

CONCLUSION

Religious anthropologists write about the "monomythic pattern" in rites of passage. In such rites one progresses from separation through liminality to return as a changed person. At the outset of this essay I reflected that monasticism is in a period of change, not decline. In fact monasticism seems to be in a "liminal" phase of development, a transitional or "between" time when the "old way" has been left behind, but the "new way" is not yet completely clear. It is not dying, but evolving, "morphing" as the young say. The difficult question at such a time is "what is essential, the chrysalis or the pupae, the worm or the wings?" *Semper reformada* is true not only for the Church, but for all her institutions. Transitional periods are uncomfortable, and strong voices like those of Jean Leclercq or Thomas Merton who

[43] Theresa Mancuso, "The Urban Hermit: Monastic Life in the City," *Review for Religious* 55/2 (1996) 138.

"saw it coming" are both annoying and helpful in the process. In times of liminality we need both the loyalists and the loyal opposition.

The etymological root of "monasticism" is *monos*, "one," not necessarily "one" in the sense of "solitary" or "alone," but "one" in the sense of focus or direction or unity. "God alone" about sums it up. St. Peter tells the Lord, "we have left everything and followed you" (Mark 10:28). This is the ideal of Christian monasticism; everything is secondary to following Christ and seeking perfection in Him to please God alone (*soli Deo placere desiderans* as per St. Gregory). This must be the polar star of monasticism in transition. Whatever is retained, whatever is changed must be for the sake of pleasing God alone because the monastery (or hermitage) is the place where life is organized so that everything *can* be for God's pleasure. Unless I have badly misunderstood it, monasticism's hope for those who undertake the life is the refocusing of every desire to make God its object. This desire for God, to surrender to God and be conformed to Christ (i.e., to be "holy") unites Christians beyond confessional boundaries. In this regard monasteries can be great ecumenical centers. When this one-focused desire for God is operative, monks and monasteries are naturally hospitable, openhearted, and remarkably attractive. "With this conclusion, the Lord waits for us daily to translate into action, as we should, his holy teachings."[44]

Suppliant

In the monastery
the note said this:
"pick up your supper tray
at the kitchen door."

Like how many million
suppliants of ages past,
I am to wait at the portal
for Benedict's brethren
to fill my begging bowl.

---

[44] *Rule* 163.

I do not know exactly
why this makes me smile,
why I am comforted
to be among the indigent
waiting for crumbs to fall
from the monastic table.

But in history's white light
I see myself just as I am,
loitering at heaven's back door
empty handed and hungry,
waiting with the multitudes
for some disciple
to bless, break and give
God's bread.

APPENDIX

The following is the essential page of the rule of life I devised.
These are not "vows" in the traditional sense, but more practical
"life plans."

The Rule of Life for The Anchorage

*"For God alone my soul waits in silence,
for my hope is from him"* (Ps 62:5).

"Be still and know that I am God . . ." (Ps 46:10).

Pro Christi, Pro Amore

I respond in love and joy to a long-standing call on my life which
I take as a gracious invitation of God to a life of greater solitude
and thus greater availability to Him.

Hermitage is dedicated to St. Mary of Egypt.

She found joy in the wilderness of repentance.

My act of repentance and renunciation is not only for my
own sin, but for the evils of the world, our inhumanity and
wickedness to each other.

I undertake the way of life:

- To be still and know
- To hear God more clearly with the ear of my heart
- To give God delight
- To give my life for spiritual balance in the universe as a place/ person of peace, calm, and clarity

The Ordering of the Life

Daily

- Morning, noon, night prayer & a period of meditation
- Study, manual labor/work, rest/recreation

Weekly

"Sunday is a day of contemplation sacred to the mystery of the resurrection." Thomas Merton

- Eucharist (twice weekly, more frequently when available)
- Service to others at least ½ day a week (work at food pantry, give spiritual direction)
- Two days in silence and isolation (except where the demands of charity intervene)

Periodically

- Spiritual direction and accountability
- Days away from The Anchorage for prayer
- One week retreat annually
- One or two months a year in relative isolation (no outside work, teaching, travel, etc.)

THOUGHTS ON MONASTICISM'S POSSIBLE FUTURES

by Michael Casey, OCSO

The monks and nuns of the future will be a degenerate lot. We may well come to this conclusion if we give any credence to the well-known *topoi* in which great monastic figures have lamented the low-level living of their contemporaries compared with the monastic giants of former times. The situation can only get worse! Because monastic life is an experiential tradition it has always seemed to its practitioners that those to whom the charism is passed are not of the same caliber as those from whom they themselves received it. On the basis of such precedents I consider it quite unlikely that I would approve of the forms with which monasticism will invest itself in the decades and centuries ahead. But I won't be around to ventilate my opinions.

The transmission of the monastic charism from person to person means that it is susceptible to non-programmatic change. In the past, the evolution of the monastic way of life has not followed an inherent logic but has constantly adapted its form to any situation in which it emerges. Its progress has been determined by the practical steps taken by charismatic individuals to make provision for the monastic impulse exploiting the opportunities offered by contemporary society and compensating for its liabilities. Desert-dwellers, stylites, imperial schoolteachers, warblers of psalms, scruffy wanderers, and cloistered mystics may seem radically unlike, yet we find them all in monastic history.[1] What makes them monks is not the specificity of their

---

[1] For a recent overview see Jan María Laboa, *The Historical Atlas of Eastern and Western Christian Monasticism* (Collegeville: Liturgical Press, 2003).

institutional lifestyle but the fact that they all share some essential "monastic" attributes.

For me to recognize a lifestyle as monastic, I would insist on four broad characteristics or components.[2]

1. Monks and nuns must be seekers of God, however the divine reality is described. They must be pilgrims of the Absolute, in search of the transcendent. In Christian circles this may be described simply as the following of Christ or, in the terms used by John Cassian in his first Conference, embracing the goal of entering the Kingdom of heaven.

2. This seeking after "something more" must inevitably involve a radical renunciation that includes a solid degree of separation from "the world," at least at the level of belief and value.[3] The more radical the monastic lifestyle, the more complete the physical sequestration. A distinctive end requires distinctive means, therefore monasticism involves the practice of asceticism: the adoption of specific practices that, under grace, facilitate the attainment of the ultimate goal.

3. Monastic life is characterized by a "blessed simplicity."[4] This is not merely the result of withdrawal from the accelerating complexity of "modern" life or the self-conscious pursuit of an inauthentic neo-primitivism. Although it is expressed externally in poverty and modesty of material goods, simplicity in its essence is the effect of sustained subjective commitment to a single objective.[5] It is a quality of will that is the result of serial choices made with a single purpose in view. Such clarity

---

[2] It is only for the sake of euphony that I will sometimes take the liberty of speaking about "monks" rather than "monks and nuns" and avoid the ugly use of the adjective "monastic" as a noun. As my argument progresses it will become clear that I believe that gender-inclusivity will be a feature of future monasticism: perhaps "monk" will become gender-neutral just as "actor," "manager," and "hero" have. A late Latin word *monacha* exists, but it is not widely attested.

[3] See M. Casey, *Strangers to the City: Reflections on the Beliefs and Values of the Rule of Saint Benedict* (Brewster: Paraclete Press, 2005).

[4] This is the title Raimundo Panikkar gives to his book: *Blessed Simplicity: The Monk as Universal Archetype* (New York: The Seabury Press, 1982).

[5] "Properly, simplicity is a will that is completely turned towards God, seeking only one thing from the Lord and pursuing it, and not walking according to the world's multiplicity." William of St. Thierry, *Golden Epistle* 49; SChr 223, p. 184.

cannot be attained quickly; it is a lifelong pursuit. This is what the ancients termed *puritas cordis:* an undivided heart. Even though he engages in multiple tasks, a real monk, at heart, cannot be hyphenated.

4. A monk is constituted as such by living within an evident tradition. Genuine monasticism is not self-generating. It cannot be the product of individual self-expression precisely because the goal of monastic living is self-transcendence. This is why Benedict finds it essential that the monastic recruits should desire to live a common life under an abbot so that "they do not live by their own judgement or obey their desires and pleasures, but walk according to the judgement and instructions of another" (RB 5:12). It is in training newcomers to go beyond self-will that monasticism most effectively serves its purpose. When the novice receives the habit from an elder it signifies the start of a process whereby the charism is slowly transmitted to a new generation. Do-it-yourself monasticism is no more than a semblance of the real thing.

Supposing that these qualities are present, the monasticism of the future will take its specificity from the different social situations where it is found. We do not know whether monasticism will have to plot its course through a nuclear wasteland, generalized anarchy, or post-capitalist freebootery. The form that monastic renunciation will take will be determined by those areas in which the ambient society expresses its alienation from or uninterestedness in God: whether these be the pursuit of wealth, power, pleasure, or entertainment. On the other hand, one would have to be a complete pessimist to believe that the future will have nothing positive to contribute to the monastic project, just as contemporary social values had made those in monasteries more aware of hygiene, good nutrition, developmental psychology, environmental issues, the immorality of war, and the inequity of discrimination. In other words any attempt to envisage the future of monasticism must surely be based on guesswork regarding the future of the world-culture that surrounds us. Maybe globalization will produce a more homogeneous world society, in which case the monastic response will be more uniform. Perhaps the globalizing trend has already peaked, as John Ralston Saul insists, and the future will belong to strong local cultures and enterprises. In any case the public shape of monastic living will be determined most visibly by the things renounced by those entering. In other words monasticism will take its definition from whatever it is that new entrants will be asked to forego in embracing the monastic pursuit.

In particular those who are attracted to monasticism may be those who prefer their reality to be non-virtual. If industrialized society continues to insulate its members from the untidiness of human existence, perhaps monasteries will draw candidates precisely because they renounce slickness in favor of the gritty imperfection typical of unaided human endeavor. Today we see an increasing number of people for whom what they see on television is more important and real than what is happening around them. There are many who self-medicate by massive doses of entertainment. There seems to be a progressive substitution of a virtual world for the earth we stand on.[6] Nature exists only to be manipulated and dressed up. We observe this, for example, in genetic modification, cosmetic surgery, psychotropic drugs, synthesized music, and computer-generated art. The monastic choir will never sound as good as the blended sounds they hear through their entertainment systems; real life will always be grittier and less predictable than the slick products of technology precisely because it is real. Maybe monasteries will be seen as centers of non-virtual reality.

Who knows what the future may bring? It is all guesswork. But perhaps there may be some indicators of future monasticism in forces already at work within the monastic world.

POST-CONCILIAR MOMENTUM

Has there been any discernible movement in monastic life in recent decades, especially since Vatican II, that may give some general indication of how monasticism is evolving? I have re-

---

[6] I do not know how much credence to place in the report that a certain monastery produced a promotional brochure using models rather than real monks, because the monks did not look "monastic" enough.

flected on this question with reference to my own Order, the Strict-Observance Cistercians.[7] My conclusion was that, generally speaking, there has been a tidal movement away from concentration on the minutiae of external observance in the direction of greater pluralism, on the understanding that fundamental beliefs and values have been internalized. This means that the emphasis has moved from external discipline to personal formation, although obviously the two concerns are not mutually exclusive. The dynamic quality of the process of formation will largely depend on the degree to which it initiates newcomers into the sapiential tradition that constitutes the monastic patrimony. It is by personally appropriating the wisdom of the past that future generations will develop the capacity to interact creatively with their own period.[8]

In a circular letter written in Advent 1982, Abbot General Ambrose Southey wrote the following description of what is involved in the process of internalization of values. He is speaking about different responses to the changes which followed Vatican II.

> Finally there is *internalization* or integration as a way of re-acting to the new situation. In his case the person adopts the new values internally and externally because they are seen to be consistent with his own value system and intrinsically capable of producing growth in that system. Internalization then demands personal effort based not on external rewards or a flattering self-image, but on a capacity to transcend oneself, i.e., on a capacity 1) to be free in the face of pressures coming from the community or from internal needs and 2) to be able to choose the monastic values for their own intrinsic worth.

People remain in monastic life because there is consonance between their particular value system and monastic *conversatio*. They feel spiritually at home. The many who fled the cloister in

---

[7] M. Casey, "How Spirituality has Evolved in the Cistercian Order of the Strict Observance during the Twentieth Century"; this is an article that, I hope, will be forthcoming in a collective history of the Trappists during the last century.

[8] See M. Casey, "El patrimonio cisterciense y el nuevo monasticismo: Reflexiones sobre la I parte de las Constitutiones," *Cistercium* 186 (1991) 521–38.

the post-conciliar period did so because they had discovered an inconsistency between their personal choices and aspirations and the values embedded in the monastic regimen. In resolving this dilemma they gave precedence to urgent and/or important personal issues over commitment to continuance in monastic life.

It would seem that, in the case of those experiencing vocational discontent, the dynamic of monastic growth had slowed. People do not usually bale out of a going concern. Either there was confusion about the goal of monastic living or there was a feeling that the goal was not in the process of being attained. Many were exhausted by work, internal politics, lack of appreciation, and internal struggles and had lost heart in confronting the future. Put simply, monastic life had not brought them closer to God at the level of experience. No wonder they were discouraged. Those who came seeking God felt themselves to have been so unsuccessful in their quest and maybe even betrayed by the community. As a result there seemed little meaning in continuing.

A quiet satisfaction in the experience of prayer is essential to perseverance. The communities that will survive in the future will be those that best form their members in handling the inevitable vicissitudes of the contemplative life. In the last analysis there is no other valid reason for embracing monastic life than to be formed according to its mystical tradition. Another way of saying this is to apply to the monasteries what Karl Rahner wrote about the members of the Church in general. "The Christian of the future will be a mystic or he will not exist at all."[9] Monasteries without a strong contemplative ambience and orientation will struggle to stay alive. Those that survive will be so grounded in contemplation that they will not be shaken.

THOSE WHO WILL STAY

The immediate future of monastic life depends on those who are its present and, particularly, whether they will still be around

[9] Karl Rahner, "The Spirituality of the Church of the Future," in *Theological Investigations: Volume XX: Concern for the Church,* translated by Edward Quinn (London: Darton, Longman & Todd, 1981) 149.

when the future dawns. The losses in monastic personnel in the last half-century have been staggering. Although it is true that monks and nuns sometimes leave because of specific issues of faith or morals, most often, as I have already noted, it is because they no longer feel fully alive in the community and are seeking greater opportunity for growth elsewhere. Perhaps we should view departures less in terms of morality and psychology and more through the lens of social dynamics. Undesired withdrawals probably indicate a dysfunction or, at least, a blindness in the organization. Many of the reasons given for leaving correspond to what is happening in large corporations, some of which are losing annually as many as one in seven employees whom they wish to retain. For many persons today, commitment lasts only as long as the organization suits individual needs; if these are not satisfied then more attractive alternatives are sought. In monastic terms, since it was the prospect of a more rewarding lifestyle that brought people into the monastery in the first place, their idealism will take them elsewhere if they begin to perceive little anticipation that in due time their dream will be realized. The stability expected of members of a monastic community has become increasingly more difficult as options multiply and societies become more and more mobile. There is no reason to believe that this trend will diminish in the immediate future.

Benjamin Chaminade has made quite an impact on the business world with his investigations of the phenomenon of employee-retention, although he prefers the term *fidélisation*.[10] He has found that people begin to look for alternative employment when they experience inept management, poor training, lack of recognition or rewards, and when there is no communication about their future prospects. His analysis of the situation is penetrating, but his solution is simple to formulate. We need to

---

[10] "*Fidélisation* is the voluntary action by which a business establishes an environment that maintains the attachment of the employees over a long period. This enduring and constant attachment which binds the employee to the business is based on shared values. . . . Putting in place a policy of *fidélisation* consists in placing persons and their expectations at the heart of the business concerns so that the professional satisfaction of the employee is assured and a relationship of mutual confidence is established." Translated from Benjamin Chaminade, "Fidélisation versus rétention," in www.focusrh.com.

create an environment of genuine listening, something more sincere than what has been termed "sponge listening" whereby management absorbs complaints and soothes aggrieved feelings but understands nothing and changes nothing. "If your talented people are not happy, you have to find out why."[11] Unwelcome though their discontent may be, it may be the harbinger of a more general malaise that is better remedied early. In which scenario the outcome may well be creative.

Communities that will survive and thrive well into the future are those in which there is a good level of communication between management and commoners. Intergenerational communication is particularly important since, as Margaret Mead wrote as far back as 1970, "Today, nowhere in the world are there elders who know what the children know."[12] According to the Scholastic axiom, receptivity is determined by the capacity of the receiver. The reception of monastic tradition, therefore, is not a function of the knowledge or enthusiasm of the formator, but of the capacity of the newcomer to monastic life to harmonize monastic principle with prior learnings. If a conflict of values occurs it is important that formators know about it; it is only by listening to the seeming resistance they encounter that they can assist the next generation in moving towards a synthesis, both at the level of theory and at the level of practice.

Good communication creates a participative community in which all feel accepted, respected, listened to, and so integrated that none are marginalized.[13] In such a situation it is possible for

---

[11] As quoted in *The Bulletin*, 10 August 2005, p. 66.

[12] Margaret Mead, *Culture and Commitment: A Study of the Generation Gap* (London: Granada, 1970) 101.

[13] Before we are swept away by utopian fantasies it is important to remind ourselves that monasticism is primarily concerned with facilitating communion *(koinonia)* with God. This is realized, as Saint Benedict notes at the end of his Prologue, only by participation in the Cross of Christ. The concrete form this crucifixion often takes is circumstantial, organizational, or emotional banishment from the community to whom one has given one's life. In such a case, belonging to the community operates at a level deeper than social interaction—presupposing that the pain of the situation does not break one's heart and cause a loss of faith or courage. Sometimes, invisibly, the "success" of a particular community is the graced result of the paschal experience of one or other of its members who have been effectively sidelined by the community, but who have kept the faith, however, and remained steadfast.

individuals to work cooperatively with a minimum of conflict. There is, however, another factor. Monastic management needs to identify talent and nurture it, even if such a priority involves diminishment for the managers themselves. Inevitably such a perspective will involve some modification of traditional monastic structures and the reduction of a style of autocratic governance that some claim to find authorized by Benedict's Rule. Without a more proactive cultivation of generativity in the ranks of the community, monasteries will soon become stagnant.[14]

MONASTIC MONUMENTS

Mediocrity is the bane of historic Benedictinism. When much attention is devoted to avoiding extremes, there is a danger that the end-product will be superlatively bland: neither active nor contemplative, neither solitary nor rigorously communitarian, neither austere nor comfortable.[15] Underneath the urbane consensus it may happen that nobody is truly satisfied that this form of monastic life is facilitating progress towards a specific and long-term goal. Inevitably mere inertia will be sufficient to ensure that some individuals will persevere and some monasteries will survive. Just as semi-dormant monks and nuns can continue to live in the monastery because making a change is too challenging so, I suppose, those monasteries with a long history will survive in some form. There will always be people who are willing to associate themselves with such a worthy tradition even if a particular monastery has long ceased to be at the cutting edge of the monastic endeavor. Such communities could easily become monuments of marvelous irrelevance: pious theme parks with *real* monks as proprietors and part-time participants in various worthy ventures located on monastic real estate. The beneficent purpose of such institutions will be the preservation of the memory that once monasticism existed in the Church. Those who are beguiled to enter them will quickly discover the shallowness

---

[14] On generativity see, *Strangers to the City*, 124–41. See also the conference of Abbot General Bernardo Olivera quoted therein.

[15] On this see M. Casey, "The Dynamic Unfolding of the Benedictine Charism," in *The American Benedictine Review* 51:2 (2000) 149–67.

of the facade and begin to disturb the ordered calm of mediocrity by clamorous demands for a more authentic form of life. Some of the dissidents will eventually quiet down and become socialized, others will give up the monastic pursuit and, maybe, a few will band together to sally forth in a new monastic endeavor. And who knows? One or other of such reforms may endure. Meanwhile the parent monastery will probably subsist, affectionately sustained by alumni and admirers of its history, beloved of producers of television documentaries and the target for the romantic projections of the piously inclined.

THE LAMBETH DILEMMA

Recent crises in the Anglican Communion may well point to a potential danger for future monasticism. Among Anglicans it has become apparent that the churches in the West have a completely different attitude to same-sex unions from that dominant in the newer churches of Africa. The more liberal principles espoused by the Church of England and other long-established bodies are seriously at odds with the sterner line adopted by the newer churches. This division has intensified to the point where continuing communion is threatened.

The same kind of conflict, although about different issues, could easily occur in monastic orders whose traditional European monasteries are steadily becoming depopulated while monasticism is flourishing in the diaspora. At one point in the not-too-distant future, general chapters may cease to have a European or American majority.[16] And although it may be true that the first post-colonial generation may mimic their mentors, those who come after them will certainly begin to speak in the accents of their own very different cultures. The result may well be a recall to a more primitive observance, which, for example, may involve a more incisive practice of poverty, specific measures to curb individualism, and a more liberated attitude to liturgical and

[16] I understand that this has already occurred with the Tutzing Benedictine Sisters, who have been so successful as missionaries that Korean members alone outnumber those from traditional monastic areas.

other regulations. This process of reverse inculturation may be a bitter pill for some to swallow, especially if it results in the enactment of legislation designed to implement a more demanding lifestyle.

One of the endearing qualities of vital monasticism is that, chameleon-like, it tends to take much of its nonessential coloration from its surroundings.[17] Over the generations, these elements of ambient culture become inseparable from the central beliefs and values of the charism and are passed on to succeeding generations as a single package. This is why making a foundation in an alien culture has always been difficult. It has become hard to determine what belongs to the substance of monastic observance and what is merely local baggage. Those formed in monasteries founded in different cultures are likely to have somewhat different viewpoints even regarding essential observances. Monks and nuns from Africa and Asia, particularly, will probably become increasingly vocal in their denunciation of what they perceive as the decadence of the established monastic centers and clamor for reform. Europe has no claim to a monopoly on deciding the forms by which the monastic impulse finds expression; probably not even on interpreting the Benedictine tradition. The future may demonstrate that the monastic center of gravity has moved further afield. The outcome of this will be a starker monastic observance until, in due course the reformed regimen becomes comfortable in a different setting and, once again, begins to cry out for reform. The changing demography of the monastic world may also lead to the repopulation of half-empty old monasteries by faraway communities and a corresponding change in lifestyle even at the local level.

The wonderful expansion of monasticism to all continents and its liberation from narrow monocultural constraints carries with it the inherent danger of discontinuity. Although we have seen in Ethiopia the perdurance of a strong monastic tradition in a non-Western and very isolated culture, mostly some linkage with the wisdom of past monastic generations needs to be maintained as a guarantee of present authenticity. The monastic

---

[17] See M. Casey, "The Rule of Benedict and Inculturation: A Formation Perspective," *Tjurunga* 62 (2002) 15–46.

sub-culture has been, for the last millennium, a literary culture. Access to its riches was facilitated by the fact that the Church continued to use Latin up to the 1960s and so there was some possibility of direct contact with the sources. Today the situation is different. Most of the young monks and nuns who are eager to absorb monastic tradition do so first through the medium of translation. This is a second-best solution, but it remains possible for those whose mother tongue is European. Outside that linguistic sphere, life-giving contact is attenuated: often double or triple translations are needed. In addition, the structure of such languages as Vietnamese, Swahili, Chinese, Malayalam, Tongan, or Indonesian is such that, beyond the simplest statements, some degree of paraphrase is inevitable. The emotional impact of the text is often weakened thereby, and with it much of its subtlety.

The future will see an increased need of a gateway language —a modern vernacular that is commonly accessible and yet is able to preserve and transmit elements of the vocabulary and syntax of original monastic texts. French, Spanish, and Italian are more "Latin" in character and so are closer to the original, but English is fast becoming a global language and is undoubtedly accessible to more people, although as a second or third language. If we accept that English is to be the language at least of the immediate future and that English translations will become normative, then we need to exercise much diligence in ensuring that these translations are such as to serve this function. This is the same issue that has arisen concerning the translation of the *Missale Romanum*. The claims of a close-to-literal translation into basic, nonliterary English against those of a more elaborate, literary translation ought to be weighed in the context of the end-user. A translation appropriate as a medium to other languages needs to be naked and free from artifice. Translators, especially those able to enjoy the Latin originals, can then enhance the bare text with a style appropriate to the target language. A translation intended for native English-speakers can afford to be more literary, and probably needs to be if it is also to reproduce the spirit and emotion of the original.

Among thirteenth-century Cistercians in Ireland problems multiplied because of a lack of general knowledge of Latin, despite Ireland's long literate history. With no facility for reading

monks soon find alternative pursuits that tend to contribute little
to their understanding of monastic life: idleness, hobbies, work,
outside interests, and various other ways of filling in time. The
future of monasticism in non-European cultures may well depend on the assiduity of the intervening generations in making
available in different languages faithful and beautiful translations
of ancient works, as well as generating a new literature that will
transmit those treasures in a different idiom. Another case of *nova
et vetera*. It will be the unanimity produced by formation in a
common patrimony that will bind together men and women from
different cultures in concord and charity. In that situation culture
clashes can be avoided.

LIMINALITY AND UNIVERSALISM

Monasteries thrive best when they are on the margins not
only of secular society but also of the Church. An enthusiasm for
hobnobbing with the hierarchy and identifying with the institutional Church brings many collateral advantages in terms of
attracting benefactors and vocational inquiries (which seem to
come more from the right than from the left) but there are draw-
backs involved in renouncing a more impartial stance. Monasteries should not easily be labeled "conservative" or "progressive";
they need to maintain their capacity to offer hospitality to both
traditional devotional Catholics and those pushing the limits of
prophetic indignation. Left and right equally should feel at home
in a monastery and find there a mirror of their truest spiritual
aspiration. In a sense the monastery needs to be catholic (lower-
case) and thereby ecumenical. Not only locales for ecumenical
and interreligious encounter and dialogue but, perhaps, proleptic
centers of Christian communion, and even intercommunion.

Christian Monasticism belongs to the undivided Church;
ideally, it should not be too blatantly stamped with the seal of its
parent sect and not too much given to proselytism. Monks are
meant to be more than arch-Catholics. This willingness to be a
universal witness to ultimate values was probably the reason why
the attraction to Taizé transcends denominational boundaries.
Catholics, evangelical Protestants, and even Orthodox believers

find there a resonance to their unformulated spiritual yearnings. Yet Taizé is not wishy-washy or without principles; it does not blur ecclesiastical distinctions. The magic of the community consists in the fact that it tries simply to be faithful to its own charism and call, and then to invite others in to share what it has. Whatever the future of enclosure walls, future monasticism, it seems to me, will need to ensure that the walls of bigotry, prejudice, and exclusivism are well and truly demolished. I cannot but believe that such monasteries will flourish in the future.

When I speak of a universal hospitality that mirrors the hospitality of God I am not restricting myself to the reception of guests and visitors. I include recruitment in that divine openness. This means, first of all, that those entering a particular monastery may well come from different faith-backgrounds and, as a result, for some people the monastic option will become the primary mode of discipleship. Protestants or Anglicans may choose to enter into a monastery without formally renouncing their previous affiliation and giving their "submission" to Rome. It will be understood as implicit in the process of becoming a monk. This is how they experience concretely the assent of faith. The same will apply to those who abandon irreligion, agnosticism, or apathy. Conversion and entry into monastic life will again become somewhat synonymous. Theoretically this will create challenges for those responsible for formation, but treating every person as unique will obviate these, as well as increase the effectiveness of the help given.[18] In the short term there may be canonical problems, but these too are not necessarily insoluble. Those who come truly seeking God will, as Cassian understood, be more shaped by their ultimate goal than by the past out of which they have emerged. At some stage the inclusiveness may pass beyond the ecumenical to the interreligious. This happens occasionally today, for longer or shorter periods. The future may see more of such sharing of life, to the benefit of all parties.

---

[18] In any case, monastic formation always has to grapple with the exact blend of continuity and discontinuity with regard to the newcomer's past. It is probably true to say that acceptance of the past, reconciliation where necessary, and substantial harmonization with a monastic present are appropriate objectives during the first phases of monastic life. Total rejection, denial, or repression will not contribute to a healthy outcome.

This passion for inclusiveness may lead to monks and nuns living chastely together in a single community.[19] I cannot see how this can be avoided once we have accepted the premise of gender-equality and have experienced the more complete integration that results from a fuller acceptance of sexual polarity within oneself and normalized relations with the opposite gender. Combined communities are probably less risky than presently considered by some, provided the architecture of the house and the choreography of the community takes commonsense account of potential threats to chastity. Some would argue that such dangers already exist to some extent, granted the presence in communities of persons who experience same-sex attractions. The cohabitation of monks and nuns would certainly require a much more comprehensive education and formation to celibate chastity than is common today, and this would represent a positive gain. Mixed communities would also require much more attention to the subtle dynamics of communal interaction at all levels: informal, official, communal, and dialogical. In case the reader has not noticed, men and women tend to do things differently.[20]

Undoubtedly such prospects may provoke foreboding among those who see only problems. Think of the potential richness of such communities, men and women, young and old, different races, different religious backgrounds. "How good and how pleasant it is when brothers live in unity." Certainly. But how much better when brothers and sisters, Jews, Greeks, and barbarians, the young, and the old, the wise and the stupid, the innocent and the repentant. That would be an even greater miracle, as Saint Aelred notes. "Brothers, see with how much peace and concord God has gathered all these in a single social unit."[21] By what possible means could God bind together such disparate characters? Surely the New Testament gives us the answer. It is love. All-embracing and unconditional charity is God's work rather than ours, but there is something we can do, by God's grace, to facilitate its growth.

---

[19] See M. Casey, "Towards the Cistercian Millennium," *Tjurunga* 54 (1998) 57–67.

[20] See Simon Baron-Cohen, *The Essential Difference: The Truth about the Male and Female Brain* (New York: Basic Books, 2003).

[21] Aelred of Rievaulx, *Sermo* 1:34, CCCM 2a; p. 11.

EFFECTIVE AFFECTIVITY

A multitalented, multigeneration, multi-ethnic, gender-inclusive community cannot flourish in an affective desert. Differences are inherently too threatening to be long sustained without firm support. A community of clones is self-legitimating. The greater the differences the more individuals feel insecure and need assurance and affirmation. The rhetoric of the monastery as a *schola caritatis* is fine but its practice is not easy to sustain over several decades of personal development and change. It is even more difficult to inculcate its values in a communal lifestyle, especially one in which individualism is rife. Complex relationships can easily become the playground of unintegrated (and perhaps unrecognized) emotions, and so emotional literacy and skill in communication will be key factors in community development. Those entering the monasteries from dysfunctional and abusive backgrounds will come in search of healing from their affective wounds. They will instinctively choose communities that seem capable of meeting their needs, and they will stay only if their initial perception is confirmed by experience.

If Freud could say that a baby who is not loved will die, surely it is true that an unloving monasticism can scarcely expect to survive a single generation, much less several. Nobody in their right mind would commit themselves to a lifetime of lovelessness, no more than they would embrace a meaningless and absurd existence.[22] This being so, it would seem that, alongside its spiritual character, humanity and attractiveness will be key features in monasticism's survival. Increasingly there will be fewer feeder channels for potential recruits. Those who enter will do so as a personal decision, perhaps following an experience of grace, crisis, or conversion. For them the evident love of the members of the monastic community will be a lodestone that points to a more abundant life.

---

[22] "In everyone there sleeps / A sense of life lived according to love. / To some it means the difference they could make / By loving others, but across most it sweeps / As all they might have done had they been loved. / That nothing cures. An immense slackening ache, / As when, thawing, the rigid landscape weeps, / Spreads slowly through them"; Philip Larkin, "Faith Healing."

WORK OF GOD AND WORK OF HUMAN HANDS

There is a strong traditional element in all liturgy that is especially marked in monastic liturgy which owes less deference to popular trends than parish worship. This is not because monks are ineluctably conservative or antiquarian but because monastic liturgy services needs are different from those in the parishes and presupposes a considerably higher level of catechesis. The Liturgy of the Hours has been, especially in the West, an integral component of the monastic pursuit of continual prayer, a concrete way of spinning the web of prayer throughout the different activities of daily life. It is hard to see an integral monastic life continuing without the ongoing use of this essential means—or its replacement by some future alternative that works as well. On the other hand, decline in the importance assigned to the Liturgy of the Hours seems to me a surefire recipe for extinction.

Full liturgical participation demands a continual expenditure of time and energy; preparation is an additional task and for a community to be liturgically creative a great deal of leisure is required. Substantial time given to liturgy and to its supporting infrastructure means that monks and nuns will never be able to put in a full day's work. Granted the importance of recollection and mindfulness to the life of prayer, the most suitable kind of work will not necessarily be the most lucrative. Monks and nuns will have to live more meanly or rely more fully on the charity of benefactors. This will certainly be the case in a post-capitalist world where investments will no longer provide a base income. If social welfare structures collapse under the weight of an aging population, the much-appreciated fillip coming from pensions and other payments may also be lost.

While it is certainly true that "the association of possessions and virtues is usually not long-lasting,"[23] there are many cautionary examples in history that indicate a connection between economic decline and the loss of the monastic spirit. The ideal formulated by Benedict was that all that was necessary would be provided within the limits of sufficiency and moderation. When this cannot be achieved within the parameters of monastic

[23] *Exordium Cistercii* 1.

observance, discipline crumbles and deviations from the way set down by Benedict multiply. When economic survival dominates the thinking of superiors and decides the priorities in daily living the liturgy will inevitably suffer. Without firm and visionary leadership, an institution that permits too much distance from monastic sources begins to drift aimlessly and is in danger of losing a monastic specificity that alone makes continuing existence meaningful.

LEADERSHIP

Will there be monastic leaders who will take us boldly into a creative future? Monastic history assures us that the answer is by no means certain. Monasteries and monastic groupings rise and fall, depending on whether they are serving their purpose in the context of contemporary society and its spiritual aspirations. This means a certain sensitivity to what is happening in the world "outside" and a continual fine-tuning of means and observances to ensure that monastic objectives are realistically pursued. This is hard work. It is much easier to shore up the status quo and hope that somehow or other the future will look after itself. It is easy for a fervent and observant monastery to become denatured in the course of one or two generations. On the other hand monastic and Benedictine history yields a surprising number of charismatic reformers who have seen the deficiencies in the existing systems and have stepped into the breach to remedy them. And followers have flocked to be part of the enterprise.

Partly the magic depends on what some scornfully dismiss as "the vision thing." Yet the great tidal movements of history are not guided by managers but by leaders who are genuine visionaries and effective communicators.[24]

> Leaders aren't necessarily good managers, nor good managers leaders. Leaders stir; managers smoothe. Leaders explore odd directions; managers stick to the broad pathways of

---

[24] "I might as well confess that I think management is the art of taking credit for other people's work." Germaine Greer speaking at a seminar for female managers, quoted in *The Age*, 18 September 2004, News p. 5.

consensus. Leaders arouse passions, for and against and don't much care if they are unpopular; managers want peace and popularity. Leaders want to make life complicated; managers want good order. Leaders are aloof, restless and impatient; managers make people feel wanted.[25]

Great monastic leaders are less concerned with crisis-management and problem-solving. Maintaining the status quo is not an absolute priority. What is most important is fidelity to monasticism's fundamental purpose and responsiveness to the ferment in the hearts of those who are led by the Spirit. "Christ . . . is now at work in human hearts by the power of his Spirit."[26] True leadership in a Christian context means following the Spirit who speaks *often*, as St. Benedict notes, through the younger and less entrenched (RB 3:3). Those who will create monasticism's future will be those who do not seek to perpetuate particular aspects of its past. They will not attempt to control a phenomenon that has, for more than a millennium, demonstrated a good capability to look after its own survival.

> When you seek to control things, you must manage all of the pieces; you must know what is going on everywhere in the organization; you must have job descriptions; you must really have your hands on all these pieces because your function as a leader is to hold it all together . . . [But] order is inherent in living systems. It is part of what makes things work, with or without us . . . there is an order that can emerge. And the order is not from telling people what to do, defining it, writing procedures. The order is inherent, and we need to allow people enormous freedom with the understanding that the principles and the values will order their behaviour. As leaders we really should focus our attention not on how we define behaviour through policies, procedures, organizational designs, but on bedrock principles and values.[27]

---

[25] Jonty Driver, review of John Rae, *Delusions of Grandeur: A Headmaster's Life* (HarperCollins, London, 1993), *Times Literary Supplement* 1 May 1993, p. 23.

[26] *Gaudium et Spes*, 38.

[27] Meg Wheatley (interviewed) in T. Brown, "The New Science of Leadership," *Industry Week*, January 1993.

Monastic history is really the history of great leaders—men and women who have accurately perceived contemporary needs, who have had the practical wisdom and gumption to reshape monasticism to meet those needs, and who have the selflessness and skill to kindle a fire in others. The future of a real monasticism depends on our generation so nurturing the talent of those who come to us that they will be able to be creative for a future that we will not see. There is no point in trying to mastermind monasticism's progress—we simply have to trust that the charism has sufficient energy to reinvent itself age after age, remaining attached to the life-giving tradition yet interpreting it and applying it according to the providential signs of the times to come.

*   *   *

As I conclude these reflections in 2005, I wonder whether someone, somewhere in the galaxy, will be reading them somehow in 2105 or 3005. If so, I who am long dead salute you. I hope my feeble efforts at prediction will bring a smile at least, and I pray that monastic life, in whatever form it may exist, may do for you what it has done for me, and more.

THE SECRET INGREDIENT

by Kathleen Norris

"I DON'T CARE"

The most prophetic thing Thomas Merton ever did was to say to a Louisville shopkeeper who asked him what brand of toothpaste he preferred, "I don't care." Merton told the story in a series of retreats he gave to other monastics at the Abbey of Gethsemani during the 1960s, later collected and published as *The Springs of Contemplation.* On that day in Louisville, Merton was on his way to check into a hospital when an ordinary errand became something more significant. For Merton was both intrigued and troubled by the store clerk's response. "He almost dropped dead," he wrote. "I was supposed to feel strongly about Colgate or Pepsodent or Crest or something with five colors. And they all have a secret ingredient. But I didn't care about the secret ingredient." Realizing that he had revealed himself as an outsider in America, Merton concluded that "the worst thing you can do now is not care about these things."

Merton's lack of concern about his brand of toothpaste was surely grounded in his experience of monastic life, in which he was expected to use whatever grooming products were supplied to the community. It also reflects his daily immersion in the *Rule* of Benedict, and the psalms, which continually remind us what is worth caring about, and what is not. Now, some fifty years after Merton's quick, honest response to being asked to choose a toothpaste, we can name it as prophetic. There is scarcely any aspect of American life that is not touched by marketing, the more-or-less dark art of making us care about "the secret ingredient." It's good for the economy when we believe that it is reasonable, and even necessary, to invest much time and energy in discriminating between brands. Which cotton sheets have the highest thread count? Which vodka has the most exotic and alluring "back story"? Which spa offers the most luxurious pampering? While the worldly like to pretend that such things matter, and many prosper by fostering that illusion, the monastic's reply is, always has been, and ever shall be, a resounding, "I don't care."

This not-caring is important to hold onto these days, and still prophetic, because the ultimate goal of the marketer is to have us see consumer products not as mere things, but as keys to our identity. When we walk down the street not as ourselves, but as "Calvin," "Ralph," "Tommy," or "DKNY" we walk a bit taller, our clothes having signified that we are important persons. To question why we have relinquished our given names, and allowed our bodies to be used as free advertising, is to be a spoil-sport. To suggest that we have willingly embraced a form of slavery is to go way over the top, but that is exactly where we need to go. Brands are marks that owners put on their property, often by painful means, and we are in perilous territory when our self-image, and even our self-worth, is founded on which brands and labels we can afford to purchase and display.

Cautionary tales abound, surfacing for a moment before being swept away in the restless cultural sea. An urban teenager—white, black, brown, it does not matter—murders another for his desirable brand-name jacket or athletic shoes. A disgraced Enron executive—a husband and father—commits suicide in a fashionable suburb, sitting in his late-model Mercedes with a custom interior. To allow things to become mere things again, we might employ Merton's "I don't care" as a mantra when turning on a television or opening a magazine. We can also call on the monastic virtue of humility to remind us that advertising does not aim to reach our better selves, but our inner idiot. When marketing works as it is intended to, we become the thirteen-year-old who desperately wants to belong, and needs to believe that the use of this shampoo, deodorant, or carbonated beverage will make us popular, and ease our passage to happiness and true love. A Sears ad campaign (the military language is no accident) once promised: "The Good Life. At a Good Price. Guaranteed."

Now, more than ever in America, monasteries are important as places where people can find relief from propagandists and marketers. People can appear on the doorstep, as postulants or retreatants, seeking "the good life," and be received. Not "taken in," or sold a bill of goods, but given respite, time to think, and the silence that makes it all possible. In the *Springs of Contemplation* Merton reminds his monastic audience that "it is terribly important for us to be clear about our silence," and also to be clear about its prophetic value in a world of noise. "The tyranny of noise," Merton observes, "always has a will behind it," and, "There is a note of supreme injustice in noisemaking: the noise made by one person can compel another person to listen." He goes on to say that the monastery's "service to the world might simply be to keep a place where . . . people might be silent together. This is an immense service if only because it enables people to believe such a thing is still possible." Silence, as Merton understood it, is foundational to human freedom and psychological well-being. He also saw intentional silence as a necessary and valuable counterweight to society's thoughtless and excessive verbiage.

"TO SAY 'GOD IS LOVE' IS LIKE SAYING 'EAT WHEATIES'"

Thomas Merton understood that people need both silence and speech. "It isn't that words or preaching are bad," he said, "it's just that people don't want to hear any more words." Even in the 1960s, Merton recognized that the ever-increasing abundance of words coming at us by ever-increasing means was endangering the human capacity for listening. "All words have become alike," he laments, "they've all been reduced to the level of the commercial. To say 'God is love' is like saying, 'Eat Wheaties.'" That dread flattening out of speech that was emerging fifty years ago, when Merton first took note of it, has surely come to fruition in our time. Merton could still assert that "people know they are expected to look pious when God is mentioned, but not cereal," but we can no longer count even on that. Our cereals promise such an abundance of minerals, vitamins, and fiber that they might be presumed to help us live for ever. And expensive shoes, handbags, and jackets are now displayed in store windows as reverently as if they were religious icons. God, Gucci, Whatever.

When an advertisement appears at Christmas featuring a model holding a beaded evening bag that costs thousands of dollars, and the words, "Comfort and Joy," our capacity for devotion is being subverted.

What are monastic people to do in such a time? Well, the first thing is to keep offering places of refuge, places filled with the silence that Thomas Merton insists is the only thing that really speaks to people. Monasteries may be about the only places left in America that still proclaim silence prophetically, without apology or explanation, the only places in which people still undergo silence in such a way that they can reflect on why it makes them restless, uneasy, and even afraid. The liturgy of the monastery, which can become so routine and boring to the one who practices it, can be as refreshing as a drink of water to the world-weary visitor. To hear words in their proper context, surrounded by silence! To be among people who are not frightened of silence! I know from experience that as the silence of a monastery sinks into my bones, it illuminates the neglected parts of my soul, and reawakens my battered sense of hope and reverence. Even as this silence makes me uncomfortably aware of just how tired I am, it promises to restore my strength.

The ordinary, daily practice of silence, then, is a prophetic stance, and one of the greatest gifts that monasteries can offer today. And Benedictines seem aware of this. They take very seriously their call to be silent and listen. They often seem less aware of their corresponding call to take extreme care with the words they do employ. In this regard they tend to reflect the culture rather than stand apart from it, readily transposing trendy phrases from pop psychology or the corporate world into their spiritual expression. This is worth our consideration. When "oblates" become "associates," do they become merely business partners, or are they still "offerings"? And what about "servant leaders"? While that term has a rich theological foundation, its weakness as English is such that I doubt it can long withstand the cultural forces— either cruel parody or co-optation—that would subvert it.

Benedictines are not alone in their susceptibility to code language and jargon. Christians in general, in attempting to be more businesslike and professional, can be remarkably careless with words, thoughtlessly tossing the baby out with the bathwater. At a church conference the booklet containing an order of service, prayers, readings, and hymns is entitled "Worship Resources," implying that just plain "Worship" is no longer enough. And when churches do "outreach," we often find mission statements such as this: "The Open Door Community Center is a center for Christian witness and service. Although sponsored by (a church), The Center is open to all regardless of race, creed, or color, responding to their needs with multiple opportunities to enrich the whole person, enabling him/her to be a wholesome and contributing member of the fellowship of the Center, the family, and of the total community, 'Caring' is the key word—caring in the name of Christ."

It all sounds lovely, but I must interrupt the reverie to ask why this Emperor has no clothes. What does this establishment *do?* Whom does it serve? In all their sputtering, the authors have not told me. I wonder why they're so apologetic about being Christians—*although we're a church,* we're open to anyone. And offering "Christian witness and service" to "enable" people can be dangerous ground indeed, if it means that those who are not in need serve those who are. Whether consciously or not, I believe that this is exactly what is implied in this muddle of words. I also object to using "caring" as a key to anything—it's the weakest form of a verb that means, at its root, to cry out, and to lament. The authors of this document could use a dose of St. Paul, and the simple question he asks of the Corinthians (in 1 Cor 14:19): "If you give a blessing in words that no one understands, how is it a blessing"? St. Paul's answer to his own question is still a useful one. He writes, "In church I would rather speak five words with my mind, in order to instruct others also, than ten thousand words in a tongue."

As people who claim allegiance to the true Word, the Word made flesh, Christians need to be more wary of relying on the tongues and codes of the professional world to convey a religious message. And they need to absolutely refuse the temptation to doublespeak, which uses words to seemingly say one thing, but convey, or conceal another. A company calls itself "Natural Solutions" to hide the fact that it disposes of hazardous waste; a politician refers to an accident at a nuclear power plant as "an event." And here is an applicant for a pastoral position in a church: "I envision a process approach in which the whole system collaborates in generative interconnectivity. I hope to be part of context making the meaning, helping others articulate the vision and mission, and ultimately live beyond the projection of 'authority.'" Excuse me, but what does this language do *except* project authority, crowing, "I'm in command of these big, imposing words and you're not!" When I was asked to evaluate this candidate, I borrowed from the evangelical phrase book and said to the pastor that I didn't allow this sort of language in my home, and that it *really* offends me in church.

I credit my gut-level response to the abuse of language both to my vocation as a writer, and my vocation as a Benedictine oblate. I have always been attracted to the way in which Benedictines emphasize both listening, and its prerequisite, silence. This double-edged awareness is of great value and significance in an increasingly polarized American society, in which language is so routinely abused. Slogans and catchphrases reduce political discourse to the level of a playground fight between six-year-olds. Trendy jargon becomes a convenient way of establishing hierarchies of status, effectively shutting out those who are not "with it," not in on the game. Thomas Merton, with his hard-edged sense about language, has become a touchstone for me, and a guide. I believe he would agree that we need to send the slithering tones of "process approach" and "generative interconnectivity" back to the devil from whence they came. A refusal to employ such jargon is, it seems to me, as much a part of the prophetic nature of monastic life as silence and listening, and would be of service in a culture much damaged by the cynical manipulation of words. But it is a calling that is all too often overlooked.

LETTING GO OF PROPHECY, AND FINDING IT AGAIN

If the monastic vocation is truly prophetic, then beware. For prophecy is a snake in the grass: if it doesn't bite and poison us, it will startle us, and trip us up. Prophecy is like humility in that the minute you become conscious of it within yourself you lose the capacity for it. To be prophetic is to lose self-consciousness, and not embrace it. It is to recognize and refuse trends, no matter how noble the intentions behind them. A prominent "Nuclear-Free Zone" sign, displayed in the midst of a monastery's brick building, is not prophetic, but hopelessly static. To understand why this is so, we need to ask, "What is being said here?" If the sign is meant to convey that this monastic community allows no nuclear weapons on the premises, well, that is something we already knew.

We need to name this proclamation of a "Nuclear-Free Zone" honestly, as bad science. No place on earth is nuclear-free, and bricks especially pack a radioactive punch. My husband, on first encountering this sign, asked, "Do they know how funny this is?" And it was both funny and sad to him, to witness such a thing on a college campus where geology is taught. This might seem like nitpicking, but it's not. That sign suggested to my husband and me (and no doubt many others who have seen it) the triumph of ideology over truth. It suggested that the people living in this monastery had the luxury of not paying attention to the basic facts of life, including the harder truths about our natural environment. This, of course, is a charge that has been made against the monastic way of life from its earliest days—*these people aren't living in the real world*—and I am discouraged when monastics themselves contribute to the stereotype.

It is important to take a stand against the proliferation of nuclear weapons, and to take a stand for peace. But this inaccurate little sign can't carry the weight. So how is a person, or a community, to do this effectively, and even prophetically? Thomas Merton lamented that, "We have to face the fact that contemplative life as set up today is not only non-prophetic; it's anti-prophetic. It's designed to prevent any prophetic reaction at all." No doubt feeling the pressures put on him after the unforeseen success of *The Seven Storey Mountain,* he told his monastic audience, "Our task is not to produce prophetic individuals . . . but to be a prophetic community." And that, of course, is much easier said than done.

Humility helps, because it forces us to acknowledge that we ourselves can never know if we are being prophetic. Only future generations will be able to decide. This is a foundational spiritual wisdom. A self-proclaimed prophet is no prophet. The same holds true of mystics. Benedictines recognize that anyone who campaigns for the office of abbot or prioress can't be trusted with the job. And while a person may obtain any number of credentials in order to be certified as a spiritual director, one does not become a spiritual director until others are willing to say that you are, and entrust themselves to you.

There is so much that Benedictines cannot claim for themselves without sounding smug or self-satisfied. But that also is a part of their prophetic calling, for even as they live the Rule as best they can, they must rely on others, outsiders, to tell them how they're doing. At times, these outsiders will seem dense or over-critical, but they will sometimes offer unexpected affirmation and blessing. One middle-aged monk, after reading my chapter on celibacy in *The Cloister Walk,* commented that he had been struggling, unable to see celibacy as anything but boring and lifeless, but that I made it sound exciting again. I had done nothing more than tell a few stories offering my perspective on celibacy as a married woman, and revealing how I had come to believe that monastic celibacy, properly understood and lived in community, is inseparable from its hospitality. In a culture that so consistently degrades the beauty of human sexuality, the celibacy of Benedictines can be a radical and prophetic discipline.

Monastic celibacy fulfills the basic criteria for a prophetic vocation, as defined by Thomas Merton. "One of the central issues in the prophetic life," he asserts, "is that a person rocks the boat, not by telling slaves to be free, but by telling people who *think* they're free that they're slaves." When it comes to sex, we are certainly free to exploit it as a marketing tool. And compulsive users of pornography are free to prefer virtual sex to relationships with other people. And adolescents are free to dress like "hos" and "pimps," with little understanding of the extent to which their attire dehumanizes them and makes them vulnerable to abuse. We are so sexually free that we have turned the very act that gives us life into our most obscene and violent curse word. The monastic perspective, honed by the practice of celibacy, can name our sexual compulsions correctly, as slavery, and remind us that choice is not a virtue. Discernment is, and freedom means discerning and choosing what is good for ourselves and others.

True freedom always arises out of charity, out of being open to love and being loved. Only in the context of such freedom can people enjoy human sexuality as the divine gift it was meant to be.

ROCKING THE BOAT

That the word "freedom" has been gutted of much of its meaning is just fine with marketers and politicians, who use it as a selling point or a soporific. The manipulators of souls prefer freedom as an abstraction. But prophets such as Thomas Merton ask us to stop and think about what it means to be free. What kind of freedom is it, he asks, that allows us only to choose from among a variety of new and improved "secret ingredients"? What kind of freedom is it to be offered any number of fancy gizmos when selecting a new car, but not to be free to live without a car? Or a cell phone? Or internet service? As technology advances, the poor who must do without such things pay more: extra service fees, for example, for the privilege of writing a check and mailing it rather than paying bills online.

Monastic people are called to be prophets in the sense that they remind us what it means to be a free people who can enjoy a holy leisure. That is difficult, I know, and monastics can feel hypocritical on this score—I recall Timothy Joyce saying at an ABA convention that these days the true Benedictine motto seems to be "ora et labora, et labora, et labora." But monastics do know the value of restorative leisure. The fact that their horarium includes time for play, as well as prayer, *lectio*, meals, and work, reminds us that the sabbath rest was given by God to a free people. If it's only slaves who cannot observe a sabbath, what does that say about us, or the businesswoman I once heard describe her day as so frantic that she was "too busy even to go to the bathroom." How do we define ourselves as free in a workaholic society that pressures so many of its most productive, well-trained, and well-compensated people to be available 24/7? Do the cell phones, PDAs, and laptops come with invisible chains, marking us as slaves?

The usual prophetic suspects—not only monastics, but poets such as Wendell Berry—are asking good and necessary questions about the meaning of work, and what it means to be human in the world today. The monastic way of life remains a challenge to contemporary culture, as it is still what Thomas Merton called "a sign of contradiction" that reminding people of the freedoms they have so readily forfeited. Simply by living as they do, monastics take on the awesome idol of being "free" to earn more for the sake of earning more, epitomized in the remark of an Internet billionaire who came right out and said that his goal in life was to die with more toys than the next guy. The very existence—and persistence—of monastic people in America puts this absurdly capitalist goal in its place. It challenges the corporate world's cruel assumption that human beings have little value as employees, or even as shareholders, but only as consumers, preferably ones who are easily seduced by effective marketing techniques such as "branding."

In contemporary America people are effectively discarded once they are ill, unless they can afford private medical insurance. And when they become old, they simply cease to exist. This of course does not happen in monasteries, because Benedict insists that the ill and the old be listened to and cared for with particular attention. In that "of course," and in this particular foundation of Benedictine life, lies a wealth of prophetic power. How is it that monastic community life so insistently continues on into old age? And isn't this a prophetic stance in a culture that routinely tolerates the abandonment of the elderly? A few years ago, in Chicago, many of the aged who died in a catastrophic heat wave had so little connection with the outside world that they could not be identified as having families, or communities of faith. They were buried anonymously, in a mass grave. In a society that accepts this as the natural result of being old and poor, the Benedictine way of life is resoundingly Other.

A LITTLE RULE, FOR BEGINNERS

I suspect that the prophetic aspects of monastic life are mostly to be found in that which is overlooked, or which seems insignificant. Take, for instance, the fact that in a monastery everyone is equally famous, or infamous, as the case may be. In a culture that is increasingly obsessed with celebrity, this signifies something radically different: how can it be that all persons are of equal value and importance? I once took a monk to a book publication party in New York City, and what struck him the most was the way some people looked past each other as they were conversing, casing the room to see if there were someone more important they might be talking to. As a Benedictine my friend found this both comical and pathetic, the antithesis of hospitality, and of monastic listening. When guests come to the monastery, they are all to be "received as Christ," with attention given to them according to their need, and not their status in the world. As far as I know, no monastery provides one retreatant's lounge for the *hoi polloi,* and another for VIPs. These days, to insist that people are on an equal footing is to be both counter-cultural and prophetic.

Monastic people, without much apparent effort on their part, often allow me glimpses into another, better, and more prophetic way of being in this world. Many years ago, I accompanied a monk to a shopping mall because he'd asked me to help find a special birthday card for his mother. Our path took us near a major department store, and I said something like—"I want to go in there, but I know I shouldn't, but I do love their shoe department." His simple question, "Why expose yourself to temptation?" stopped me in my tracks, and has been of use to me ever since, even if I often recall it in the breach.

Sometimes I think that the only cure for consumerism is a dose of monastic formation. I have noted in my sister-in-law, a former Episcopal nun, that her long-ago formation still defines her. When she began working as a stockbroker, she needed business attire, but hated shopping. Giving her gift certificates didn't help, because months later she'd need to be reminded to use them. My family was then living in a three-generation household, and my mother hit on a solution. Periodically, she would go through my sister-in-law's closet, remove any clothing that was worn beyond repair, and replace it with items she had purchased. Most of the time, my sister-in-law would dress in the morning without noticing that she was wearing a new skirt, or shirt, or blazer. This, like the monk's question about temptation, is a sign to me, a question, and a challenge. And the best way to answer it is by re-forming myself, by adopting my own "little rule." If I buy something new, it is to replace something I can no longer use. If it might be of use to someone else, it goes to charity. Even children can learn this rule. One six-year-old friend knows that acquiring a new toy means giving up an old one. Her mother tells me that the road to acceptance has been rocky, but now the girl insists on accompanying her to the homeless shelter with her outgrown clothes and the toys she has selected to give away.

THE SECRET INGREDIENT—REVEALED

As one who has so often been on the receiving end of Benedictine hospitality, I have no qualms about naming it as prophetic, a quiet but potent "speaking out" of God's word and will. For me, visiting a monastery is the ultimate in luxury travel, and the joke is that the communities don't have to do anything out of the ordinary to provide it. These days, in a booming market for affluent travelers, resorts compete to offer the most unique and exclusive experiences. A Waikiki hotel recently hired a fashion designer to remodel an oceanfront suite that rents for as much as $5,500 a night. Demand for the room is strong, and I suspect that for that price a kind of hospitality is provided: a staff that calls you by name, if you prefer, and brings fresh flowers, or a teddy bear for your child. But it can't compare to the hand-lettered "Welcome, Kathleen" sign, penned by an arthritic hand, that I find on a monastery's guest room door. It can't hold a candle to the radical hospitality that is offered free of charge, with no expectation of return. The prophetic nature of hospitality is one of those things that monastic people themselves can't see, as they scurry to find clean sheets and towels for an unexpected visitor. But in my experience, hospitality is the one thing most commented on by a monastery's guests, and is most often cited as a reason they want to return. Benedictines are formed in hospitality, and it shows.

Increasingly, as retreat centers provide necessary income to monasteries—often the lion's share of the income for communities in remote rural settings—monastics will need to be especially deliberate and intentional in their hospitality. Spirituality, like everything else in America, is easily co-opted and commodified, made into just another product to be consumed. I can pay good money for advice on the prayer method that best suits my needs, be it centering prayer, angel-channeling, or getting in touch with my past lives (or just that old, familiar inner idiot). Catalogs and shops carry items intended to promote spiritual well-being, and people have been known to pray over such things as finding the right color scheme and carpet, the right pillows, candles, images, and incense, as they seek to create the perfect meditation space. People do have a great need to establish private spaces in a crowded and threatening world, a phenomenon that marketers term "cocooning." And monastics are well-suited to help people put this need into perspective.

Monastics are on the front lines here, and I trust that they will be resolute about refusing to allow spiritual practice, which traditionally has been aimed at sharpening our awareness of the legitimate needs of the world, into becoming just another layer of insulation from it. They will do well to continue to welcome people as they are, and listen well as retreatants let go of the frustrations they feel in trying to gain a better hold on faith. But monastics are called, I believe, to resist the teaching of prayer as mere "technique." Instead, they must reveal it as a way of life. Somewhere, in every retreat house—not over the entrance, as it might be deemed inhospitable—but over an exit, as a reminder of the challenges facing the retreatant who is returning to everyday life, a notice might be posted, a quotation from a character in Graham Greene's novel, *A Burnt-Out Case:* "People have prayed in prisons, in slums, and in concentration camps. It's only the middle classes who demand to pray in suitable surroundings." Proclaiming this truth would not violate Benedictine hospitality, but could offer the visitor the fresh breeze of humility, and deeper insight into the prophetic nature of prayer.

In a tired and despairing world, prayer itself is prophetic. It summons hope, it insists on hope, and is yet content to seem to many like a hopeless, useless mumbling. Love, of course, is the secret ingredient that makes prayer possible, and gives it potency and strength. The love of God, of the neighbor, and the self, is the only "secret ingredient" worth caring about. Life is too short, and too valuable, for anything less.

THOUGHTS ON THE FUTURE OF WESTERN MONASTICISM

by Terrence Kardong, OSB

AUTOBIOGRAPHICAL PREAMBLE

When I was asked to contribute a paper to this collection of essays on the future of monasticism, I was quite hesitant to do so. Normally, I cheerfully accept invitations to contribute talks and papers on monasticism, because those challenges stimulate me to do things that I might not get done on my own. Moreover, I usually don't have much difficulty organizing my ideas and getting them down on paper. I tend to finish these projects well ahead of time—sometimes years ahead.

But this particular topic is in a different category. I have spent much of the present summer thinking about it, and an equal amount of time putting it off. Maybe for the first time in my life, I am finding out what a talented procrastinator I can be. There is always another letter to be written, another book to be reviewed, and if all else fails, well, the filing system needs to be weeded. In addition, I have spent a good deal of time asking myself why this topic is so hard for me to address.

Some of the reasons are not too hard to find. Since I am basically a researcher on ancient Western (Latin) monasticism, I spend most of my time looking backwards. Of course, I try to do so in order to make sense of the present, but I rarely venture beyond that into the future. There is a good deal of comfort and satisfaction in dealing with the past, since it does not require of us any decisions or commitments. But it can also be a trap that robs us of the courage, or even the ability, to face the future. We need to understand the past in order to cope better with the future, but in no sense is the past a blueprint for the future.

As the editor of a major monastic journal *(The American Benedictine Review)* I have observed this same dynamic at work throughout the monastic world. Our understanding of the monastic past becomes richer and richer, while our vision of the monastic future becomes murkier. Compared to fifty years ago, we are much better informed on the history and literature of Western monasticism. But fewer and fewer writers concern themselves with the monastic future. This does not mean that they are not *thinking* about it, but they certainly are not writing about it.

It was not always this way. When I think of my own case, once upon a time I thought I could see what the monastic future would be. I remember writing little essays on what needed to be done. I even started a file folder labeled "The ideal monastery." I wrote a letter to Merton (which he even answered). Of course it was idealism, but what is youth for, if not for idealism? Besides, my own youth just happened to coincide with the "youth of the world." That is to say, I was a young man in the 1960s, a time when a lot of people were eager for a new order. It was a time when one was not afraid to dream dreams.

Now, of course, I am much older and no longer find myself thinking so much about the monastic ideal. Part of that is natural. Aging has a way of stripping a person of illusions. One has seen too many ideals and idealists crash and burn. Besides, dreaming takes a lot of energy, and there is not too much of that commodity left over when one has accomplished one's daily work. Still, it is not an entirely comforting thought that one has ceased to have visions for the future. There is always that nagging line from the Bible: "When vision ceases, the people perish" (Prov 29:18).

But this is not just a matter of personal history. The fact is that 2005 is a very different time than 1965 for monasteries. A tremendous amount of cultural and spiritual change has intervened, and we find ourselves in a very different place. In 1965, we were riding high. Almost all monastic communities were bursting with energy. Novitiates were full; new physical plants were being built to accommodate our numbers. The liturgy was being renovated, theology was suddenly exhilarating, and everything seemed possible. Like the rest of the Church, we were full of fervor and enthusiasm for the new future that Vatican II seemed to promise.

I remember a conversation I had with my brother about that time. He is five years younger than I, and he was also a young monk in our monastery. He came to me one day and said that things had to change. He then proceeded to tick off a whole laundry list of monastic ideas and practices that he felt were obsolete. And he added that these things needed to be changed very quickly. My reply was that I agreed with him about every single point, but that it would take about ten years for such a transformation. I assured him it was coming, but he said he could not wait. So he left.

Perhaps the reader expects me to report that things did not change and that is why we are in the shape we are now in. But in fact, things *did* change; within less than ten years most of the necessary changes were accomplished. So at least I can report that there was a time in the distant past when I really *did know* what was needed. Maybe it was just obvious and everybody else saw the same problems. But this leaves us with a further question, and it is truly disconcerting. If we got what we wanted, then how come things are not better? Is this just another proof of the old cliché, "The only thing worse than not getting what you want—is getting what you want"?

Probably it is not necessary to spend too much time detailing how "things are not better." Most of the problem comes down to recruitment. By and large, people are no longer joining our monasteries. My own congregation, the largest in the Benedictine male world, has about half as many members as it had in 1965. Given the demographic laws, it is going to get much smaller, and it will not take too long. Granted, a St. Bernard and his whole family could show up at the door tomorrow and turn this trend around. But overall, the monastic world is shrinking.

Someone may interject that not all monasteries are shrinking. In the developing world, there is no lack of novices. A few years ago I spoke to a whole roomful of African novices (over 50) in one convent, and there were that many on the waiting list. In reply, one can only say that the social conditions in those places are very different from our own. For a multitude of reasons, monastic life still appears attractive to many people in the developing world, while it is much less so in our own society. This is a given we must work with, not something we can change.

Someone else may add that it appears that the monasteries that have changed least are getting the most novices. To judge from the few cases I know, that is apparently true, but it could well be that these monasteries are simply flourishing in a "niche." That is to say, there are a certain number of people out there who are looking for a very traditional form of monastic life. They are not much interested in adapting to the times; they want something timeless. Still, it is hard to see how this could be the future of the *whole* monastic body.

At any rate, it is easy enough to see why I have become somewhat chary of monastic visions and especially of future projections. The future that I hoped for actually has come to pass, and it hasn't prospered. How wrong can you be? Let me get more specific.

The local situation that I faced in 1965 was a common one for Benedictines. I was completely immersed in our school. It was work that I loved, but there was one problem: it left little or no time for monastic life. As a teacher and prefect of teenage boys, all my time was consumed in serving their needs. As the school grew larger, and the standards rose higher, I found myself almost completely absorbed by the apostolate. To me, it was very apparent that the school was the tail wagging the monastic dog.

This situation was not at all unusual for American religious. From their very immigration in the 19th century, almost all the religious Orders were invited into the dioceses of this country to serve the Catholic people. This was an adolescent nation, and the needs of the Church were enormous. Given the ghetto mentality of the Church at this time, great emphasis was placed on Catholic schools. If the Benedictines were willing to operate them, they were welcome. Besides that, there was a real need for Benedictine pastors and also for Benedictine hospitals. Beyond that, there was not much interest in the particular monastic charism of Benedictine monks and nuns.

Yet my reading of church history, and especially American church history, suggested to me that this situation would not continue indefinitely. Eventually, the state would take over the schools and the hospitals, and the diocesan clergy would take over the parishes. Then where would we be? With our vague, shaky understanding of our particular monastic charism, we would be "out of a job," as it were. Things have not worked out quite that way, but I still think that my analysis (which is by no means original with me) was accurate.

What has come to pass is not that different from the above scenario. Many of our schools and hospitals have already closed, not because the state or secular forces have taken them over, but simply because we have run out of monastic personnel to operate them. Some of these institutions still bear Benedictine names, and the lay personnel make brave efforts to understand the Benedictine ethos, but without nuns and monks, they are no longer truly Benedictine institutions. As for the parishes, the bishops will employ almost any monk who can still remember his own name.

Rather than continue on an autographical note, let me try to address the specific questions that were asked in the original prospectus for this book.

WHAT ARE THE PROSPECTS OF SURVIVAL FOR MONASTICISM IN THE WEST?

This is a painful question, isn't it? Who would have even thought of asking it fifty years ago? And yet it is not a particularly unhistorical or ridiculous question. There has never been a time in the history of the Catholic Church when there was no monasticism. True, Christian asceticism was not highly organized before the fourth century, nor did it seek remote places to dwell. But there have always been monks in the Church. Indeed, they are such an intrinsically important part of the Eastern (Greek, Syrian, Coptic) Church that Catholic life there is almost unthinkable without monasteries.

That, however, is not quite the case in the Western Church. For one thing, there is something about the West that is just not as contemplative as the East. And that means that there is often less comprehension of the meaning of monasticism in the Latin Church. In the East, in places like Athos (Greece) and the Wadi

Natrun (Egypt), you still find the common people flocking to the monasteries. They seem to think that the monks are a special locus of the divine. To talk to a monk, even to touch a monk, is sure to bring blessings. Whether this is good for the monks is beside the point. In the East, people still know what monks are.

In the West, it is not necessarily so. True, monastic guest-houses are fuller than ever, but it is not always clear why people go there. Of course they are looking for quiet and order and peace, and they usually find it there. But there are all kinds of other retreats that offer those things, and they are not monastic. As long as the West remains marked by the Enlightenment and the Industrial Revolution, we should not expect its incomprehension of monks to improve much. In a sense, this is good for monks because it forces us to try and try again to explain our monastic ethos to the public. But it is not an easy thing to do when it clashes so violently with the prevailing culture.

Will monasticism survive in the West? The numbers are no comfort, since they seem to tend toward the zero point. Nor should we assume that the extinction of monasticism in the West (or anywhere else) is unthinkable. For one thing, Napoleon came within an ace of closing down all the monasteries in Europe in the period just after the French Revolution. Of course, there will be some fire under the ashes. The Russian Communists closed down most of the monasteries, but they have begun to spring up again since 1989. So the present Western malaise in recruitment, which is not caused by any obvious governmental interference, nor by famine or plague, but simply by changing social and religious aspirations, may be unprecedented, but it is not unthinkable.

Maybe it is worthwhile to ask ourselves whether the demise of monasticism would be contrary to the mind of God. It is easy to get confused on this point, since, at least to a certain mentality, there are so many wonderful aspects to monasticism. What would we do without all the great spiritual writings, the fabulous monastic architecture and art, the cultural enrichment generated by monasteries? But that in itself does not mean that God wants monasticism to survive. The Church, yes. "The gates of hell will not prevail against it." But monasticism? There have been whole zones and eras of Christianity that have flourished very well without monks and nuns. We have to admit that. We should not get taken in by our own rhetoric. We are dispensable.

Someone might say that I have not answered this question. I don't believe that a yes or no answer would be of much use. Sometimes all one can do with a question is to try to sharpen it. If we can properly situate the question, we move toward an answer.

WHAT COULD THE CHURCH AND THE WORLD EXPECT FROM AN AUTHENTIC MONASTIC WITNESS DURING THE 21ST CENTURY?

This question could be construed in many ways, but I will take it to mean something like this: What do people expect from us nowadays? Let me first ask a counter-question. Why should we care? There is a whole branch of pop psychology that seems to be devoted to the proposition that we should not care a fig what people expect from us. There is that saying from Fritz Perls that you sometimes see on little plaques on people's desks: "I am not in this world for you; you are not in this world for me." The idea is that we have to decide for ourselves what is important, what is worth living for. So, too, we monks have to decide what will be an authentic witness for the 21st century.

Let me rush to say that I do not believe this in any absolute way. In fact, we are placed in the world with other people and we derive a good deal of our meaning from them. Even though *monos* means alone, monastic life is not solipsistic. The monk does not authenticate himself in any absolute way. "Monk" is a universally recognized cultural/religious archetype, and one either conforms to that template or one is not a monk. Further-more, a Catholic nun or monk is first of all a member of the universal Church, and only secondarily a monastic person. We have to care what the Church expects of us.

Having said that, I would also contend that no one knows better than the monks themselves what their witness should be. Consequently, it is quite possible that monks or nuns could be asked by this or that bishop to perform a role that they should not accept. We spoke earlier about the historical fact that the

Benedictines were pressed into active apostolic service as soon as they came to this country. Actually, this process had begun even earlier in the Austro-Hungarian Empire where the monasteries were disbanded unless they ran schools or parishes. Perhaps the Benedictines had no choice in those situations; it was either do what the state or the church asked, or cease to exist.

Yet there can be circumstances where monks may have to refuse to meet the expectations of society. Obviously, that may make some people unhappy. It may even make our own development office, if we have one, unhappy. It is hard to keep everybody happy all the time. In a country like ours where public relations are deemed so important in all aspects of life, we may find ourselves thinking in patterns that are not necessarily compatible with monasticism. One of St. Benedict's aphorisms on this issue reads like this: "You should become a stranger to the world's ways" (RB 4.20). Not much about p.r. in that verse! But rather than discussing the expectations of others as an independent question, let me do so in connection with what I think we have to offer the 21st century.

WHAT IS YOUR MONASTIC VISION AND HOW DO YOU THINK THE MONASTIC CHARISM SHOULD BE INCARNATED IN THE NEW MILLENNIUM?

Under this rubric I will talk about what I perceive to be some of the main issues before us as monastic persons at this time.

Community

Let me tackle the hardest question first. To put it bluntly, I think community is the toughest problem we have to deal with today. I assume here that community is essential to the Benedictine vocation. It is true that the Rule of Benedict makes provision for hermit-monks, but I am not qualified to discuss that vocation. At any rate, the essential Benedictine ethos is cenobitic, which refers to community life. Benedict defines cenobites as "those who live in monasteries and serve under a Rule and an abbot" (RB 1.2).

I do not want to spend time arguing here whether a monk or nun must always live in a monastery. Nor do I want to talk about the Rule or the abbot. I want to deal with the simple phenomenon of people living together in community. A quick perusal of Benedict's Rule shows that he understands Benedictine life as a life in common. Indeed, he does not even provide people with private rooms, and one is astonished by the apparent fact that people in the Rule are together virtually all the time. No doubt some of that was a product of the sixth century itself, since monks and nuns did have private cells before that time, and also in later centuries.

To the person coming to the novitiate today, such a prospect is utterly foreign. People come to the monastery today from a background of extreme privacy. Often they have maintained their own apartment, owned their own car, plus all kinds of appurtenances that enable a person to live independently. But it was not so very long ago that many religious, or at least those in formation, lived in dormitories without much apparent discomfort. Clearly, life has become increasingly privatized in our time. Part of this no doubt comes from modern affluence. The richer a society becomes, the more privacy it provides.

It seems significant that Western society, or at least American society, has moved so far from what it was at the time of Vatican II. The 1960s and 1970s were a period when there was an explosion of communal experiments. Indeed, never since the 1840s had the nation seen so much communitarian idealism and so many communes. True, most of these efforts ended soon after they started, but at least people must have been experiencing an intense yearning for human solidarity.

Today one hears very little talk like that. No doubt there are still some communal experiments, but nobody seems interested in them. The focus now seems to be on the self, not the social body. Individualism seems to be the dominant thrust of our society, so much so that the famous book, *Habits of the Heart*, which lays bare the American psyche in such a revealing fashion, is essentially a study of extreme individualism. We are not the first society with this characteristic—the Plains Indians were also highly individualistic. But it is doubtful whether this trait has ever progressed further in human history than it has among us.

It is not only secular society that has become less and less communitarian. The same holds true for our monasteries. Of course, we should not expect those coming to us to teach us basic things like community, but when something like community is utterly foreign to them, it will impact us very much. Granted, community means different things to different people. A monk once told me that "No one is a monk of X unless he comes to recreation!" But another monk told me that his monastery, a very respectable one, has no recreation period at all.

In my observation, it is precisely the communal dimension of our life that is hardest for newcomers to handle. Most of them are quite pious, so they do not find our schedule of elaborate liturgy much of a burden. In fact, they often urge us to introduce new devotions like public recitation of the rosary. But we also find them piously meditating in church when they should be participating in recreation. Granted, our recreation conversations and games are sometimes quite raucous and nothing that would edify the more delicate sort of soul. Nevertheless, living the common life means that one presents one's body at various times at events that one does not particularly relish.

Someone will point out that formal exercises like recreation do not necessarily guarantee a genuine community life. I would be the first to agree with that. They are largely symbolic of a whole world of behavior and attitudes that promote human mutuality. Certainly, the essence of Christian communal life is willingness to serve one another. And the deepest way to do that is to open oneself to others in a spirit of transparency and trust. The monastery is not just another apartment house where you hardly ever speak to your neighbors. It is not a boarding house for ultra-private persons. It is a good framework for authentic Christian community.

Celibacy

Another area where a healthy monastery has something to offer the contemporary church and the world lies in the practice of celibacy. Of course, this is a highly controversial subject in current Catholic life, and many people feel that the Church is making a serious mistake by requiring celibacy of everybody it ordains. But there is no controversy about the celibacy of monks and nuns. Celibacy is of our very essence. There is no such thing as a married monk or nun. When married people claim they are really "monastic," they are simply contributing to the confusion already surrounding celibacy.

Some priests now insist that they only accepted the yoke of celibacy as a rider to the priesthood because there was no other way to get ordained. That is an unfortunate situation, but no monastic person can say the same. The vow of celibacy is at the core of her or his vocation. Indeed, it is the most personal of the vows, since nothing is closer to our selves than our personal sexuality. Those who claim, mistakenly, that Benedictines really do not vow celibacy, but obedience, stability, and *conversatio morum* are misinformed. In fact, anyone who does not promise celibacy is simply not a monk.

Celibacy is not just a discipline for us. It is by no means just a rider that we accept in order to be accepted into the monastic community. Celibacy is an ancient name for our personal relation to Jesus, to God himself. We may not understand our own feelings fully when we enter monastic life, but if we mature as monks and nuns, we will arrive at a place where we can truly say that there is no room in our lives for a spouse because of our relation to the Lord. That does not mean that a spouse makes married folk more distant from God. It just means that a monastic celibate feels unable to marry.

This certainly does not mean that spouse and children are something that we find unattractive. Of course, not all of us yearn for such a life, but there are times when most monastics are acutely aware that they have indeed given something up. They have also avoided a peck of trouble, but they know very well that they are missing a primary human experience that is in some way irreplaceable. Yet no one can live more than one life, and the life of one called to Christian celibacy is a full one. To be a happy celibate is to live without regrets.

By now we are well aware that celibacy does not mean living without relationships. No one lives without human bonds, no matter how chaste or virginal they are. Far from being merely a question of genital activity, relationality is a basic human component to the extent that we can say that the more successful the celibate is, the better developed her or his relationality. There are many corollaries to this, but one is simply this: fear of sexuality is no motivation for celibacy. And where fear and hostility to the other sex are what drives a celibate, then the whole vocation is called into question.

If there is one thing that can be said about the tone of our present Western culture, it is "pan-sexual." Whereas the Victorian Age specialized in hushing up everything to do with sex, we today seem determined to explore the subject at every possible opportunity. It is now almost impossible to turn on the television without seeing erotically explicit material. Our vocabulary is now laced with suggestive terms, even when we have no intention of discussing sexuality. Perhaps due to the influence of Freud, we now seem to agree that sex is the most important subject for the human psyche.

Like it or not, this is the atmosphere in which celibates now live. To say that it is not very supportive of our vocation is a blatant understatement. It is hard to imagine a more negative atmosphere in which to practice monastic chastity. Still, the thing is not impossible, and in fact there are some good aspects of the present climate. Since sex is no longer swept under the rug as a topic, it is necessary for all of us to come to terms with it. There is no more place to run and hide. If our celibacy is not a flight from sexuality, we need to be able to deal with it matter-of-factly.

This does not mean that we go looking for compromising situations, but it does mean that we become solid enough in our personal celibate commitment that every slightest breeze of sexual innuendo will not blow us over. If we really have a vocation to be celibate, then we will not be easily threatened. Furthermore, a grownup approach to sex will teach us that, contrary to what Hollywood and Madison Avenue suggest, sex is only a small part of a healthy human life. It does one good to hear married people tell us that. Our own monastic witness to celibacy should also proclaim (quietly) to the world that sex is not such a "big deal."

But of course in some ways it *is* a big deal, as the Catholic Church has found out to her intense chagrin. The whole world is now well aware that some Catholic celibates have not been able to live up to their calling. And in fact some of them have violated their vows and violated innocent people in outrageous fashion. One might say that those who have promised to live a life of extraordinary sexual purity have sometimes not been able to maintain even an ordinary, healthy relational life. It is a case of "the corruption of the best is the worst."

In a sense, the Church has caused some of its present problems by her own obsession with sexuality. For whatever reasons, the Church has allowed its moral vision to become narrowed down to the sixth commandment. Those who studied the old moral theology remember the principle that when it comes to sexuality, there is "no parvity of matter." That means that all sexual sins are mortal. Not many confessors still accept that principle, if they ever did, but it has had the effect of playing right into the modern over-fascination with sex.

In this atmosphere, it seems to me that monastic celibates can contribute a calming influence on the Church. You don't hear celibacy discussed too much in the monastery because we take it for granted. Therefore, when the Church finds itself convulsed over sexual issues such as abortion, single-sex marriage, and so forth, monastic celibates need to remind people that there are also other issues of some importance. Anybody who reads the New Testament and the Church Fathers regularly, as monks are supposed to do, knows that they say far less about sexuality than about feeding the hungry, clothing the naked, and turning the other cheek to our enemies.

Even though St. Benedict says little about celibacy, he says a great deal about humility. Therefore, when monastic celibates talk about their own sexuality, it behooves them to do so with humility. We should admit that we don't understand our own sexuality very well, and we certainly don't know much about the sexuality of married people. A fitting modesty in this regard would be a salutary witness to the official Catholic Church, which has never had any hesitancy about telling people how to conduct their sex lives. The present crisis of priestly celibacy might be a good time to tone down our rhetoric in this regard.

Lectio Divina

This subheading may not be immediately intelligible to non-monastics. And who can blame them, since the term was hardly ever heard among monks until about 25 years ago. It appears in the Rule of Benedict (RB 48.4), but even there it is not particularly lucid. In arranging the daily timetable of his monastery, the author leaves about three hours a day for *lectio divina*. But exactly what the monks are to do with all that time, he does not say. He leaves indirect clues, but he never spells out the exact content of the term.

Granted, the words have a commonplace meaning: holy reading, divine reading, reading from God. Therefore, it has something to do with perusing books, and probably *the* Book, namely, Scripture. The traditional translation "spiritual reading" is not useless, but it hardly conveys what actually went on during *lectio divina* in ancient monasteries. Very likely, this time was partially spent memorizing the words of the Bible, so as to stock the memory with material for "meditation." One could then "ruminate" the biblical verses, no matter where one was.

Lectio divina was also a time for learning biblical texts to be used in the Divine Office. Benedict tells the monks to use the time between Vigils and Lauds for this purpose. The scarcity of books in those times made it necessary for people to know the texts by heart. In contrast to our own book-glutted society, people in those days relied mostly on their prodigious memories for most spiritual purposes. Obviously, a person who knows considerable Scripture by heart is much better prepared for the Christian spiritual life than someone with no biblical memory.

But *lectio divina* did not fare very well in later monastic history. Actually, it *never* was easy for monks, as is obvious from RB 48.17-21, which warns monks not to fritter away this period of the day. Clearly, it was hard for some of them and the problem was not laziness but rather a form of *acedia* or spiritual boredom. Today we would call them "hyperactive." Later on in monastic history monks filled in the time for *lectio* with more work or more liturgy. Rarely did they ask for more time for *lectio*.

What has this esoteric discussion got to do with modern monks or nuns? We are no better than our ancestors at *lectio*, and yet we need it at least as much as they did. Of course, our psyches are somewhat differently wired than were theirs. Now we have plenty of books, but we have proportionately smaller memories. This is inevitable, for people only memorize what they need to possess. Most do not memorize for pleasure and never did. But we are not therefore incapable of *lectio divina*. We can engage the Scriptures just as fruitfully as they ever did; we now have private rooms, multiple Bible translations, and many other helps for this task.

But my point in this section is not to teach people to do classical *lectio*. I would contend that *lectio* must be biblically based, but I doubt if Benedict would have excluded the commentaries of Church Fathers or other solidly scriptural books on the spiritual life. I think Benedict would be delighted by Heschel or Brueggemann! But he would *not* be so impressed by some other things that now pass for *lectio*. I do not think he would be too happy with those who watch videos or listen to CDs for their *lectio*. But I may be wrong.

This is a huge topic and a very difficult one for monks. A particularly tough question for monasteries right now concerns the media. What do we do about television and the internet? Some monasteries solve this matter quickly and easily: they exclude all such electronic contacts with the world. Other monasteries, such as my own, allow the brothers to find out for themselves what is good and bad about these things. Such experiential learning is probably more solid than mere prohibitions, but there are casualties along the way. There are awful things on the internet, and some monks have succumbed to them. Their lives have been virtually ruined.

The mass media has a legitimate function in our society and it can also be of use to monastics. Certainly it can serve as a valuable medium for the communication of the fine arts. And it can offer a decent form of relaxation for tired minds. My point here is that it should not become a virtual way of life for Benedictines. Our profession commits us to *lectio divina*, which is a very different form of spiritual and intellectual life.

I am well aware that not everyone will agree with this, but I am convinced that it is not possible to be a happy monastic without solid reading habits. Actually, I am not even sure we should be accepting people into our monasteries who have an aversion to reading. Anthropologists have pointed out that celibacy rarely appears in nonliterate societies. Can we conclude that celibacy cannot flourish in monasteries where reading is languishing? This whole question becomes more difficult as the electronic media become more and more prevalent. Recent research shows that young people who spend time with video games are not less intelligent than those who read. But what *kind* of intelligence do video games promote? Problem solving, which is quite different from a contemplative outlook toward the world.

The nicest thing I think I ever heard about monastic *lectio* came from a lady in a parish where the pastors were monks. She said that she considered herself privileged, even spoiled, by the presence of the monks. Every time they climb up in the pulpit, she said, you can expect to hear something thoughtful, something nourishing. You can just tell that they are reading serious stuff and pondering it over. What better advertisement for *lectio divina?*

CONCLUSION

And so it is time to end this essay. For a fellow who was reluctant to start, I almost had trouble ending. I could have mentioned many other ways in which monasticism could be of help to a century that seems to have little use for it. If I seem a bit pessimistic, I am unrepentant. Some of this is temperamental, some of it is situational. After all, I have been somewhat disappointed in my past hopes for the monastic enterprise. As I admitted, *my* plans have largely come true, but they have not turned out to be what many other people want—or perhaps what God wants!

Still, it would be rash to conclude that monasticism has nothing more to offer the Church or the world. Its history during the last two millennia indicates something quite different. And there is always the possibility that the problem is not with the institution itself, but with its practitioners. In other words, as Chesterton said of Christianity, it is not that monasticism has been tried and found wanting. It has just not been sufficiently tried. Therefore, to the monks and nuns of the world, I say, "Let's try it and find out!"

MONASTICISM AS A SCHOLA: SOME REFLECTIONS FROM THE IVORY TOWER

by Lawrence S. Cunningham

INTRODUCTION

As Christians we say, in obedience to the words he himself gave us, that Jesus Christ is the Way. The earliest description for those who followed Jesus Christ was that they were Followers of the Way.[1] Nonetheless, as the subsequent history of Christianity clearly demonstrates, there are many ways of following the way of Christ; in other words, there are many ways of joining the One who says "I am the Way." Every Christian, in a sense, responds to the gospel invitation to follow Christ and, in that response, assimilates the way of Christ according to his or her age, education, state in life, disposition, personality, and cultural condition. This diversity in the following of Christ is so true as to be almost a truism.

In the long history of the Christian tradition there have been certain moments in which a person or a group of persons have so discovered a way of being Christian that they not only found that way satisfactory but have served as a point of reference or a template for others in subsequent ages to emulate their insight into the Gospel life. In a classic work written a generation ago Gustavo Gutierrez provided a plot line for understanding such a development. He set out three stages:

---

[1] See: Acts 9:2; 18:26; 19:9ff.; 22:4; 14:22.

1. Someone (or a community) has a powerful experience of the Way of Jesus;

2. Those (and others) reflect theologically on the experience to formulate a general paradigm to explain the experience(s) and, in the process, seek to emulate that experience and, as it were, codify it. Such reflections are a second-level appropriation of the originating experiences;

3. The fruits of those experiences and the reflections on them becoming a tradition are then offered to the believing community, which then become one of many spiritualities that come down through the centuries and "continually serve as appropriate ways of following Jesus."[2]

The trajectory described by Gutierrez when it becomes a recognizable way of life found in the tradition can be described as a "school of spirituality." Hence, it has become and remains common in the Catholic tradition to speak of "schools of spirituality." "Schools" can stand generically as a pedagogical reality and "spirituality" is to be understood as living in the Spirit after the manner of Christ (see: Rom 8:9-17). A school has certain defining characteristics that would include the following main features:

In the first place, schools of spirituality privilege certain texts from sacred scripture. They dwell on a "canon within a canon." It is not that they reject the rest of scripture, but a given school tends to focus on those texts from which they draw special nourishment as the school attempts to perform and shape their following of the Way of Jesus.

Second, every school of spirituality develops a certain pedagogy of prayer which becomes characteristic of that school. Persons who learn from that school are initiated into its way of prayer in various ways. Thus, to cite a conspicuous example, those who follow the Ignatian school "make" the Spiritual Exercises of Saint Ignatius of Loyola under the guidance of a director to be initiated into that form of prayer and then themselves remake

---

[2] Gustavo Gutierrez, *We Drink From Our Own Wells: The Spiritual Journey of a People* (Maryknoll, NY: Orbis, 1984) 53.

the Exercises over time and may have the charism of guiding others into the Exercises.

Third, each school of spirituality articulates the charism of the school which then gives shape to the school as a whole. The "canon within a canon" and the pedagogy of prayer is in service to the guiding charism of the school whether it be to serve the poor in the name of the poor Christ (Franciscan) or to hand on to others the things already contemplated in study (Dominican), etc.

Fourth, each school has as its final *telos* not acquisition of mere intellectual sympathy for the teaching of the school but, rather, deep religious experience of conversion, religious zeal, identification with Christ, awareness of the indwelling of the Trinity, etc.[3] The monastic writer Cassian, for example, says that the practices of monasticism are only proximate; the goal of life is to achieve "purity of heart" for in that purity, as Jesus says in the Beatitudes, we will see God. Hence, the *telos* is not an idea or cluster of ideas but authentic religious experience.

There is one final aspect to be noted when considering the concept of schools of spirituality. In a recent intense study of the character of schools of spirituality, Kees Waaijman has correctly noted that schools are born within specific cultural matrices. The originating intuition which gave a particular school its original impetus remains alive in that cultural matrix as long as there is no blockage which prevents the original source experience from flourishing and remaining open to the future. When such a blockage occurs it becomes necessary for a reforming element to enter or the school ossifies and loses its significance. Historical examples of such reform impulses are not difficult to find in the Jewish-Christian tradition; they are as ancient as the deuteronomic reform in the Old Testament (or the rise of Pharisaism for that matter) and as modern as the *devotio moderna* which was a reaction against a certain common static externalism of late medieval piety with the *devotio moderna* (or better: its remnants) reformed by the scriptural and liturgical renewal of our own day. Most

---

[3] On the nexus between the term "school" and "spirituality," see: Lawrence S. Cunningham and Keith Egan, *Christian Spirituality: Themes from the Tradition* (New York: Paulist, 1996) 5–28.

commonly, such reforms in our own age have taken the form of *ressourcement*.[4]

THE MONASTIC SCHOOL

If there is any stream within the Christian tradition that deserves to be called a "school" it is the monastic tradition. Indeed, the prologue to the Rule of Benedict adopts the word itself in a justly famous formulation: "We intend to establish a school for the Lord's service" (Prologue 45). As many commentators have pointed out, that simple phrase captures the core intention of the prologue and, by extension, of the entire rule.[5] School, in Benedict's sense of the term, meant the community who came together for the "common purpose specified by the Rule: to seek God, to imitate Christ, to obey his commands, to persevere in his teaching."[6]

The history of monasticism is a long and complex one whose development is outside the purview of this essay. Nor is it pertinent to set monasticism into the template outlined above to describe the notion of a school of spirituality. Suffice it to say for our purposes that monasticism arose in the Church as a "way" of being Christian and has existed since its inception as one fruitful way of living out the Christian life. It is a hallmark of both Catholic and Orthodox Christian life, not for everyone but as one way to be a Christian in the world. For our purposes it will suffice to mark out some of its salient characteristics as well as indicate ways in which it has enriched Christian life both in the past and, it will be argued, for the future.

While the popular stereotype of monasticism usually involves imagining a hooded figure gliding down a cloister walk while Gregorian chant plays softly in the background, the fact is that monasticism is a complex historical phenomenon with contemporary monasticism only the end product of a long historical

---

[4] The full story can be found in Kees Waaijman, *Spirituality: Forms, Foundations, Methods* (Brussels: Peeters, 2002) 116–211.

[5] See the commentary on Prologue 45 in *The Rule of Saint Benedict*, ed. Timothy Fry (Collegeville: Liturgical Press, 1981) 165.

[6] Fry: 365.

process in which many layers of monastic experience have been distilled into the current picture. As I pointed out in another work, when Thomas Merton entered the Abbey of Our Lady of Gethsemani in 1941 he entered a milieu which had been shaped by a seventeenth-century reform (La Trappe) of a twelfth-century monastic movement (Cistercian) which was a re-visioning of a late antique monastic vision (Rule of Benedict) which was based on earlier models acknowledged in the Rule of Benedict itself. Merton's abbey, on top of those many layers, also was shaped by the paraliturgical piety of the Catholic Reformation of the sixteenth century.[7] Such accretions, of course, are common enough in the Catholic tradition. The eucharistic liturgy described by Justin Martyr in the second century is fundamentally structured like the Tridentine Mass of the sixteenth century, but the accidental accretions, additions, and emendations are conspicuous.

Despite the complex evolution of monasticism in the West, one can still detect constants which distinguish monastic life from other ways of being a Christian. These constants may be enumerated in different configurations but most would agree with the following:

Countercultural community: Monasticism arose as an alternative way of living from the majority culture in order to seek purity of heart which, as the Gospel says, frees one to see God.

Sharing of Goods: If there is any foundational text for monasticism it is the insistence in performing the sharing of goods reflected in the Acts of the Apostles where personal possession and acquisition is abandoned in favor of nonpossession.

Communal Prayer: It is a given that the common recitation of the psalter is a hallmark of monastic prayer.

Life under a Superior: Freely chosen familial living under a superior (and Abba/Amma).

Chastity/Celibacy: A life committed to sexual liberation and the free decision not to marry.

---

[7] Lawrence S. Cunningham, *Thomas Merton and the Monastic Vision* (Grand Rapids: Eerdmans, 1999) 19–21.

Work: Monasticism has put a premium on work with the hands as both a way to support the community and as a strategy for maintaining a simplicity of life.

Asceticism: A certain askesis with respect to food, drink, clothing, ambition, nonaffluence, etc. not as an end in itself but as a means towards the greater end of following Christ in order to achieve that purity of heart which He holds out as the way to see God.

To be sure, others might well indicate other characteristics of the monastic life[8] but the ones cited above are surely representative. They are not discrete items; rather, the ones cited above interpenetrate in a symbiotic fashion. Asceticism, for example, is implicated in the willingness to work without personal reward while such work is also crucial for the well-being of the community which, in turn, only functions ideally when the community lives harmoniously under a superior. Similarly, work is not to be conceived as an end in itself; the asceticism which undergirds work makes it possible for that leisure *(otium)* required to permit one to live a life of prayer and work itself.

Monasticism is not only a school of spirituality rooted in a countercultural impulse but also, as a consequence of its countercultural impulse, reflects both a prophetic and an eschatological message. To be a monk is to exercise a critical judgment about the relative value of ends more highly prized in society: status, acquisition, power, self-promotion, self-enhancement, rugged individualism, and so on. Similarly, the monastic school points to the "not yet" of the *Eschaton*. It is not without interest to note that monks rise before dawn to pray at a service called "Vigils" —monks are watchers and the watcher lives in anticipation of what will or may transpire: "My soul waits for the Lord more than sentinels wait for the dawn / More than sentinels wait for the dawn, let Israel wait for the Lord" (Ps 130:6-7a).

Shaped in the monastic school of spirituality allows the monastery and its living community to be a seedbed from which

---

[8] See the lists in Michael Casey's *Strangers to the City: Reflections on the Beliefs and Values of the Rule of Saint Benedict* (Brewster, MA: Paraclete Press, 2005) 179–80.

diverse gifts come for the building up of the church.[9] Historically monks have done this by their hospitality, by their spiritual direction; by missionary activities, scholarships, the founding of schools, pharmacies, hospices, scholarship, the ministry of hospitality, and other forms of outreach as cultural conditions so required. Most of all, monasteries, especially those whose primary *telos* is the contemplative life, have acted as a prophetic sign and as a reminder of the fundamental Christian theme that God is manifested in Christ and it is as Christ that all are called to live.

Obviously, not everyone is called to be a monk but, obedient to the point we made at the beginning of this essay, it is one way of Christian living and if that way were not present certain insights of the Gospel would be lost. As Aidan Kavanaugh so well put it nearly a generation ago: "A Christian need not be a monk or nun, but every monk and nun is a crucial sort of Christian, and there have been too many of these people over the centuries for their witness not to have considerable theological importance."[10] Indeed, it could be argued that what distinguished both Catholicism and Orthodoxy from the Reformation is its continuing interest in and exaltation of monasticism as a valid manifestation of the apostolic nature of the Christian Gospel.[11]

MONKS AND THE CHURCH

The New Testament word *ekklesia* which we ordinarily translate as "church" more correctly means an assembly or a congregation. That is the meaning of the word every time Paul uses it in his letters. Paul often enough distinguishes the assembly *(ekklesia)* from the place where it assembles *(oikos – house)* just as Benedict will distinguish the place *(monasterium)* from the community that

---

[9] Speaking of the monastic life Vatican II says that monastics "should so adapt themselves to the present-day needs of souls that monasteries will, as it were, be seedbeds *(seminaria)* of growth for the Christian people." *Perfectae Caritatis* #9.

[10] Aidan Kavanaugh, *On Liturgical Theology* (Washington, DC: Pueblo, 1983) 7.

[11] Recent monastic communities like Taize, Grandchamps, etc. are an indication that at least some elements of the Reformation see that clearly. The increasing numbers of Protestants who come for retreats, etc. at monasteries is another indication but which cannot be pursued in depth in this paper.

dwells within it *(congregatio)*.[12] The monastic tradition has never hesitated to use the word in that profound sense. Saint Bernard of Clairvaux often refers to his monastery as a church—the church at Clairvaux. Similarly, it was common enough for solitaries to call their hermitages a "little church" *(ecclesiola)*. When we think of monasteries today it might be helpful to think of them as little assemblies who are part of the vast skein which makes up what the Fathers called the "Great Church" or the "Catholic Church."

Monastic life, then, has a profoundly important ecclesiological value in that it models not only a certain way for a Christian to follow the Way but it also reflects a certain separate way of being "church." Monastic life attests to the pluriform character of Catholicism not only as a spiritual path but as an alternative enfleshment of Christian community. However, like every local congregation *(ekklesia)* its richness and fullness comes because it is part of a skein of communities which make up the whole. To be a local church is not to be sensitive to and ready for service to that greater whole. That is what Paul had in mind in his enduring metaphor of a body; not only is the body organically constituted as a whole but each part, through that organicity, affects the whole (see: 1 Cor 12:12-16).

This rapid excursus into ecclesiology is prelude to an important point which points in two directions: from the monastic community to the larger church and, conversely, from the larger church to the monastic community.

Even though the monastic community is self-contained as a community it is not and cannot be self-isolating; it is also part of the Great Church. It has an obligation to share its gifts with the entire church according to its own discernment and with respect to the integrity of its own charism as was made clear at Vatican II: "While preserving, therefore, the nature of their own institution they should renovate their ancient holy traditions and should so adapt them to the present day needs of souls that monasteries will, as it were, be seedbeds of growth for the Christian

---

[12] "As often as anything important is to be done in the monastery *(in monasterio)* the abbot shall call the entire community *(congregationem)* together . . ." RB 3.1.

people."[13] How, and by what modality, that renovation is to be done is not amenable to a general law but particular to each monastic family. Monastic communities with which I am familiar have taken the Council's charge seriously and have sought ways to serve the church (often through thinking boldly about how to imagine the traditional monastic characteristic of hospitality in expanded ways) creatively while observing fidelity to the essence (and not merely the epiphenomena) of the monastic school.

From the perspective of the larger church vis-à-vis the monastic presence it seems clear that here the church has the obligation (and opportunity) to be a listening church to learn what the monastic school can contribute to its spiritual and temporal betterment as well as to the larger world. In fact, it seems that over the last century or so the church has been enriched greatly from what it has learned from the monastic school. It is not hard to adduce evidence. The contemporary liturgical renewal would be unthinkable without the pioneering work originating from monastic centers like Mont Cesar in Belgium; Maria Laach in Germany; Solesmes in France; Saint John's Abbey in the United States. That work, of course, has nineteenth-century roots again in largely monastic circles (e.g., Beuron or Solesmes). The enrichment of Catholic spirituality both before and after the Council has benefitted by the writings of monastic authors who reflected the deep liturgical and biblical roots that shaped their own lives (Columba Marmion, Hubert von Zeller, Eugene Boylan, Thomas Merton, et al). In the period after the Council the intense dialogue between Christian monastics and other religious traditions (especially the Buddhist tradition) has been an ongoing and fruitful enterprise. Finally, it is crucial to remember that many Christians who are heirs of the Reformation have mined the monastic tradition for elements of the Christian life which monastics have always treasured but which have been latent in the Reform.[14]

---

[13] *Perfectae Caritatis* #9.

[14] Monastic contributions to the visual arts and architecture are well covered in Kevin Seasoltz's *Senses of the Sacred: Theological Foundations of Christian Art and Architecture* (New York: Continuum, 2005); for the contemporary scene, see especially 289–342 on monastic architecture.

MONASTIC AFFILIATION

Since religious life is one way to be a Christian it is obvious that not everyone is called to that life. Nonetheless there is an ancient and honorable tradition of people who choose, either informally or formally, with the aims of the religious life. Under the charismatic influence of Francis of Assisi, for example, many people were tempted to leave their state of life and follow in the example of the Lesser Brothers. Some of them were bound to family or as an integral part of their society so to forestall an impromptu enthusiasm for a life of mendicancy. Francis argued that people should stay where they were and learn from the Gospel values of the friars and apply them to their own state of life. We even possess two versions of an exhortation that Francis wrote to "the faithful" encouraging them to a life of penance and a strict observance of the mandates and stipulations proposed at the reforming council of Lateran IV. It was from this proposal that arose the so-called "third order" of secular Franciscans.[15]

This practice of affiliation is widespread today. There are "third order" affiliates of many different religious communities. Many laypeople join as oblates of Benedictine monasteries and, more recently, the Cistercians have developed "associates" under the aegis of specific monasteries.[16] Many religious congregations of both men and women encourage associates who join in their apostolic work. Such affiliations are not designed to create monastic "wannabees" but to allow laypeople to learn and assimilate some of the characteristic practices of the monastic school such as *lectio*, simplicity of life, the use of the psalter, and so on. Each school of spirituality, as we noted in the beginning of this essay, has a characteristic pedagogy and it is through oblate and association programs that the pedagogy moves out to a world wider than that of the monastic community itself. In so doing, the

[15] Both the "Earlier Exhortation" and the "Later Exhortation" may be found in volume one of *Saint Francis of Assisi: Early documents*, ed. by Regis Armstrong et al (Hyde Park, NY: New City Press, 1999) 41–51.

[16] Dom Bernardo Olivera, the current Father General of the Cistercians of the Strict Observance, has devoted a number of reflections on these associates; they may be found in his *The Search for God: Conferences, Letters and Homilies* CS 1999 (Kalamazoo: Cistercian Publications, 2002).

church is enriched and made more catholic in that it universalizes spiritual values which are part of the tradition and makes them available as a gift to the wider church. In that way monks are faithful to their own vocation, but their lives and their witness carries with it a "surplus of meaning" which becomes a resource for those who are not *ex professo* canonical members of a monastic community.

It is not necessary, of course, to formally affiliate with a monastic community as an associate or an oblate in order to learn from and make present in one's life some of the lessons that come from monasticism. Writers as diverse as Paul Evdokimov (Russian Orthodox), Esther de Waal (Anglican), and Kathleen Norris (Presbyterian)—to name just a conspicuous few—have written lovingly of their own assimilation of monastic values into their own lives while highlighting the ways in which others may be encouraged to do the same. In some conferences given to religious women a few years ago Protestant exegete and theologian Bonnie Thurston noted that the traditional three vows of poverty, chastity, and obedience should be seen in terms of the ends for which they are intended. When thus envisioned they teach every Christian crucial lessons for living. Poverty is oriented towards detachment which helps us understand how to live in a consumer-driven society, just as chastity is oriented towards *caritas* which should undergird the whole of life while obedience demands the most radical countercultural value of all: to take ourselves off center stage to point to "something other than ourselves."[17] One, of course, can multiply those transformations of monastic values and some of them bear lessons that are crucial for our times. It has always been my contention that what made Thomas Merton into such a powerful witness to his age and ours is precisely the ways in which he could mediate monastic values to a larger world on topics as diverse as monastic peace and the contemplative root of human life.

---

[17] Bonnie Thurston, *Religious Vows, The Sermon on the Mount, and Christian Living* (Collegeville: Liturgical Press, 2006) 3. I quote from the galleys of this forthcoming volume.

A PERSONAL REFLECTION

I am not a monk and have never been one although my interest in monasticism has been long and abiding. Speaking to monastic communities has been part of my "ministry" as an educator and, as such, has brought me into close contact with various communities. I have been honored to spend time with the wonderful community of Trappistine Sisters in Arizona (and, through them the Benedictines in Tucson) over the past years and I have looked forward to my stays with the Benedictine community at Saint John's University in Collegeville, Minnesota, where I have taught in their summer school program. Perhaps my most natural monastic "home" has been thanks to the hospitality afforded me at the Abbey of Gethsemani in Kentucky on my frequent visits there.

Chaucer says of his scholar that he "would gladly learn and gladly teach." Even though I sometimes "teach" in a monastic setting, I have been more of a learner than a teacher. Looking back over the learning experiences afforded me by my monastic sojourns, certain lessons have been paramount in that education.[18]

First, monasticism privileges the priority of listening as the opening word of the prologue to the *Rule of Benedict* insists. To listen deeply is the first step on the contemplative way since in order to listen one must erase the static, the noise, the gabble of the ephemeral, and the vagrant in order to hear the Silence which is God—that silence which rests beneath all of our human striving. Slowly it has dawned on me to be attentive to what really stands behind my professional work and study, and teaching, and writing—namely that More which is God. It has taken me a long time to grasp fully what Thomas Merton so brilliantly describes in the opening pages of *New Seeds of Contemplation*, namely, that "contemplation is more than a consideration of abstract truths about God, more than affective meditation on the things we believe. It is awakening, enlightenment, and the amazing

---

[18] I elaborate here thoughts I wrote a generation ago in "The Life of Thomas Merton as Paradigm: The View of Academe," in *The Message of Thomas Merton*, ed. Patrick Hart (Kalamazoo: Cistercian Publications, 1981) 154–65.

intuitive grasp by which love gains certitude of God's creative and dynamic intervention in our daily life."[19] Without the education in the contemplative life afforded me by my contact with monastic sources my life as a teacher and scholar could have easily become merely "professional" and devoid of any spiritual depth.

Second, monasticism values tradition precisely because it is the *regular* life. The term "regular" means life under a rule (Latin: *regula*). Monastic life tests itself constantly against this criterion: is this monastic community faithful to the spirit of the Rule to which it binds itself? Such fidelity requires that those who aspire to the life must learn to understand the Rule, absorb it into their life, and exhibit it in their way of living.

There is an analogy between this understanding of the monastic way of life and life in the university. The university is, in the first place, a stable community, a *universitas*, whose aim is study and the initiation of others into the life of study. To be an authentic professor is not only to bind oneself to the way of study but, simultaneously, to uphold the *universitas* and to initiate others into it. If there is one thing that has helped me to understand my life as a professor while, at the same time, giving me an ideal to strive for it is that to undertake the vocation (I do not hesitate to use that word) of a teacher-scholar one must somehow combine the pursuit of study in a community which nourishes that aim not only for me as an individual but as one who has a responsibility to those who wish to enter that community. It is for that reason that I have always treasured the Dominican motto of *contemplata aliis tradere*—to hand on to others the things contemplated. Further, such an understanding of my profession, aided by my links to monastic life, has made me aware of how true the title of Dom Jean Leclercq's classic study of monastic learning is: "The love of learning and the desire for God."[20]

In the past year I had the opportunity to spend some days with the monastic community of Bose in Northern Italy. A young

[19] Thomas Merton, *New Seeds of Contemplation* (New York: New Directions, 1962) 5.
[20] Jean Leclercq, *The Love of Learning and the Desire for God* (New York: Fordham, 1961).

community now in its fourth decade, it is a mixed lay community of about seventy men and women who focus on the life of prayer and study. Not yet canonically recognized as a new order (they operate under canon law with the full approval of their bishop) they have accepted in their community some members who come from the Reformed Church and part of the year they offer hospitality to a retired Greek Orthodox bishop. Their outreach is devoted to the encouragement of biblical study and the practice of *lectio*. In some ways their monastic practice is very ancient with its emphasis on the praying of the psalms, work, and contemplative withdrawal. On the other hand they are "new" in their ecumenical character, their mixed community of men and women, and their essentially lay character.

What they taught me in the short period I spent with them, beyond the traditional values of prayer and hospitality, is that the monastic life can, like the good householder, draw forth "old things and new." They are living out a vision of the church in the monastic mode which draws from the wellsprings of tradition as well as utilizing the energies made possible by the reforms after the Second Vatican Council. The fact that they draw thousands every year to their retreats and conferences and the fact that they have had great success in attracting members (the average age of the community is about forty) testifies to the perennial vigor of the monastic charism. They are a laboratory example of the latent forces within monasticism.[21]

Bose is only one of a number of experiments in monasticism today. Some of the experiments will fail while others may be a harbinger of things to come. What all have in common is a sense that the ancient tradition of monasticism contains tried insights into that way of life. At the same time, so as not to merely turn monasticism into a museum piece, those insights must be lived in the particularities of time and culture.

Finally, to repeat the distinction between means and ends already noted by Cassian, monasticism, in both its traditional and experimental forms, has taught me that the one thing neces-

---

[21] The fullest account that I know of about the community of Bose is Mario Torcivia's *Il segno di Bose* (Casale Monferrato: PIEMME, 2003). Dom Andre Louf has a beautiful preface to this book. There is nothing comparable in English.

sary—the *unum necessarium*—is to find my way back to that Source from which I first came. By anchoring myself in an interwoven life of prayer and work and leisure and living in a social community (all those activities fundamental to monastic life) it has been possible to integrate my life into one which has made me dimly aware that there is a *telos* to existence which is that yet undiscovered land towards which everyone is drawn. If my life has not in any sense been a monastic one it has been monastics, nonetheless, who have been my fellow travelers and, not infrequently, my guides. As a consequence, I say, using a phrase sometimes attributed to Saint Thomas More: what the world needs is more housing for the poor and more monks.

OLD VISION FOR A NEW AGE

by Joan Chittister, OSB

The story of Monte Cassino and its Coat of Arms touches every Benedictine heart. *"Successa Virescit,"*—Cut down, it ever grows again—we remind ourselves interminably: *Successa Virescit* as the novitiates empty. *Successa Virescit* as monasteries merge. *Successa Virescit* as the number of members everywhere shrivels to half the volume of the last 30 years. *Successa Virescit* we say as the world changes around us and we change very little at all.

Clearly the question we need to ask is whether, in our complacent assurance of eternal institutional life, we are living in myth or in reality. Reality, if we are willing to face it, can teach us things about growth. Myth, on the other hand, if we take it literally rather than seriously, may simply drive us, like lemmings on the way to the sea, to our own destruction.

The point is not whether or not monasticism is renewable. Hundreds of years of history tell us that it is. It is obviously not unreal, then, to expect a monastery to be able to negotiate change as well as multiple other social institutions around it do. The point is whether or not we are willing to renew it. The number of now-extinct communities tells us that to expect renewal without being willing to pay its price is sheer myth.

The question of renewal is, in other words, not philosophical alone. It is psychological as well. To change an institution in which we have been formed, of which we have no other image, requires more than fidelity; it requires the emotional maturity and the living faith to believe that the vision that spawned it lives on even after the structures which expressed it are in need of replacement.

We search everywhere for the kind of answers that can possibly explain the present moment to ourselves in ways that make future directions clear as well. Why the loss of membership? Why the apparent loss of public interest in an institution that has, over and over again, been its mainstay, its *avant-garde* in a shifting universe of change? It is Benedictines who honed the educational system, saved the manuscripts of Europe, created a hospice system for travelers, developed a welfare system for the poor, were the judges, the teachers, the agronomists of the time. And they did all of it out of a vision shaped daily, hourly, by the call of the prophets and the image of Jesus. So what can possibly be the problem?

We have some favorite shibboleths to explain our own situation, of course. It's not that the answers we give ourselves are not plausible. It is simply that they are not as defensible as they may appear at first glance.

In a highly secularized world, religion has lost its impact, we say. But religion has never been more prominent in world culture than it is right now. In fact, religious fundamentalists from the center of the United States to the center of the globe are fighting fierce culture wars to save the soul of the system as they see it.

The world breeds materialism, we say, and families no longer encourage their young into altruistic or low-paying vocations. But the Peace Corps, the Greens, international aid programs, and social volunteerism attract young people by the thousands. The truth is that the one great life choice to which young people are not giving their lives is religious life.

It's just a bad period, we say. We just need to go on doing what we've always done until this period is over and things will be normal again. But this "period" is already almost 50 years in the making and not only are the signs of growth not getting better, they are, by and large, getting worse. Nor do we ask what "normal" is supposed to be for those who claim to be following the Jesus who walked from Galilee to Jerusalem curing the sick, raising the dead, feeding the hungry.

The image of ostriches comes far too readily to mind.

One thing we seldom do is to look for the answer to the present situation in ourselves rather than in the world around us. What is it, in a lifestyle we love, that fails to communicate itself to the world around it?

Or does it?

The fact is that people young and old, married and un-married, flock to our monasteries even now, even yet. They come for retreats, for programs, for prayer, and for community projects. They help us in our works, contribute to our existence, join our activities, and revere our elderly. But they do not come to stay. Clearly the purpose of the monastic lifestyle as lifestyle simply does not appeal to them, lacks meaning to them, fails to engage them in the great human enterprise of the spiritual life. What they hear when they get to our monasteries does not magnetize them, does not keep them, does not draw them into the effort itself. It does not excite their hearts enough to make staying worthwhile. But it is only purpose now, not the old self-aggrandizement of salvation, not the fear of hell, that can possibly enthrall them.

The situation reeks of the most frustrating kind of simplicity: Monasticism is obviously in transition. Some, if numbers mean anything, would say declining, in fact. Over 1500 years of history, however, gives no small witness to the fact that monasticism is a hardy but flexible institution that has weathered age after age. Other major lifestyle forms, both secular and religious, have disappeared forever in even less amount of time—the Knights Templar, the Shakers, the feudal system, Puritanism among them—but not Benedictine monasticism.

If any group ought to be able to translate from one moment in history to another, then, surely monasticism would seem likely to be one of them. Even more convincing, perhaps, is that, with the exception of Judaism, for which family life is taken to a divine mandate, every major religious tradition—Hinduism, Buddhism, and Islam—has nurtured the image of the single-minded seeker of the divine for whom communal life was an important part of the search. Serious researchers even presume that as human beings we are as wired for religion as we are wired for language, in which case it is, it seems, part of the human condition for some people to give their lives to the search for the ultimate in life.

Add to that the stirrings of religious revival generated by a world at war in the last century and it is not surprising to see that Benedictine monasticism which had withered under the antireligious, anti-Catholic movements of 19th-century Europe flowered again in the 20th. Monasteries grew in membership.

More than 250 foundations took root in areas outside the Western world. Schools and colleges everywhere flourished.

What seemed like a new flowering of monasticism did not last 500–1000 years this time, however. Nothing does anymore. Communication is too continual; ferment is too persistent; change is too constant. Now, it is stability of purpose, not stability of systems that counts as the world shifts around us. And shift it did.

By the mid-twentieth century, the whole world was embroiled in an even more impacting kind of social cataclysm. Technology, social mobility, feminism, globalism, scientific advancement at unheard-of rates, space travel, individualism, the sexual revolution, and an ecumenical council that opened the church itself to critical reevaluation turned the world and its long-standing assumptions upside down.

It was a time of unparalleled newness. The convergence of science, democracy, social consciousness, technology, and theologies of liberation swept away just as many systems in their wake as the world up to now had taken for granted. With them went all the social absolutes upon which the whole Western system had been based: that women were secondary creatures, for instance, that people of color were less than fully human, that nation states were inviolable, that the U.S.–European West was the center of the universe, that Catholicism was the only major religion on earth.

New ways of living and being alive, new ways of relating to one another, new horizons in the face of the breakdown of bygone boundaries unleashed new social systems and led to the reexamination of old ones. The new world began to eclipse the past, to bring it into question, to smother it. Only the memories of those who yearned for the older, more stable, more secure, less challenging world preserved it. Only the memories—and in their midst—the questions that emerged in the shadow of them: What was monasticism really supposed to be?

It was the beginning of a new moment in time, not all of it good but all of it powerful. The 20th century was a crossover point in history at least as major as the rise of nationalism in the 13th century, the discovery of the New World in the 15th century, the religious reformation in the 16th century, the scientific revolution of the 17th century, and the democratic revolutions of the 18th century.

Every major institution felt the shock waves of it all: marriage, government, economics, and, of course, religion.

God, in a period of quantum physics and space travel, became an idea to be clung to passionately or an idol to be destroyed. God was not dead; God was irrelevant—a state far worse than the first.

Women discovered their abilities and claimed their personhood as moral agents, as full members of the human race, as shapers of every dimension of it. White men discovered their limitations and strained to understand what it means to be simply equal members of the human race, not definers of it. Couples struggled to discover new ways of being together that did not depend on the invisibility of one for the sake of the other.

Young people—both young men and young women—had a world to explore. Gone were the days of limited roles and narrow options. New possibilities opened for them from one end of the globe to another. Women could be pilots; men could be nurses; women could be executives; men could be stay-at-home-husbands. Options became the name of the game.

Science had a world to create, animals to clone, birth to alter, life and death to reconfigure. The clash of consciousness that such meteoric and total reinterpretations of what had, for generations, been seen as immutable human processes might create for society as a whole never entered the picture. What Marshall MacCluhan had once named "culture shock"—the inability of a group to absorb the meaning of rapid change—became a commonplace of the human condition.

Business had a world to rape and ravage for its own profit, whatever cost to anyone anywhere, and in the doing of it, changed the lives of peoples and villages and countries from one end of the globe to the next.

Technology had at its fingertips now a whole world to connect and engage in great common questions, in new global works. Satellite towers went up in Peoria and Peru, in Kentucky and Kenya, in Appalachia and Afghanistan. Technology made international voyeurs of us all. We could no longer plead that we didn't know, didn't see, didn't have anything to do with the poverty, the oppression, the impossible life situations which our lifestyle had imposed on others. The "world village" had come home to us all with a vengeance. None of us were innocent anymore.

This was not the world of Benedict of Nursia. Or anything close to it.

And yet in the world of Benedict of Nursia there is surely a model, a vision, of what must be done to exist in a world such as this one. The Benedictinism that stabilized Europe, that gave a center to its villages and a spiritual glue to its systems, has never been needed more.

The problem is that those of us who now carry the ideals of the last century into this one straddle both of those worlds. We have one foot in a formation model that was local, agrarian, and hierarchical. We have the other foot in a global, urban, technological, science-centered democratic world in flux.

The question with which such a situation faces us as we try to foresee the future of monasticism, to recommit ourselves to its lasting vision, is a major one, a fundamental one, a dangerous one. And it is all the more dangerous because the question is so basic and the answer is so simple. What becomes of monasticism in such a shifting universe, now and in the immediate future, depends on how this generation understands the essential purpose and nature of monasticism itself?

It is not how we pass judgment on the nature and character of the world around us that will determine whether or not monasticism can once again be a vital force in a world that often confuses the practice of religion with the soul of religion. It is how we see ourselves functioning in that world that will make the difference.

The question that confronts our time is very much the question that confronted Benedict himself. What exactly does it mean to be religious in this world now? What does it mean to be "contemplative"? What exactly is "the contemplative life"?

The answer to those questions, and the vision of monasticism that develops out of it, depends on whether or not contemplation is described as an active or a passive dimension of the spiritual life.

If we understand contemplation to be the energy that drives us out of ourselves, into the mind of God, and from there into a world waiting for the Word, we will have one vision of the monastic life.

If, on the other hand, we define contemplation as the magnet that draws us away from the questions of this life, into space unsullied by "the world," we will have another perspective on monasticism.

Whichever we choose—immersion or distance, transcendence or transformation, incarnation or intellection—will determine the nature of the communities in which we live.

History has not always benefited the discussion. The tendency over time has been to make the terms "contemplative" and "cloister" synonymous—as if place were the determining factor in the making of a contemplative, as if Jesus was not a "contemplative," as if all of us are not called to be "contemplative." As a result, where we did what we did came to be more important than what we did and who we cared for and what we said and to whom we said it. In fact, it circumscribed life to the point that there were boundaries to what we could and could not see, could and could not address. We came from a contemplative tradition and arrested the process of our contemplation in mid-flight.

But not all. Some of our most contemplative figures—Catherine of Siena, Thomas Merton, Hildegard of Bingen—have been our most active. Some of our most active figures—Theresa of Avila, Dorothy Day, Ignatius of Loyola—have been our most contemplative.

If the contemplative, then, is the one who comes to see the world as God sees the world, the one who puts on the mind of Christ for the world, the one who cries out the will of God for the world, in the cloister and out of it, out of it as well as in it, then the vision of monastic life changes radically.

A basic principle of group formation is that every group attracts what it is. If we ourselves are passive in a world that cries out for both the spiritual life and the redemption it brings to the sordid and the unholy, then we will attract the passive. If we ourselves cry out loud with the prophets for the redemption of the world around us, then our prayer is true and our contemplation is real and the monasticism we live is a firebrand in the midst of the world.

It is that vision of monasticism, the monasticism that saved Europe, that brought peace and order, yes, but brought challenge and voice, as well—to the sick on the sides of the road, to the poor in the fields, to the illiterate in the streets, to the oppressed in the cities, to the dispossessed on the highways, and to the unemployed in its villages. This is the Benedictinism that re-forested Europe, reclaimed its swamplands and made rules to keep the Peace of God in the midst of its wars, employed the serfs, taught their children, and housed their sick. This is the Benedictinism that came out of the cave to attend to the shepherds in the fields.

That is the Benedictinism that young people and old are waiting to see again in us, to hear again from us, to live again with us if Benedictinism is to save the best of this world and, at the same time, give witness to the new world that they are waiting to see here and now among them.

The monastic community, historically a center of life and stability in a reeling world, exists to provide a vision of a new world lived in harmony—with one another, with the community of nations, and with the planet. It is not Rome, now, that needs to be confronted with a clear, prophetic voice of justice and peace. It is Washington, the World Bank, the IMF. It is sexism, racism, clericalism, and materialism that are strangling the life out of people. It is elitism, militarism, and nuclearism that are really terrorizing the world. And it is Benedictinism with its accents on a community of equals, the common voice, stewardship, peace, individual needs, sabbath, work, openness to the world, and immersion in the mind of God that has the language for it.

In order to meet that potential in this age, when the world is steeped in social chaos, economic uncertainty, international tension, institutionalized injustice, secularism, sexism, and the sense of futility that comes with a feeling of powerlessness in the face of major forces, monastic communities must become signs of hope.

Monastic communities of the future need to give new meaning and bold shape to whole new ways of being a public voice in a world deafened by the social bedlam in which it exists.

To be a living model of the scriptural foundation of the Rule of Benedict, monastic communities must begin to develop new ways of addressing these new issues rather than simply of ignoring them. The painful truth is that by ignoring them, we perpetuate them in the name of having removed ourselves from responsibility for them by virtue of the contemplative dimension of our lives. Worse, by ignoring them, we identify ourselves with them by our silence in the face of them.

On the contrary. To be a new voice in the world again, to be a new model of Benedictine life in a new world, a new vision of the Christian life in the world today, monastic communities must devise new methods of outreach, new ways of sharing the fruits of their contemplation with the world around them. The tools and skills, the insights and professional expertise to deal with each are already alive within us and our monastic communities. It is simply a matter of doing consciously and with Gospel commitment what the Liturgy of the Hours calls us over and over again every day to be.

We must become centers of reflection, centers of conscience, centers of spiritual development, centers of human service, model of interfaith interaction, model of equality.

MONASTIC COMMUNITIES MUST BECOME CENTERS OF REFLECTION ON THE FAITH

The purpose of prayer in the life of a monastic community is not simply to say it; it is to be shaped and formed by it, excited and troubled by it, challenged and confronted by it in those empty spaces in our own lives where the voice of God is yet to be heard. Those for whom prayer is the center of their life must be prepared to enable others to search out its implications for themselves, as well—not as teachers who have all the anwers but as disciples who are not afraid of the questions.

Monastic communities that create faith-sharing groups aimed at applying the scriptures to life as we know it today build bridges between the private prayer life of the average individual to the aching hearts of the whole people of God. Like the psalmist, they enable people to hear the cry of the poor.

One of the most common temptations of the spiritual life is to use it to justify our own disinterest in the life of the world around us. Isolated monastics attend peace vigils—but their own communities do not hold them. A few members of the community sign petitions in an attempt to save the rain forests but the community itself has no policy on organic gardening. Individuals read articles on current affairs but they are never used for table reading, never included in community prayer, never become the subject matter of retreat discussions or chapter decisions.

We become communities without a beating heart. And we call ourselves holy for it.

People come to our monasteries to celebrate the liturgy but join other groups to find a way to live a holy life in the middle of the city. They do not look to monasticism to be the spiritual light that enables them to choose between alternatives.

MONASTIC COMMUNITIES MUST BECOME CENTERS OF CONSCIENCE

The monastic community that stands for nothing but itself is soon of little value in the lives of others. How is it that we expect other people to live differently, to speak out on issues of the day, to examine the moral implications of legislation that takes from the poor to give to the rich but never do it ourselves?

There was a time when we gave ourselves and everything we had to educate a deprived Catholic population in a society unduly hostile to Catholics. We paid the price for doing it and never considered the action "political"—though hardly a more political action could have been devised in the heydays of anti-Catholicism in this White Anglo-Saxon Protestant country. Now we tell ourselves that a community commitment to support small farmers in the area in which we live, to eliminate racism in our schools, to eliminate sexism from our textbooks and public prayers is somehow or other improper, while those made poor of body, poor of spirit by those things languish at the gate.

To talk about the Rule and not to talk about a peace that is broader than ourselves may be, if history is any guide at all, the most unmonastic witness we could possibly give.

To live in the world as if being contemplative gives us the right to ignore the gospel we preach and teach and make the sign of our lives, however well-meaning we are in the process, may well be a distortion of the vocation which, the Vatican documents remind us, is "the prophetic dimension" of the church.

Small wonder, then, that the world looks again at monasticism as having run its course.

In 19th-century Germany, monasteries were permitted to reopen as long as they performed some useful service for the society around them. Surely, one of the useful services the world has the right to expect from those whose lives are centered in prayer and contemplation is the fruit of that contemplation.

Who may we expect to expose the effects of social legislation on the poorest of the poor if we do not?

Who will see it as part of their lives to counter the kind of pious moralism that passes for religion with a spirituality that is co-creative, if that kind of thinking never comes out of Benedictine monasteries? Who can we hope will dignify women in their liturgies, their language, and their project planning if not communities of Benedictines, for whom discrimination of any kind was foreign to a Rule written in the most discriminatory of societies?

MONASTIC COMMUNITIES MUST BECOME CENTERS OF SPIRITUAL DEVELOPMENT

The days of a flourishing Catholic school system where the smallest towns in the United States of America had a Catholic church or school on all four corners of the main street are long gone. Where will the next generation get its training in spiritual development if not in the monasteries themselves?

Early monastic communities took children into their midst to train them, to educate them, to teach them the essentials of the faith.

Some of those who became oblates of the community stayed there for years. Others linked themselves to the spirituality of the monastic life by public promises and lived and died faithful to the lay Benedictine life.

Perhaps it is time to reinstitute those temporary live-in programs so that men and women of all ages can find in the monasteries of the country what they cannot find in their parishes: full immersion in a spiritual tradition that enables them to see life through the filters of the gospel.

It may be time for us to see ourselves more as spirituality centers for the people of an area than simply degree-granting institutions. Or worse, empty remnants of an era that was once highly productive but which is now largely past. These kinds of programs have been the mainstay of Buddhism and Hinduism. Monasteries, served by a core community of perpetually professed members, provide at least a year's training for every member of the society. This cadre then becomes both the mainstay of the monastery and the ongoing light of the tradition in the center of the system. They become the lay carriers of both the tradition and the spiritual life. Unless and until Christian monasticism finds some kind of similar integration of monastic values and spirit with the larger society, the light that was once the undying torch of European spirituality can only become dimmer and dimmer by the year. In fact, if we examine the flow of young people in and out of monasteries these days who come for a while and then leave, aren't we simply doing what we fail to institutionalize and, therefore, do better?

THE MONASTIC COMMUNITY MUST BE A CENTER OF PUBLIC SERVICE

The Rule that welcomes strangers every hour of the day or night, the tradition that taught Europe to farm and read, the institution that responded to slavery with the practice of entrance-based rank rather than hierarchy is a tradition of service.

Clearly, monastic service is not simply the creation of some sort of product like farm produce or diplomas or hospitality. Monastic service is meant to highlight what is not being done in a society. It is meant to bring the attention of the world to what is not being done by raising it to consciousness itself. When the poor are hungry, it may be soup kitchens. When the excluded are women, it may be inclusion. When the forgotten are the sexually abused, it may be psychological help. When the public disease is violence it may be programs on anger management.

The point is that it must be more than business-as-usual if society as it is now is to be healed of its sicknesses, exposed in its political nakedness, brought to consciousness about its hidden evils. Good people don't want to spend $150 for sneakers that were made by an Indian child for $.06 an hour. But someone has to organize good people to respond to such things in the name of God or they will never be seen to have moral value. "After all," the corporations rationalize, "they're better off with us than without us, aren't they?"—a loose translation of which must surely be, "They're better off with our injustice than without it, aren't they?"

The cloistered community which—in the name of cloister—does not choose the books in its library carefully to make the connection between personal and public spirituality, that has no posters saying "Nuclear bombs are a sin against humanity" (Pope Paul VI), that never calls attention in its mailings to the needs of the poor, fails the very concept of cloister itself. The purpose of cloister is to focus our attention on the things of God. Since when were the poor, violence, oppression not the things of God? "I have heard the voice of the poor," God says to Moses, "and I am sending you to deliver them."

The message may be as apt for monastic communities today as it was for Moses then. Monasticism is not an excuse for inaction. When it is used to create an image of piety acceptable to the powerful, the wealthy, the secure who have the power to make a difference in the lives of the forgotten ones, monasticism has failed. When it cares more for its own acceptable public image than for the concerns of the poor, it has surrendered its prophetic voice to religious niceties and the prophets of the court.

MONASTICISM MUST BE A MODEL OF INTERFAITH INTERACTION

With the world on the brink of culture wars masking as religious commitment and wide enough to engulf the entire globe, monastics, of all people, must move into the public arena to extend hands, to show respect, to listen, and to learn about the word of God to the other, about the experience of life from the perspective of the other, about the spiritual insights of the other.

Only religion can possibly stop the violence being used in its name. "The world cannot find peace," Kofi Annan said, "without

the cooperation of the religions of the world." Monasticism pre-
dates the religious ruptures of the West. In its contemplative
dimensions, it is the one authentic bond between East and West.
It is the link between the spiritual mind of one and the spiritual
heart of the other. In monasticism, all the religions understand
one another, speak the same language, seek the same God, hear
the same message of peace and transcendence, of unity and
human wholeness.

Monasticism has a great role to play in the present age—if
only we can see beyond our past successes to become again what
once we were.

MONASTICISM MUST BE A MODEL OF EQUALITY

The order that traces its origin and growth, its insights and
impulse to both St. Scholastica and St. Benedict—to the twin
instincts of both women and men—needs to claim that joint heri-
tage more clearly, more courageously than ever. We must be to
one another what we wish for all the women and men of the
world: equally visible, equally respected, equally involved in the
articulation and expression of this thing we call "monasticism."

We cannot be bastions of sexism in a world where half the
population of the human race has almost nothing to say about
their own lives. In monastic communities of this age, special
attention must surely be paid to the needs and development of
women in faith, in liturgy, in spirituality, and in public voice.
Benedictines must respect and publish the work of both male
and female writers. We must include on our altars both men and
women. We must make room for the spiritual expression and
moral agency of women as well as the theological history of men.
We must support in the church those things that assure the full
spiritual participation of women, as well as of men.

Without doubt, the world in which we live now needs, as it
did in Benedict's time, reflection, conscience, spiritual development, human service, equality, ecumenical interaction, and social
critique. To be seen as significant enough to attract others to such
a life, Benedictines must spend their own lives to make it real.

It may not be so much the discovery of a "new" vision of
monasticism we need as a rediscovery of the old one—the one

that turned peasants into thinking monastics whose opinions were valued and whose thought was encouraged, the one that gave new dignity to commoners and showed Europe how to rebuild itself, the one that guaranteed that the light of learning would not go out as the world searched again for light.

We have new needs now but the light is no less threatened by them, the dignity of many is still at stake, the ideas of the masses are still being ignored. The financial nobility is back in charge. Where is the new vision monasticism must bring of what it will take to be truly human, truly equal, truly holy now? Where are the new populations on which we are spending our lives?

The fact is that we cannot live in the world as if we were not here, as if tending the Garden were not as much our responsibility as it is the responsibility of others.

We cannot be centers of authoritarianism in the name of obedience when half the world is demanding to be included in the decision-making processes that involve them. Instead we must begin by developing environments that bring our own members to full adult agency and participation and then including others in our projects, our statements, our concerns, as well, so that we all grow to full stature together.

Fulton Sheen is said to have remarked once, "My concern for religious life is that its members will be fit only for the sandboxes of heaven." Apocryphal statement or not, it is a prescient one. We cannot use religion and contemplation, Benedictinism and obedience as an excuse for not growing up.

We cannot continue to model hierarchical models of dependence and underdevelopment in our members in the name of God's will while whole peoples struggle for the right of self-determination.

We cannot be centers of withdrawal from the questions of the world and purport to be steeped in the word of God, truly contemplative, totally aware of God's will for the world.

We cannot sanctify self-centeredness in the name of a contemplation that hears but sows no seed, bears no fruit, nurtures nothing.

In its dedication to a new vision, monasticism itself will become new again. Structures will change. Ministries will change. Community organization will change. And yet, they will certainly remain emphatically, effectively the same.

Trees are cut down, pruned, in order to cut away the old growth so out of the same roots new life can spring. When we do that, we have the right to assure ourselves that "cut down, it will grow again." *Successa Virescit,* indeed. But only if we ourselves are willing to prune the old growth so that the new growth can be as strong, as vibrant, as clear as in the past. That's the reality of the thing, not the myth.

MONASTICISM:
A POETIC PERSPECTIVE

by Robert Morneau, D.D.

INTRODUCTION

I write as an outsider. My only direct experience of monastic life involved a short retreat at the Cistercian Abbey of Our Lady of the Holy Cross in Berryville, Virginia, and conducting a weeklong retreat for the monks at the Abbey of Our Lady of Gethsemani in Kentucky. Although I participated in the daily liturgical life of these monasteries, my exposure to monastic life is obviously very limited. So a significant part of my perspective on monasticism comes from my study of Church history, my reading of those who lived the life, and my understanding of the Catholic tradition.

My conviction is that monasticism is a unique call within the sacrament of baptism. No matter what lifestyle is chosen (more accurately, responded to), everyone—be they married people, those called to the consecrated life, singles, or those ordained—everyone is called to five specific "vocations": to maturity, to holiness, to community, to service, and to generosity. Those in the monastic life attempt to respond to these five calls in their own unique circumstances and within a specific tradition. At the deepest level, every Christian is called to discipleship (following Jesus) and to a life of stewardship (a way of life based upon conversion of heart as an expression of discipleship).

I have chosen as a mentor for these reflections the Anglican priest-poet George Herbert (1593–1633). His poetry captures well the various dimensions of our faith journey and provides an angle of aperture regarding our baptismal calls. Herbert's insights through his prayer-filled poetry might shed a ray of light on our attempt to deepen our understanding of the mystery of monastic life.

MATURITY

It is no more than right that we thank God unceasingly for you, brothers,
because your faith grows apace and your mutual love increases; so much
so that in God's communities we can boast of your constancy and your
faith in persecution and trial.

(2 Thess 1:3-4)

The Pulley

When God at first made man,
Having a glass of blessings standing by;
Let us (said he) pour on him all we can:
Let the world's riches which dispersed lie,
    Contract into a span.

So strength first made a way;
Then beauty flow'd, then wisdom, honor, pleasure:
When almost all was out, God made a stay,
Perceiving that alone of all this treasure
    Rest in the bottom lay.
    For if I should (said he)
Bestow this jewel also on my creature,
He would adore my gifts instead of me,
And rest in Nature, not the God of Nature:
    So both should losers be.

Yet let him keep the rest,
But keep them with repining restlessness:
Let him be rich and weary, that at least,
If goodness lead him not, yet weariness
    May toss him to my breast.

George Herbert

It was St. Ignatius who said that we came from God, we belong to God, and we are going back to God. What a mature perspective of the Christian journey the founder of the Society of Jesus had. George Herbert was aware of this insight and captured it well in his poem "The Pulley." Our creator God is wily. In gifting us so bountifully there is one gift that is withheld, one that, if given, could make us permanently immature. That gift is the false peace of resting in the created world. We are made for infinity and eternity; our knowledge and love seek Ultimate Reality. Thus, our restlessness. To the extent that we see life in a mature way will we be able to enjoy all the created graces of life with joy while being keenly aware of Uncreated Grace, God Himself, our true country.

Spirituality is about growth, the realization of our potential. The Gospel seeds are to produce fruit, thirty-, sixty-, a hundredfold. Between the drama of birth and death (as the poet Pablo Neruda states), we are called to development and maturity. According to one framework (cf. James and Evelyn Whitehead), that growth can be charted to some degree by our deepening sense of identity and destiny, our ability to love and be loved, and the exercise of responsible stewardship. Obviously, this is a lifelong process but no one is exempt from this universal challenge.

Monastic life provides circumstances to nurture maturity: a rule of life, support of a community, ongoing formation through study-reading-retreat, daily celebration of the Eucharist and the Liturgy of the Hours, participation in ascetical practices, work, and a sense of being part of a universal Church with its broad mission of evangelization. Members of the monastery who are open and cooperative with these means come, however gradually, to a deeper awareness of who they are, the importance of receiving and giving love, and a commitment to use their unique gifts for the well-being of others.

The call to growth and maturity can be short-circuited. Routine can be deadly, even narcissistic. Living in a confined space can lead to a malaise or to a blatant (if somewhat silent and passive) orneriness. The eccentricities of one's neighbor are there to stay. One's personality can be of a very different temperament than superiors and has the potential to stunt one's development. In other words, the walls and enclosure of the monastery cannot keep out the human condition. The monastic enclosure is ambiguous in that it has the potential to develop or stunt one's growth.

The goal here is that expressed in John's Gospel. Jesus came that we might have life, life in abundance (John 10:10). We are to bear fruit, mature fruit that nourishes others. A petition in the Divine Office captures it well: "Lord Jesus, you are the true vine and we are the branches: allow us to remain in you, to bear much fruit, and to give glory to the Father." The monastic task is to stay connected to Jesus and his Mystical Body, indeed, to God's whole world. In so doing maturity will be achieved and we will bear much fruit. The fruits of the Holy Spirit—love, peace, joy, patience, kindness, goodness, trustworthiness, gentleness, and self-control (Gal 5:22)—will give evidence that growth is and has taken place. What results from all this is the glory of God. God is glorified when each person becomes an authentic agent of light, love, and life.

HOLINESS

May God himself, who is our Father, and our Lord Jesus make our path to you a straight one! And may the Lord increase you and make you overflow with love for one another, and for all, even as our love does for you.

(1 Thess 3:11-12)

Love (III)

Love bade me welcome: yet my soul drew back,
    Guilty of dust and sin.
But quick-ey'd Love, observing me grow slack
    From my first entrance in,
Drew nearer to me, sweetly questioning,
    If I lack'd anything.

A guest, I answer'd, worthy to be here:
    Love said, You shall be he.
I the unkind, ungrateful? Ah my dear,
    I cannot look on thee.
Love took my hand, and smiling did reply,
    Who made the eyes but I?

Truth Lord, but I have marr'd them: let my shame
    Go where it doth deserve.
And know you not, says Love, who bore the blame?
    My dear, then I will serve.

You must sit down, says Love, and taste my meat:
So I did sit and eat.

George Herbert

Holiness is about love, the perfection of charity. Christians put all their eggs in one basket, a dangerous economic policy but the only one for authentic discipleship. The poet William Blake captures well the essence of life: "And we are put on earth a little space / That we may learn to bear the beams of love." Failure here is the only ultimate tragedy in life. Monasticism is a chosen way to respond to the universal call to holiness.

The Second Vatican Council, in chapter V of *Lumen Gentium*, speaks of this universal call to holiness:

> *The Lord Jesus, the divine Teacher and Model of all perfection, preached holiness of life to each and every one of His disciples, regardless of their situation: "You therefore are to be perfect, even as your heavenly Father is perfect" (Mt. 5:48). He Himself stands as the Author and Finisher of this holiness of life. For He sent the Holy Spirit upon all men that He might inspire them from within to love God with their whole heart and their whole soul, with all their mind and all their strength (cf. Mk. 12:30) and that they might love one another as Christ loved them (cf. Jn. 13:34; 15:12).* (#40)

All of this is possible because of one thing: God first loved us. Monasticism must be a school in which that lesson, begun hopeful in early childhood, is relearned and daily appropriated. Yet original sin touches all of life. There is something wrong. There is a major block to the reception of this extravagant love, so much so that millions upon millions of people refuse or are unable to say "yes" to this eternal grace. If monasteries are not houses of love, geographies of deep concern and respect for God and one another, they are hellholes. Love unites. Unloving individuals and environments separate and divide, casting us into isolation and destructive loneliness.

We need return always to our image of God. Our personal and communal concept of God is seminal and conditions not only our prayer life but the very meaning of existence as well as our self-understanding. John's Epistle declares unequivocally:

"God is love" (1 John 4:8). The possibility of holiness, becoming recipients and transmitters of God's charity, is dependent upon our embracing this revelation. St. Augustine did and gives this marvelous description of grace: "Quia amasti me, Domine, fecisti me amabilem" ("Because you have loved me, O Lord, you have made me lovable").

Herbert's poem "Love" captures well aspects of holiness, our call to love as deeply and fully as possible. It all begins with God's initiative, the offer of divine hospitality. And is not faith a warm, gracious welcome of God's self-offering? Yet a problem arises: self-knowledge. We are made of dust—indeed, according to Shakespeare, "the quintessence of dust"—and, in all honesty, we are sinful. How then accept the call to dwell in the light of God's love? But the God revealed in Jesus is a quick-eyed love, One who notices everything including our temptation to flee by making excuses based on unworthiness. Herbert's God is not harsh and confrontational; rather, God questions gently what the problem may be.

Again, we see the temptation of separation. Our unworthiness, based upon being unkind and ungrateful, as accurate as that self-evaluation is, does not stop "this tremendous Lover," this "Hound of Heaven," from constant pursuit. So God reaches out and takes us by the hand—TAKES US BY THE HAND! Again, another question. Are we unaware of who made the eyes that find it so difficult to look upon the divine light, the smiling face of God?

The poem concludes with a strong imperative. God will not be put off by the humiliation of our guilt and shame. His mercy, that is, His love in the face of our sin, only grows brighter and more expansive as the invitation to sit and eat turns into a command. God, the divine lover, is insistent that we turn from self to His all-encompassing compassion and affection manifest in Jesus, the one who bore our blame.

The call to holiness is universal though its implementation/ achievement is unique. In summary, ". . . holiness consists in one thing only, namely, in faithfulness to God's plan—an *active* fidelity, insofar as we accomplish as best we can the duties of our state of life, a *passive* fidelity insofar as we accept and suffer with love whatever divine providence sends us" (cf. Aelred Squire's

Asking the Fathers, Westminster, MD: Christians Classics, Inc., 1973, 217).

THE CALL TO COMMUNITY

You, then, are the body of Christ. Every one of you is a member of it. Furthermore, God has set up in the church first apostles, second prophets, third teachers, then miracle workers, healers, assistants, administrators, and those who speak in tongues. Are all apostles? Are all prophets? Are all teachers? Do all work miracles or have the gift of healing? Do all speak in tongues, all have the gift of interpretation of tongues? Set your hearts on the greater gifts.

(1 Cor 12:27-31)

Trinity Sunday

Lord, who hast form'd me out of mud,
   And hast redeem'd me through thy blood,
   And sanctifi'd me to do good;

Purge all my sins done heretofore:
   For I confess my heavy score,
   And I will strive to sin no more.

Enrich my heart, mouth, hands in me,
   With faith, with hope, with charity;
   That I may run, rise, rest with thee.

George Herbert

In baptism, all of us are baptized into the Trinitarian life and into the Christian community. We are not to travel alone even though some, anchorites for example, choose a solitary life. Yet we are all in a web of relationships no matter how isolated. The mystery of our God is revealed to us through scriptures and our tradition as a triune life. God is our Father, Son, and Holy Spirit; our Creator, Redeemer, and Sanctifier; our Light, Love, and Life; Lover, Beloved, and Loving (a la St. Augustine); Primordial Being, Expressive Being, and Unative Being (a la John Macquarrie); Giver, Given, and Giving (a la Michael Downey). Language fails to express the fullness of the divine mystery, the God who creates and came among us in Jesus and who remains with us still through the gift of the Holy Spirit.

George Herbert's "Trinity Sunday" gives us five activities of our loving God. God forms us out of our muddy human condition, redeems us in the passion of the Christ, makes us holy that we might do good, purges our misguided desires and burns away our sins, and enriches us with the theological virtues. This triune God, to whose image we are made, is ever present in being with, for, and in us.

Monasticism is about community. It is a participation in the triune life of God and in the life of the universal Church. Even for those monks who live in seclusion, they are bound to the community of their order as well as to their brothers and sisters throughout the Church. The communal life is one of sharing and caring. The *communio,* so emphasized by Pope John Paul II, is at the heart of monastic life. We are made for intimacy, for oneness of mind and heart with God and one another. Prayer, asceticism, and service are means to accomplish this marvelous oneness.

There is a glorious mutuality that underlies all existence. Within God there is the dynamic of Lover, Beloved, and Loving that St. Augustine articulates. Within each of us there is a mutuality of the cognitive, affective, and behavioral components seeking integration and wholeness. And within the human family, we are made for mutual interdependence. Self-reliance, understood literally, is a great falsehood. Even Ralph Waldo Emerson in his classic essay "Self-Reliance" is not speaking of a narrow autonomy. Social in nature, human beings need one another and a "higher power," so aptly described in AA spirituality.

The communal nature of monasticism cannot be overemphasized especially in a world culture that highlights individualism. Whether the activity is one of liturgy or work, of eating or retreating, monks are in their life together. If love does not govern this way of life, aggression will. If communal activities do not draw monks together, they will pull them apart. The underlying attitude in this way of life must be that of sacrifice, a surrender of one's own particular will to the will of God and the community.

One last word about the call to community. An integral, healthy community is based on communication. It may seem strange that those monastic traditions that emphasize silence and solitude are well practiced in the art of communication. But such is the case. There can be no authentic community without knowledge of one another based on communication. This need not be a paradox since there are so many forms of communication besides words or personal dialogue. We communicate by the way we walk and look, by the way we lift up our voice in common prayer and do our work, by a smile or a frown. Sometimes silent dialogue is more forceful than explicit speech.

We are made for serious conversation that leads to a strong community. And, of course, we find that serious conversation in the liturgy wherein God speaks to us and we respond in prayer and song. It is here, in the "opus Dei," that community happens or fails. Full, active, conscious participation in the Eucharist and Divine Office foster authentic community.

THE CALL TO SERVICE

Peter was hurt because he [Jesus] asked a third time, "Do you love me?" So he said to him: "Lord, you know everything. You know well that I love you." Jesus said to him, "Feed my sheep."

(John 21:17)

> Sum up at night, what thou hast done by day;
> And in the morning, what thou hast to do.
> Dress and undress thy soul: mark the decay
> And growth of it: if with thy watch, that too
>   Be down, then wind up both: since we shall be
>   Most surely judg'd, make thy accounts agree.

(cf. George Herbert's "Perirrhanterium," 451–56)

We all have our work to do; we are all called to service. Be that work tilling the land or baking bread, healing the sick or instructing the ignorant, preaching the word or engaged in the contemplative prayer, no one is exempt from expending energy on his/her unique vocation. And, obviously, behind the service is a need. As Jesus mandated Peter: "Feed my sheep." Whatever the hunger, be it for food or health or intercession, God's people are to be fed and each of us is called, through baptism and confirmation, into that service.

At the end of the day monks are to examine their souls and the work of that day. What was the quality of prayer and manual work? What were the interior attitudes toward fellow members of the community and one's superiors? What needs were perceived and addressed in chance exchanges? Was God glorified by the work done?

Again, to quote from his excellent book *Asking the Fathers,* the Camaldolese monk Aelred Squire states: "And conversely, a man without work at all would be shallow and sick and his narcissism, aggressiveness, and erotic energy could express themselves in subhuman and antisocial form" (Westminster, MD: Christians Classics, Inc., 1993, 97). Elsewhere he states that working too little, working too much, or working in the wrong way are injurious to one's spiritual well-being and that of others. Good, solid work does keep at bay boredom and narcissism, aggressiveness, and various forms of deviance.

Robert Frost, in his famous verse "The Road Not Taken," highlights the importance of our life's work. The road we do take does make all the difference. The monk's road appears from the outside, by the postmodern culture, to be unproductive, unpragmatic, and a "waste." From the inside we know that such an evaluation is simply false. Monks have made a major difference in the lives of others through their witness of transcendence and their writings, through their fidelity to prayer and their "white martyrdom," through their focus on the mystery of God and their compassion for the world. This less traveled road is the road that Jesus walked in his own unique way.

That having been said, there is a danger in cloistered living where one's needs are provided for in a fairly secure way. At times there is a want of accountability in religious communities as there is in every walk of life. Monks, like doctors or teachers or parents, can cut corners and, comes day's end, fail in accountability. Slackers dwell in every profession, religious or secular. And the price paid for such a choice—a lack of peace.

In our postmodern culture that experiences the forces of hurriedness, consumerism, and muddleness, monasticism renders a unique service. There is in the monastic tradition a witness to a spiritual tempo that refuses to be rushed; a witness to that holy poverty that refuses to get caught up in the acquisition of all kinds of "stuff"; and, a witness to a faith clarity that says that God is first in the commitment of time and energy. Such a service provides an alternative way of leaning into life. For that witness and choice, we, on the outside, should be grateful.

THE CALL TO GENEROSITY

He [Jesus] glanced up and saw the rich putting their offerings into the treasury, and also a poor widow putting in two copper coins. At that he said: "I assure you, this poor widow has put in more than all the rest. They make contributions out of their surplus, but she from her want has given what she could not afford—every penny she had to live on."

(Luke 21:1-4)

Teach me, my God and King,
In all things thee to see,
And what I do in anything,
To do it as for thee.

(cf. George Herbert's "The Elixir")

At the very heart of monastic life is the Eucharist. In that sacrament the extravagant love and mercy of God is made present and manifest in Jesus. The response to this divine generosity is twofold: praise and thanksgiving. More, an authentic celebration of the Eucharist leads to an attitude of radical gratitude and a commitment to a life of generosity. The gift received must be shared. A lack of generosity means that a person has failed to appropriate the inner dynamic of the eucharistic life.

Monasticism, therefore, is about stewardship. Stewardship is what a person does after he or she says they believe. Stewardship is summarized in four infinites: to receive God's gift gratefully, to nurture those gifts responsibly, to share God's gifts justly and sacrificially, and to return those gifts to God in abundance. Stewardship is an expression of discipleship and is based on conversion of heart. What has been freely given is to be shared.

The haunting stewardship question comes from Psalm 116:12: "What return can I make to the Lord, for all the good the Lord has done for me?" God has poured into our lives so many blessings: the gift of time and existence, the gift of talents and treasures, the gift of family and friends. We are not "absolute" owners of anything or anyone. Rather, all has been given in trust and will one day demand an accounting.

The cornerstone of generosity is gratitude. A constant giving of thanks, day in and day out, establishes an interior attitude that overflows into a life of sharing, a sharing not just of time and talent and treasure, but a sharing of one's very self. That is why Mary is the model of stewardship: she was totally obedient, she was totally self-giving. In fact, that rhythm describes the Eucharist. In the liturgy of the Word we are to be obedient, true listeners: in the liturgy of the Eucharist, we enter into Jesus' self-giving, yes, even unto death.

The stewardship dimension is crucial if we are to address the problem of joy. Is monastic life a joyful way of existence? The claim can be made that unless gratitude and generosity are present in one's soul then joy is impossible. Joy is the by-product of generosity. So much sadness and depression can be attributed to our acquisitive mode of existence. And one additional factor. Besides joy flowing from generosity there will also be deep peace.

Monks are disciples/stewards. They have been given countless gifts over the centuries and have left the Church with a rich legacy. That inheritance comes in the forms of masterful writings, creative art work, a witness to transcendence. Like a beacon of light, monasticism has and keeps reminding us of the mystery of God and the meaning of our existence. In exercising good stewardship, the careful tending of gifts given, monks have earned a merited crown.

CONCLUSION

There is yet another poem by George Herbert that might help us to understand the vocation to monasticism. He entitles it "Matins," and indeed what a morning prayer it is. Beginning with the faith conviction of God's abiding presence, the soul raises the question of the nature of the human heart. It is the heart that God woos; it is the heart upon which God pours so many gifts and so much love. And although God is present and giving, yet we fail to do our "theology" having been distracted by our finite world. So the poet makes *the* great request: to be taught the mystery of God's love. For if we are graced with love we will come to know God the Creator and the mystery of Creation. Then all that we need to be united to God is a sunbeam, or a butterfly, or a bumblebee. This is more than a poem. It is prayer of the heart that asks for the most important gift of all.

Matins

I cannot open mine eyes,
But thou are ready there to catch
My morning soul and sacrifice:
Then we must needs for that day make a match.

My God, what is a heart?
Silver, or gold, or precious stone,
Or star, or rainbow, or a part
Of all these things, or all of them in one?

My God, what is a heart,
That thou shouldst it so eye and woo,
Pouring upon it all thy art,
As if that thou hadst nothing else to do?

Indeed man's whole estate
Amounts (and richly) to serve thee:
He did not heav'n and earth create,
Yet studies them, not him by whom they be.

Teach me thy love to know;
That this new light which now I see,
May both the work and the workman show:
Then by a sunbeam I will climb to thee.

George Herbert*

* The poems of George Herbert quoted in this article are taken from *George Herbert: The Country Parson, The Temple,* edited, with an introduction by John N. Wall, Jr. (New York: Paulist Press, 1981), and are reprinted here with permission of the publishers.

In his biography *Silent Lamp: The Thomas Merton Story* (New York: Crossroad, 1992, p. 257), Fr. William H. Shannon offers this reflection on the monk. He captures well the essence of monasticism:

> The monk is distinguished from other people (whose lives are also a search for God) by the fact that the monk gives himself exclusively and most directly in the seeking of God. Others seek God in the midst of responsibilities to society and family. Other (active) religious seek God by seeking to help others in their search for God. This does not mean that the monk's exclusive concentration on the seeking of God makes the monk a better person (or better Christian) than these others; it is simply that he treads a path that most others do not choose: not necessarily a higher or safer or more dedicated path, simply one he knows he is called to follow.

FRAGMENTS FOR A VISION OF CISTERCIAN LIFE IN THE 21ST CENTURY

by John Eudes Bamberger, OCSO

INTRODUCTION

To formulate "a vision of Cistercian life for the 21st century" is to engage to some degree in a form of prophecy, though it makes no claim to be inspired. A prophecy that is over-precise and fixed in detail is hardly compatible with life as lived in the world of our time. Since our concern here is with Cistercian life in the years ahead the detailed content of this vision remains fluid, open to modification and responsive to fresh insight, that is to say, interactive. But the major elements of this way remain in continuity with the tradition, that is to say, it remains Cistercian life. Rather than attempt to depict the whole of the Cistercian way for our times, I shall focus on those areas of the tradition which call for further adaptation than they have received in the past. For that reason I offer fragments for a vision; I make no attempt to supply a full description of Cistercian life in the concrete.

My view of what should characterize Cistercian life in the present century takes its origin in Scripture. It also is based on the conviction that, while continuity with the basic structures and practices of our Order is essential, yet certain teachings of our Fathers need to be elaborated further in order to make them more accessible to our times. In antiquity a popular name for the monk was "a philosopher." Eric Voegelin has observed that "the philosopher has to find men of his own kind in a community that comprehends both the present and the past."[1] It is such a community

---

[1] Cited in "Why Philosophize?" *Communio* 28 (2001) 877.

of contemplatives who take the mystery of Christ as their philosophy that I envisage for our times. In particular the practical application of the doctrine of the creation of the human person in the image and likeness of God which was fundamental for the early Cistercians should be given greater prominence. None of the early Cistercian authors, or any others at the time or since, has indicated in sufficiently concrete detail how the doctrine of the image and likeness affects the organization of the monastic observances nor, except in the most general way, given a detailed account of how it enters into the experience of the individual. In modern times we are provided with some useful aids that contribute to this task. In the course of this article I hope to indicate some of the practical implications of this doctrine for monastics by pointing out how this basic doctrine can be brought into relation with pertinent modern insights and thereby be applied more effectively to life experience.

We live in a culture where many scientists are so taken up with the very real achievements of recent times, that they are distorting its human significance by interpreting the data to fit the ideology of materialism. Cistercian life has a contribution to make to society as well as to the Church in this context by assuring that spirituality is rooted in the reality of the created cosmos precisely by using such discoveries to implement the contemplative program outlined in more general terms by St. Bernard and his associates.

While monks cannot be expected to do such technical exploration themselves, I hope to indicate how some of the very recent studies in areas pertaining to the concept of the human mind and body, and in particular the passions and emotions, can contribute to a fuller appreciation of the continuing relevance of the doctrine of the image and likeness with its emphasis on free choice *(liberum arbitrium)* and further indicate the role of the spiritual senses in the process of divinization that gives meaning to Cistercian life in our century as it has done from the time of our monastic Fathers.

St. Luke in the Acts of the Apostles sets forth with a few masterly strokes of the pen a vision that was to serve as a model for the Church. He used as his model the concrete life of the Christian congregation in Jerusalem in the primitive period, prior to the evangelization of the Gentiles (Acts 2:42-47). His concise wording is a sharply outlined vignette: "They persevered in the teaching of the apostles, in fellowship, in the breaking of bread and in the prayers." These four features have remained integral to the vision that the Church has held up as normative for its well-being. Fidelity to the teaching of the apostles includes obedience to their authority as well as belief in the dogmatic truths they preached. Fellowship, or communion *(koinonia)*, among the faithful is referred to in a second passage where Luke describes the fervent way of life of the Church again with admirable brevity: "The multitude of the believers was one heart and one soul . . . and all possessions were common *(panta koina)*" (Acts 4:32). The Eucharist and liturgy are here referred to as "the breaking of bread and prayers," and ever since the celebration of the mass and the hours of the office have been at the center of the Church's life.

John Cassian saw in this rendition of the life of the primitive Jerusalem Church the origins of the monastic way and in particular he stressed communion of mind, heart, and goods. When the sharing of all possessions in common no longer proved practicable for the Church as the faith spread, yet the vision was never forgotten. He passed it on through his writings to St. Benedict. Eventually the Cistercians of the twelfth century were guided by their understanding of this same conception. Modern historians have shown that Cassian was mistaken in seeing a direct historical continuity between the primitive Jerusalem community and the monks of Egypt. However, he correctly perceived that there was a moral identity that established a bond between the monastic way and the Primitive Church, both of which shared the same vision: a community of believers united in heart and soul in the witness to the Gospel. Monastic life in this century must make this heartfelt collaboration and unity of spirit a major concern that permeates all the various expression of its life. In order to assure that this oneness of heart is achieved and maintained considerable attention must be paid to the practice of dialogue that is frank, honest, and sincerely in the service of the common good. Such exchanges require a considerable level of emotional maturity and a genuine desire to contribute actively to the discernment of God's will rather than insisting on one's own views and preferences. This formation to dialogue which is provided for in the Rule of St. Benedict only in very general terms, should be a consideration in the manner of teaching and exercising authority.

Stimulating individuals to think for themselves, to pursue those particular interests for which they are best suited as far as compatible with community needs and possibilities, welcoming questions, and learning from disagreement and criticism are attitudes that are essential for the unity in truth that only a climate of honest dialogue can achieve and preserve. The self-denial, effort at self-knowledge, the requisite study of issues and topics important for the community are modern forms of asceticism that are to be taken no less seriously than bodily mortification and fasting.

The original vision of unity among the faithful was adopted wholeheartedly by early cenobites and was preserved for the benefit of the whole Church. Where it is achieved and given adequate expression it will not only strengthen the local Church but also be a sign for others outside the faith as it was in primitive times. "See how they love one another!" was said by pagans, "See how they honor one another, how they assist, care for, support one another!" will be no less on the lips of modern persons where such attitudes are cultivated and practiced in our times. They are highly valued in our day where they are encountered.

All these features of the Church as singled out by St. Luke—full acceptance of the Church's teaching, communion among the faithful, attending the Eucharist and the liturgy—remain essential for us who live the Cistercian life in this 21st century. Cistercian life, to fulfill its role in the Church of our period, must give prominence to making dedication to the value of unity of heart and mind united as manifested in the common life and the observances that nourish it. Simplicity of life, regularity at liturgy and common meals, manual labor, together with silence, are traditional ways in which Cistercian monks created a high level of fraternity and at the same time maintained a climate favorable to contemplative prayer. These practices are no less necessary for us in these times, though they are more countercultural than in an earlier age.

Community spirit is not only to benefit its own members but it will extend itself so as to assure, as far as is compatible with the solitude essential for our life, that this way offers these benefits to the Church at large. This entails receiving guests in such a way as to encourage active participation in the Liturgy, providing spiritual assistance and giving support for living a more communal life with like-minded faithful, even organizing such groups living a form of monastic spirituality adapted to life in secular society. This outreach makes special demands on the community in the way of providing adequate teaching and guidance. At the same time, it serves to give the moral support of the larger community and contributes to a healthy realism in dealing with issues of current society as encountered by persons living the faith with dedication.

In recent years the rhythm of cultural development has become so marked and rapid that the process of change itself is now a prominent feature of modern experience. Multitudinous elements shift and reorganize to form new structures even as one speaks of them. In a world where a certain dynamic quality colors the whole of modern culture, the appropriate mode for a vision of Cistercian life as it takes form on its advance into our present century is best conceived as interactive. Accordingly, formation to Cistercian life for this century will consciously strive to impart a modality of openness to appropriate adaptation while remaining rooted in the unchanging values of the tradition, rooted as they are in the vision described in the Acts by St. Luke.

NEW DEVELOPMENTS AND THE IMAGE OF GOD

Among the more obvious and acknowledged causes of recent increase of the rhythm of social and political change is the regular advance of the sciences and their application in the form of new technology. The most significant of these took place in the mid-twentieth century. The great advance in physics that resulted in the atom bomb in 1945 followed shortly after, in 1953 when the highly complex and intricate structure of DNA was accurately described. This discovery has led to a new understanding of the relation of the human body to all forms of life from mosses, plants, bacteria, and viruses to chimpanzees. With this achievement, great impetus was given to the study of living organisms for the sciences of chemistry and biology, which fused to create the new field of molecularbiology. As a result, just fifty years later, in 2003, the project of accurately determining the structure of the entire human genome was successfully completed for all of the roughly 25,000 genes found in every somatic cell of the body.

Not surprisingly, these findings are being widely interpreted as indications that the human person is nothing but a variant, more highly developed form of organic life. Like all other organisms he/she will perish as a personal being at death. As further advances in molecularbiology occur such claims are made with a show of greater plausibility.[2] In this interpretation the belief that man is the image of God is considered at best irrelevant and belief in the eternal soul is held to be superfluous.[3] This materialist philosophy is now penetrating into the field of psychology where it exclusively is applied to interpret human experience. To cite but one instance, dreams are interpreted by some to be merely associations and memories resulting from the excitations caused by random neurochemical processes.[4] This interpretation of the data is being popularized and already exerts formative influence in scientific and university circles. Many working in the fields of neuroscience and molecularbiology are propagating interpretations of the new findings that are radically opposed to the traditional Catholic doctrine of the image and its significance for faith and the spiritual life. This influence was recently illustrated in a report of an interview with a young North American girl who came to Rome for the funeral of Pope John Paul II. Asked why she attended the services she stated that she loved the Pope and wanted to do him honor, for he was such a good and great man. She then added: "But, of course, I am not a believer, for I studied science."

Such a materialist concept of man throws into high relief the necessity of giving prominence to the Cistercian teaching on image and likeness and showing its relevance for the experience of God in the world as disclosed by the established findings of

---

[2] As I write this a study comparing the genome of the chimpanzee with that of humans announces that 96% of their respective genes are the same. The author of the study comments that it is one of the clearest proofs of the validity of Darwin's theory of origin of the species by random variation. Of course, what theological significance attaches to evolution remains an open and much debated issue at present.

[3] Michael Shermer, "Monists [that is, the author and those who live by faith in science] contend that body and soul are the same and that the death of the body spells the end of the soul," *Scientific American*, September 2004, 38.

[4] Jonathan Winson, "The Meaning of Dreams," *Scientific American*, vol. 12.1, 2002, 55.

physics. In a culture where, literally, every week fresh scientific discoveries reveal new understanding of the workings of nature, monks do well to incorporate into their thought and prayer those assured insights that are pertinent to the concept of the human person and the nature of the world.

When St. Thomas assimilated Aristotle's natural philosophy, he initiated a new phase of theology that had spiritual as well as dogmatic consequences; his worldview entered into his spiritual practice and that of his followers. Today contemporary science furnishes concepts and terms that must replace views that are archaic. One of the more neglected and little understood practices of monastic doctrine on contemplative prayer has been *theoria physike*. It has not proved easy in the course of the tradition to follow Evagrius Ponticus in his contention that the contemplation of the logoi of created things, of Providence, and of the invisible world, that such engagement with creation is purifying. It represents an essential approach to the loving experience of the Blessed Trinity in contemplative, mystical prayer, which gives spirit to the vision I propose of the Cistercian life in these times.

However, neither Evagrius nor anyone else in the Patristic period or in the early Middle Ages had been able to describe in a way that is helpful to moderns, just what this entails concretely, and how to go about it. On the whole such limited discussion as is found in his better known works remains too general to prove of much practical use for those endowed with less intuitive genius than he possessed.[5] Yet in practice this manner of contemplative prayer has large contributions to make in purifying the heart and in the cultivating of the spiritual senses. In recent years there are certain developments in the physical sciences, and psychology, that provide us with particular helps to utilizing this form of contemplation in a more effective manner.

---

[5] It seems to me that Thomas Aquinas, on the other hand, devoted a great deal of his synthesis to carrying out this program. As Polyani has noted, the worldview that prevailed in his day and which he necessarily shared and his scholastic manner in presenting his thought and findings, however, render the use of his writings less accessible than they were to an earlier generation. Many of his insights, of course, remain valid and helpful. Michael Polyani, "Faith and reason," *Communio* 28 (2001) 874.

To profit from the opportunity created by recent studies that affect the concept being formed of the human person requires a rather thorough knowledge of the doctrine of the image and likeness as worked out by its main exponents, as well as some familiarity with the findings of modern physics and biochemistry. Since it is fundamental to my vision the doctrine of the image and likeness will be presented here while indicating at what points it would profit from a confrontation with certain of the established data of modern psychology and to some extent biological sciences so as to demonstrate that it remains a plausible and eminently pertinent basis for the spiritual life. The developments unforeseen by our 12th-century Fathers are occasions for applying their teaching with enhanced insight into the more precise operations of the faculties in the process of recovering the likeness. As we shall see, one of the characteristics, in fact, of a theology adapted to the new century is its stress on God as author of the unforeseen and unpredictable. He who created us also calls forth new forms of life and reveals unexpected pathways for realizing his plan that surprises. As a theologian who specializes in the relation of science to religion observes: "A saving future invades the present unpredictably."[6] This principle has guided Catholic exegesis of the Hebrew Bible from earliest times: the past does not explain the full meaning of the text; it must be read as preparation for the future who is Christ.[7] All Christian spirituality is open to the new, being ordered to the future when Christ Jesus will come in glory to make all things new while remaining in continuity with the truth already grasped.

FRAGMENTS FOR A VISION, WITH RUNNING COMMENTARY

The dominant, ruling concept in my vision of Cistercian life for the 21st century is the monastery as a school of charity where all the essential, practical skills for attaining to union with God

[6] John Haught, "God After Darwin," Boulder, Co.: Westview Press (2000) 94.
[7] Cf. Joseph Ratzinger (Pope Benedict XVI), "In the Beginning," tr. Boniface Ramsey, op, Grand Rapids, MI: Eerdmans (1990) 17.

are acquired. Fidelity to this concept taken directly from the tradition engages us to present it in a more dynamic manner than was perhaps as necessary or as possible as is now the case. The first characteristic of this school that I would stress is that its program is ordered primarily to experience; knowledge, to be sure, must be imparted, and done so, as far as possible, profiting from the many valuable insights of the last decades of scholarly studies of the tradition. Not only the final goal, which is union with God in the kingdom of heaven, but also the immediate aim, the *scopos*, as Cassian calls it, is practical. *Both the lifestyle, that is the structures, the horarium, and the various observances, are to be in the service of a process of lifelong transformation.* This principle has not always been kept in view or even understood as fundamental for the contemplative life. In our history, even our recent history, the immediate purpose has been viewed variously as a life of penance for personal sins, of reparation for sins of the world, as a life of intercession for others, for instance.

As good and essential as these purposes are, they do not represent an adequate realization of the Cistercian spirituality imparted by the early Fathers. The perfection of love requires an inner transformation of the inmost dispositions, even of the inner senses. We are to keep learning by listening to what the Spirit says through the Scriptures, the Fathers, and the signs of our times. "Without knowledge there is no wisdom" (Sir 3:25). At the same time this knowledge is to serve as a guide in the disposition of our time and energy; our manner and measure of relating to others, in short, all our activities; as far as possible, are to be undertaken in light of the requirements of this inner remaking of the heart. This school takes the requirements and possibilities of charity as its living subject, convinced of the transformative power of divine love that enters only the pure of heart. St. Maximus the Confessor spoke of the present age initiated by the resurrection of the Lord as existing "for the realization of the mystical and ineffable deification of humanity."[8] He adds elsewhere that the will "has yet to be wholly endowed with the Spirit

---

[8] "Ad Thalassium 22," "On the Cosmic Mystery of Jesus Christ: Maximus the Confessor," tr. Paul M. Blowers and Robert Louis Wilken, Crestwood, N.Y.: St. Vladimir's Seminary Press (2003) 116.

by participation in the divine mysteries . . . For the Spirit . . . converts the willing will toward deification."[9]

Cistercian life will flourish in the measure that this dynamic conception effectively bears upon actual ascetical and contemplative practice. The concept and vocabulary of *transformation* is taken directly from the Pauline Epistles where the expression occurs five times. It is the spiritual analogue of *evolution,* the concept that dominates in biological and cosmic theory today. Such an evolutionary view is at once rooted in the tradition followed by our Cistercian Fathers and connects with current conceptions of biophysical science as well as with the insights of depth psychology. Many of the findings in both these fields, in fact, can be placed at the service of this spiritual process when they are properly assimilated.

This dynamic manner of understanding the spiritual life is the polar opposite of the reductionist thinking practiced by the purveyors of current materialism. At the same time it readily accommodates one of the more critical recent insights of science: higher-level emergents cannot be completely accounted for by lower-level components. What gets lost in the reduction is among other things "information," that is to say, "the overall ordering of entities—atoms, molecules, cells, genes, etc.—into intelligible forms or arrangements . . . information itself slips through the wide meshes of science's mechanistic nets."[10] A convincing illustration of this point is the fact that the DNA code depends on the specific sequence of the four amine bases. That sequence is not a function of physico-chemical laws but adds a decisive, real element to the living cell that determines the specific proteins produced and determines the concrete forms assumed by matter. Analogously, the action of the Spirit of God operates upon the human mind (gnome in Maximus) enabling free will to order its various activities so as to result in divinization of the subject.

---

[9] "Ad Thalassium 6," *op. cit.* 103, 104.

[10] Haught, *op. cit.,* 70ff. Interestingly, Henry Adams, toward the end of his life, understood the place of some such real energy as this concept of information. In describing his "Dynamic Theory of History" he speaks of "supersensual forces" that account for the otherwise chaotic and unforeseen happenings of history. *The Education of Henry Adams: An Autobiography,* Boston: Houghton Mifflin Company (1988) 487, 488.

This means in practice that the formation given involves a discernment of the concrete state of the individual monk, his dispositions, possibilities, and attractions as seen in light of the integration of the emotions and memory. Such insight renders effort more efficacious because it is directed at the proper level and applied in the appropriate area of the interior life. Understanding this process contributes to facilitating the appropriate ordering of monastic practices and the manner of prayer so as to bring the monk to the desired goal of divinization. This perspective then assists greatly in avoiding the rigidity and alienation that all too readily has resulted from a more static and narrow conception of Cistercian life.

There is a distinct advantage for our times in giving a decided prominence to the explicit cultivation of the love of God through the ascetic practice associated with contemplative prayer centered on Christ. For widespread in our times is a decided reluctance to speak of the love of God. A few years ago, Father Vacek, a Jesuit professor of theology, noted this absence of any direct reference to personal love of God and upon making a survey of his students, of priests, and theologians—found that few persons are willing to speak of their love for God or give a satisfactory response to the question: "What do you mean by love for God?" He concluded from his study that in our times there is an eclipse of love for God which calls for a correction that remedies this deficiency.[11] Cistercian life will fill a serious need for our times when the monks make it their primary and explicit aim to grow in love for God himself and for his glory and are able to speak of it to others, introducing it in conversation with familiar ease.

The young Bernard of Fontaines was able to identify the spirit of the founders as charity, the perfection of love. Not long after the new foundation was made, he gave explicit expression to the primacy of love in his formal teaching. He brought out the fact that the energizing force operative in the Cistercian experience is not chiefly expended in fidelity to the integral observance of the Rule, rather it carries out this observance in view of deepening

---

[11] Edward Collins Vacek, sj, "The Eclipse of Love for God," *America*, vol. 174, no. 8: March 9, 1996, 13–16.

and purifying love. One way Bernard expressed this prominence of charity was by assigning a new title to the Cistercian monastery. St. Benedict had referred to the monastery as "a school of the Lord's service"; St. Bernard designated it as "a school of charity." In addition, he wrote an entire treatise "On the Love of God," which is among the first in monastic literature dedicated formally to that subject.[12]

This work is constructed on the concept of the transformation of human love, describing the characteristics of each stage of its evolution. The last eighteen years of his life Bernard took love as the dominant theme of his Sermons on the Canticle of Canticles, interpreting this book as an inspired description of divine and human love in process of growth. He spoke there (Sermons 49 and 50) of monastic life as the "ordering of love" *(ordinatio charitatis)*.[13]

True love including the love of God, considered as an attraction, is integral with human nature as St. Basil teaches in his Long Rules.[14] The purity and fullness of love, however, is acquired by art; art is the result of training. "Training" is the proper translation of the Greek word *"askesis."* Love that is true and pure is acquired only by an art requiring *ascesis,* that is, training and discipline, with all that implies of teaching, strenuous effort, self-denial, and practice. This was consistently preached by our Lord who summed up the whole of the Scripture in the commandments of love and affirmed that its practice entailed carrying the cross daily. Monastic literature remained very reticent concerning the topic of love. The Rule of the Master does not encourage the monks to cultivate fraternal relations; while the Rule of Benedict devotes a chapter to this topic, he confines himself to exhortation and brief description; he does not analyze it as

[12] William of St. Thierry, "On Contemplating God," somewhat earlier, is entitled "On Love" in some manuscripts, a title which corresponds more accurately with the content of this treatise.

[13] *"ordinatio charitatis,"* cf. *"Sermones super Cantica,"* 49 and 50. St. Augustine had already used the expression *"ordo charitatis";* the abbot of Clairvaux elaborated on it.

[14] "Learning the love of God is not from anything exterior but a seed-like word is implanted from the time the living man is established in being." *Regulae Fusius Tractatae,* II, PG 31:908.

an interior experience. St. Bernard changed this. The troubadours and practitioners of courtly love were introducing a new understanding of love and devising rules for its practice in his times. His doctrine, while based on Scripture, took up certain of the tender humanistic strains of that courtly love, which flourished in the aristocratic society of his times. But, though he encouraged St. Aelred to write on love as human friendship, Bernard himself wrote of it only in occasional letters to those with whom he had close ties of friendship. He preferred to focus on the love of God, and love of the Savior as spouse of the soul, adopting some of the noble ideals of the secular literature of his time while transposing them to another mode, in the service of spiritual union with Christ. More particularly he realized the significance of affect in his relation to the humanity of the Savior, thus introducing the theme of emotions into spirituality without, however, in the least yielding to sentimentality.

The spirituality of Bernard and Aelred especially is notable for its sensitivity to the humanity of Jesus. This establishes a point of contact between the Cistercian tradition and the Hesychastic tradition of the Eastern Church. It is a legitimate development to include in the expression of Cistercian life some of the features of this contemplative movement centered on the glorified Christ making use of the recent studies concerning the emotions. The finding of the neurochemical pathways, their complex influences on memory, imagination, and the functioning of the senses have resonances affecting one's self-image. They bear upon such issues as distractions in prayer, image-free prayer, the proper role of emotion in personal relations, and a variety of other issues pertinent to contemplative life. Bernard's works gave more attention to indicating prayerful contemplation of our Lord's life and passion. Along with the ascetic practices that the Cistercian life entails, this contemplation serves to transform the innate love of self, narcissistic eros as Freud was to term it, into a more selfless affection for the Savior. With continuing fidelity to these practices and under the influence of the Spirit, this psychic energy is further purified and eventually leads to as full a union as is possible in this life.

This analysis of the process of inner development lends itself readily to further elaboration in that it is based on experience.

Rather than simply reject those passions which are disordered, as is commonly done, Bernard encourages an attitude that is more objectively accepting of their reality. *This crucial, realistic, and objective admission is the point at which theory and principles are converted into experience.* Bernard points to this need but only in the most general terms of self-love; nowhere does he analyze it or elaborate upon it. Such elaboration was undertaken centuries before by a brilliant monk living in the Egyptian desert, Evagrius Ponticus. His work on the analysis of the passions not only organized them into a coherent system but sought to establish their dynamic relations up to a point. Further, he pointed out the necessity to identify precisely the nature of passionate thoughts to deal with them effectively and wrote a book to that end; the *Antirrheticus* unfortunately was never made available in Latin or English.

That Bernard grasped this fundamental law of psychology is one of his most genial insights. Its usefulness, even its necessity for a full engagement in the process of transformation, has not been adequately recognized and elaborated upon. I consider that in our time it is at this very point that today we can insert into this Cistercian spirituality the many aids to dealing with emotional conflict afforded by modern depth psychology and psychodynamics. In this connection as well some of the more recent findings concerning the neurochemical basis of the emotional life can prove useful, helping individuals to accept as an objectively given certain emotions that are problematical or challenging for their spiritual life.

All too often it happens that at some stage of the monastic life, a person has spiritual insights that bring into consciousness some emotional stress arising from a little-understood conflict. After repeated resolutions to overcome this difficulty the tension persists or even increases. It is not enough to accuse oneself of pride or self-will; the same pattern of impatience, or anger, or discouragement recurs. A whole body of knowledge and the techniques employed to apply it in the service of healthy human and spiritual growth is at hand to be used at this point to discern the concrete cause of such conflict. In order for it to prove effective one must first recognize and then acknowledge the precise emotionally charged feeling giving rise to it for any direct approach to prove helpful in advancing beyond the obstacle. Just as Bernard, and Evagrius before him, had incorporated such insights as they were given and made them a part of monastic formation and spirituality, so in our time we should profit from these modern helps.

"Does not the unity of love permit that there shall also be diversity?"[15] said William of St. Thierry. Communities flourish only when its members are inspired by a clear vision worthy of the nobler aspirations of the human mind and heart and assisted as far as possible in living it out in keeping with their personal gifts and attractions. The understanding as well as the affections must be engaged in any human project in which humanity and the spirit might flourish. The formulation of such a vision must be sufficiently detailed to prove of practical use as a guide as well and so to inspire hope; it should be of such a scope as to situate the individual and the community in relation to society and to the cosmos. To this end I shall describe in more elaborate detail certain contents and some immediate aims of the abbot's teaching and the formation programs that he arranges for and supervises. While assuring fidelity to the essential observances to be described below, the style of life and attitudes of the monks must not assume too rigid a structure but remain flexible. The Rule has never been lived simply as a written document; from the time of Benedict to the present it has always been interpreted and applied by the abbot. A chief duty assigned to the abbot is that of adapting its provisions and his teaching to the needs and gifts of each monk of his community.

I mentioned above that the art of love requires training, that is *ascesis* in Greek. The practices of Cistercian life are those prescribed by the Rule of Benedict. They were agreed upon and put in place from the earliest days of the Order. Our Cistercian life in the 21st century must include these same observances in order to be faithful to the ideals and practices of the founders of this tradition; maintaining the Cistercian spirit is possible only where these basic observances are honored in the practice.

---

[15] William of St. Thierry, "On Contemplating God," n. 6, CF 3, Kalamazoo, MI: Cistercian Publications (1971) 46. St. Bernard makes the same point in his *Apologia*.

Bernard fully entered upon this life with its markedly ascetic observance. He infused it with a fresh spirit that gave more prominence to contemplative experience and imparted a new tone by adding to it a developed doctrine on love of God and of the Word made flesh, the Spouse of the soul. Today fidelity to our life can best be realized by cultivating this same view of the primacy of a loving, contemplative prayer centered on the Lord Jesus, and terminating in union with the Father in the Spirit. Bernard's disciple, St. Aelred, understood well the centrality of this vision. He responded wholeheartedly when encouraged by the Abbot of Clairvaux, to develop in writing his attraction for friendship in the service of charity and of the common good of the Cistercian community. At the same time Aelred emphasized to a higher degree than the other Fathers what he called "the necessary exercises of the Order" (*"necessaria ordinis exercitia"*) and the "disciplines of the Rule" (*"regulariae disciplinae."*) He considered these essential to the contemplative life. Specifically he has in mind *"vigiliae, labores, jejunia"* (vigils, manual labor, fasts) which, he taught, represent the active life of the cloister. They are accompanied by *lectio, meditatio, et oratio,* the occupations of the contemplative dimension. Establishing a certain equilibrium among these *"Sex illa generalia exercitia, quae nobis instituta sunt"* ("these six general exercises that are set up for us") constitutes the art of the full Cistercian life of which Aelred was a master.[16] His charm along with assured confidence based on his knowledge of men and affairs as well as of the tradition, allowed him to apply these with outstanding effectiveness.

These six practices, adapted appropriately to contemporary needs, must remain integral to the Cistercian life in this century. The art of employing them effectively is much facilitated by familiarity with the doctrine of the spiritual senses which I shall treat at length below. It also requires that the abbot in consultation with the brothers, discerns what emphasis to place on each of these essential elements and what content and modality to employ in their practice. Regularly such decisions depend on the particulars of any given community, notably its economy, the

16 Charles Dumont, "Sagesse ardente," *Pain de Cîteaux* 8, Quebec: Abbaye d'Oka (1995) 15–17.

capacities of the individual monks, the needs of those newly coming from the current society among other factors that are always in flux. Evidently such decisions and arrangements will continue to be left to each monastery of the Order within the supple framework of the Statute on Unity and Pluralism which should continue to be the legislation for the foreseen future.

The program implemented by the Founders, in fact, was worked out in keeping with a new spirit that was beginning to take shape in the hearts of some of the more ardent contemporaries. Before long it proved to be attuned to the aspirations of many. The early Cistercians managed to interpret in a practical manner the spiritual needs and aspirations of their times so that the educated and the nobles, the simple and poor as well, responded to their witness. This same task of interpreting the legitimate aspirations and spiritual needs of our times and devising ways of meeting them within the framework of our Cistercian Tradition is one of the major challenges of charity. Understanding our times with its needs and hopes is itself an expression of love and not the least important. It is a condition for finding adequate ways of communicating the Gospel and the monastic tradition and setting up effective formation for the community as well as providing for guests and society in general.

Concern for this task will have to involve judicious contacts and studies in various areas having a fundamental impact on the values, tastes, and philosophy of our times. Already in 1957, for instance, Thomas Merton in the course of his multitudinous writings made major contributions by elaborating a modern language that explained such important monastic practices as prayer, contemplation, silence, and solitude. He showed by example how it was possible effectively to speak to his times while remaining faithful to the cloistered life of his community. This has become all the more necessary in recent decades when language itself reflects the absence of objective norms. Not absolute principles but personal feelings and 'political correctness' dominate speech and behavior especially in the press and in the University.[17] In the same spirit of grasping the spirit of his time and addressing

[17] John Leo, "Double Trouble Speak," *US News & World Report,* July 4–11, p. 30.

his contemporaries more effectively, Merton came to appreciate the new understanding of the cosmos and of the earth's place in it that results from the findings of modern physics. He was prompt in recognizing its significance for the monastic life and for theology. "I must get to know something of modern physics," he writes . . . "Modern physics has its repercussions in the monastery, and to be a monk one must take them into account . . . there are things one has to think out, all over again, for oneself."[18] In the years since his death the data supplied by molecular biology and astronomical physics are giving rise to altered conceptions of human nature and of the cosmos in which we live. These data are being interpreted for popular consumption, commonly by writers who are skeptics or atheists. As a result, some fundamental teachings have become murky for numbers who profess the faith; moral and spiritual confusion is openly acknowledged by many. As a result this confrontation with physics has become more urgent. As Cardinal Ratzinger points out, in our day we may not conceal faith in the doctrine of creation; and I add, especially of man as the image and likeness of God. He discusses at length the ways in which the pretensions of natural sciences undermine the basis of Christian belief and morality through the denial of the creation of the world and so of the creation of the human person. Our nature is the product of chance in that system which is being affirmed with increasing insistence.[19]

Since the impact of this view grows in strength and scope as new findings result in reappraisal of familiar concepts rapidly communicated to the public, I believe this issue requires much more attention in our formation and spirituality than it has received until now. For the concept we form of our cosmos, or matter, of our bodies and its functions obviously has widespread implications for the ascetic and contemplative practices of mo-

---

[18] *The Intimate Merton*, eds. Patrick Hart and Jonathan Montaldo, San Francisco: HarperCollins (1999) 118, entry for November 2, 1957.

[19] *Op. cit.*, Appendix passim, 92 especially. More recently, however, at a meeting in Cambridge, England, the neo-Darwinists who are very vocal in their materialist interpretation of evolution have been strenuously criticized by biologist Lynn Margulis. She points out that the actual evidence gives no support to the view that evolution of species occurs by random changes in DNA. She announces that neo-Darwinism is dead.

nastic life. As a prominent element in our society the new data supplied by the physical and biological sciences should be included in monastic teaching insofar as it bears on the life of prayer and contemplation as well as on the moral and dogmatic theology. Not only physics, as Merton came to realize, but also molecular biology and neuroscience are having an ever increasing impact on the modern concept of man and of the world he inhabits. The philosopher F.S.C. Northrop considers that, "It is the coming together of this new philosophy of physics with the respective philosophies of culture of mankind that is the major event in today's and tomorrow's world."[20] Some of the findings of physics and neurochemistry allow for application in the study and treatment of living organisms including the human body and its functions, thus contributing to the rapidity of discoveries that are interpreted by a majority as providing a fresh image of man that is incompatible with Christian faith.

In dealing with the whole field of purifying the heart of images caused by disordered passions today some knowledge is highly desirable of the neurochemical basis of emotions, the dynamics of the passions, and the neurological pathways that relate perception to memory. Recent discoveries concerning these matters are increasingly influencing the concept of human nature including such fundamentals as free will, the central faculty of the image of God according to Bernard. They are also altering the ways of understanding the nature of emotions and the passions which form the chief matter of the ascetic life. The monastic teacher can profit from the new findings to explain how the emotions and affects, so prominent in early Cistercian doctrine, fit into the view of man as made in the image and likeness of God and show, in a more helpful manner, their nature and the place they have at present for the monk especially in the life of prayer.

The fundamental doctrine of the image as conceived and applied by St. Bernard and the Cistercians is more than a theoretical construct: it is activated by faith and experienced in prayer. This spiritual experience of its very nature influences the consciousness and the dispositions of the monk who comes to know

---

[20] *Physics and Philosophy*, Werner Heisenberg, London: George Allen & Unwin (1958) Introduction, 30.

himself as essentially related to God, without intermediary as St. Augustine has taught. The human person is not only created by God; he is made for God himself. William of St. Thierry expresses well the thought of the Order when he puts on the lips of the Spouse these words: "Know then yourself, o my image! In this way you will be able to know me of whom you are the image. You will find me at the bottom of yourself."[21] He later sums up the tradition concisely: "This is the perfection of man, likeness to God."[22]

The Cistercian way of life took form, was propagated, evolved, and flourished to the extent that it gave practical scope for a fuller human development and support to the engagement of mind, heart, and spirit in the search for union with God. The vision that guided the founders of Citeaux in fact contained the seeds of a broad humanism as the event showed in time; however, it was perceived by the majority of their contemporary monks as too narrowly focused until St. Bernard and William of St. Thierry, by their analysis of love and their dynamic concept of man the image in process of regaining likeness to God, established a humanistic basis for contemplative life that contemporaries experienced as addressed to their needs and aspirations.

SPIRITUAL SENSES

Already in the early years of monastic life in the desert of Egypt, the concept of monastic practice considered as a dynamic psychological system leading to restructuring of the emotions culminating in purity of heart found a vigorous and detailed expression in the writings of Evagrius Ponticus. His teaching was to exercise a strong if largely hidden influence on monastic spirituality through its propagation by Cassian especially, who, however, for reasons of prudence, does not indicate its source. Asceticism, Evagrius points out, is much more than simply a disciplined practice that assures self-control. That is its initial aim and an essential attainment. However, accompanied by contem-

---

[21] Cf. *Sermones in Cantica*, 1.5 Cited in *Dictionnaire de Spiritualite* VII.2:1431.
[22] *The Golden Epistle*, II.3.16 Cited in *Dictionnaire de Spiritualite*, VII.2:143–144.

plation, it has a more positive and higher function, namely, its contribution to the transformation of our being. This includes not only the control of the body through elimination of vices but also its integration with the psyche in the service of the spirit through the cultivation of virtues. This attainment cannot be achieved without that purification and elevation of the interior senses, to which certain of the Fathers so often refer, from the early centuries in the life of the Church.

This doctrine of the spiritual senses and their role in monastic spirituality with few exceptions has received relatively little treatment in recent centuries. Yet it is so fundamental to the contemplative life that monastic teaching in our time would profit by giving greater prominence to the role of the interior senses in the life of prayer, making use of some of the tools of modern depth psychology to develop further and apply the traditional doctrine. A fuller appreciation of the significant place assigned to this doctrine by the Fathers and by certain Cistercian authors and a more detailed understanding of its nature and role has much to contribute to monastic formation. In particular it contributes to the process of discernment by indicating more concretely the immediate aim of ascetic observances and by describing a specific manner in which contemplative prayer contributes to the restoration of likeness to the image of God in the human person. For that reason it seems useful to indicate at least the highlights of the Patristic and Cistercian tradition concerning the five spiritual senses so as to draw attention to this doctrine. The most prominent development in the field came from the work of Origen. He elaborated a fascinating theory of anthropology which can provide the conceptual basis for a more integral approach to the inner life. In a recently rediscovered work, he speaks of a very broad theory of the correspondences between the inner and the outer man, basing himself on the Pauline doctrine of the two men in a comment on a text of St. Paul: "No longer lie to one another, putting off the old man with his acts and putting on the new, the man who is renewed in the knowledge according to the image of him who created him" (Col 3:9, 10).

Origen concludes from this passage that each of us consists of two men, each having a correspondence with the other: "For just as the exterior man has correspondence for the interior man as like-named, so is the case with its members. We can assert that each member of the exterior man is found, under the same name, in the interior man. The exterior man has eyes; the interior man also is said to have eyes . . . in observing the divine precepts we acquire, in the order of the spirit, a more penetrating vision. The eyes of the interior man are more penetrating than we are."[23] Origen elaborates his thought in considerable detail for each of the bodily senses, but in addition, for other bodily parts: "There exist spiritual bones as well as corporal; when Jeremiah cries out that his intestines are in pain, he refers to those of the heart that we also feel when the Church suffers in childbirth. When Isaiah refers to those who have lost their heart, he surely refers to the spiritual, not the bodily heart."[24]

This model of the five spiritual senses in Origen is derived from both the New and the Old Testaments. He saw Proverbs 2:5 as an explicit affirmation of their existence. The Greek text that he cites is unique in that it does not correspond to the original Hebrew or to the Septuagint or any of the other ancient translations, it should be noted. But he must have found it in some manuscript and accepted it as an authority. Here is the passage in which he cites this text: "You discover the divine sense of perception." This sense, however, unfolds in various individual faculties: sight for the contemplation of immaterial forms. . . . This sense for the divine was discovered by the prophets. . . .[25]

The New Testament text he cites is taken from the Epistle to the Hebrews, and has often stimulated discussion by preachers and exegetes: "Solid food is for the perfect, those who have by habit trained their senses for the discernment of good and evil" (Heb 5:14). Origen's interpretation of this text differs from other commentators, who see in these words a reference to the faculty of moral discernment, quite distinct from the spiritual sense of taste. Few perhaps will agree with Origen that this text serves as a demonstration of the validity of his theory of the spiritual senses. On the other hand, it does provide one plausible theory

[23] *Entretien D'Origene avec Heraclide*, ed. Jean Scherer, Sources Chretiennes 67, Paris: Cerf (1960) 88–90.
[24] *Op. cit.*, 96, 98.
[25] "Contra Celsum" I.1.48., Sources Chretiennes 132, 203–04. Rahner discusses it, p. 81.

which seeks to account for the Scriptural image of doctrine that can be ingested as a kind of food by those with pure hearts, for their sense of taste has been rendered more sensitive and subtle through the elevating and purifying operation of grace. There is an analogy here, as I see it, with the functioning of our bodily senses that is of considerable interest for the life of prayer and of ministry. The external senses function with comparative rudeness in those persons who have not disciplined them in the course of mastering some skill or applied art. Experience shows, however, that the senses can be trained and sharpened by appropriate disciplined practice and, as they undergo this education they are modified and, in certain cases, even radically transformed. Each of the senses has been studied in this connection and been shown to be capable of a surprising range of improvements.

In the course of the centuries, this doctrine was often referred to in connection with spiritual experience by authors dealing with prayer and the inner life, usually only in passing, without any intent to give a further development to it. The Cistercians of the twelfth century often refer to the spiritual senses, with conviction. A particularly moving passage is found in William of St. Thierry's *Commentary on the Canticle.* ". . . illuminating grace is the virtue of all virtues, and the light of good works, without which even virtues are without effect and good works have no good fruit. Or if on occasion they should seem to have some, yet they are without vigor, they give no cheer, they lack the oil of joy, they teach no unction, they have no flavor of divine sweetness, no odor of eternity, no efficacious experience of the spiritual senses.[26]

In an earlier work he had developed a more elaborate doctrine of the spiritual senses at considerable length, becoming the first author since Origen to evolve a consistent and rather complete system.

> For as the body has its five senses by which it is joined to the soul, by the instrumentality of charity so, too, the soul has her five senses by which it is joined to God by the instrumentality of charity. This is why the Apostle says "Be not conformed to this world, but be reformed in the newness

---

[26] "Exposé sur le Cantique des Cantiques," 47, Sources Chretiennes 82, p. 138.

of your sense, that you might test what is the good and acceptable and perfect will of God" (Rom 12: 2). This demonstrates how we become old through the senses of the body and are conformed to this world. But through the senses of the mind we are renewed to the recognition of God, in newness of life, according to God's will and pleasure.[27]

As he developed his teaching further in the course of time, he describes the manner in which the functioning of the spiritual senses is experienced by the contemplative in the course of the higher stages of the monastic search for union with God, and gives an explanation of the experience that is at once psychologically and theologically satisfying.

The Bride was sitting, cast back on herself, waiting for the return of the Spouse, having a pledge of the Spirit that he will soon return, weeping, desiring that he should return. And suddenly she seems to herself to hear first what she does not see, and to sense with her interior sense what she does not understand, the presence of the Divinity, and thus she exclaims: *the voice of my beloved*. All the senses of the faithful soul grow cheerful; she eagerly goes to meet him as he comes leaping to her, that is, hastening. . . . Seeing him coming to her, she recollects herself so as to receive him, sensing him drawing near and standing behind the wall.[28]

St. Bernard in his turn treated at some length the way in which the various kinds of love are related specifically to the five spiritual senses. "There is therefore life, truth, sense, and charity of the soul. . . . There is, if you observe carefully, to be found a variegated love that is perhaps divided into five kinds corresponding to the five senses of the body."[29]

Baldwin of Ford, however, is another of the very few who dealt formally in a fairly extensive treatment of the doctrine of the five spiritual senses, showing his awareness of the importance

---

[27] *On the Nature and Dignity of Love*, 15, tr. Dom Thomas Davis, CF 30, Kalamazoo: Cistercian Publications (1981) 72.

[28] "Expose sur le Cantique des Cantiques," Texte latin, Introduction et Notes. J.-M. Dechanet o.s.b.; tr. M. Dumontier, ocso, Sources Chretiennes 82, #166 Paris: Cerf (1962) 346.

[29] "Sermones de Diversis," X.2, PL 183:568.

of attending to the cultivation of these faculties that condition the subject for sensitivity to the loving presence of God. He very probably was familiar with the passage from Augustine cited above, and was influenced by it. He may well have had some knowledge too of William's work or, more likely of St. Bernard's treatment of this topic.

> When it is wonderfully united to God by the love of obedience, the soul lives and senses in him and by him, and it draws a sort of analogy with the things it knows through the bodily senses. Thus, by the grace of a most inward inspiration, it senses God within itself and touches him spiritually by faith, smells him by hope, tastes him by charity, hears him by obedience, and sees him by contemplation.[30]

Baldwin here indicates *that obedience* is more than a moral virtue or a practical expedient. Rather, it is so to be enjoined and carried out as to contribute to a higher sensitivity enabling one to practice pure prayer with enhanced readiness. This dynamic and affirmative manner of conceiving one of the more significant virtues makes its practice more palatable to modern men. Baldwin's whole development displays considerable literary virtuosity and poetic imagination. He does not, however, engage in an extensive theological analysis of this topic. St. Bernard, on the other hand, in a later work of his, brought the doctrine of the spiritual senses to a new height of significance in his insights into its bearing on wisdom, *sapientia*. In deriving this Latin word from the noun meaning taste, *sapor,* and defining wisdom as a taste for the good,[31] he made of this virtue the guiding concept of spiritual striving and experience. In this view wisdom is the perfection of the sense of taste so that wisdom includes not only the aspect of insight and good judgment but also embodies sense experience and affection.[32] The Abbot of Clairvaux repeatedly insists that Christ himself is the wisdom of God (cf. 1 Cor 1:24), so that his

[30] *Spiritual Tractates*, vol. I, tr. and annotated by David N. Bell, Kalamazoo: Cistercian Publications (1986), Tractate IV, 118.
[31] *Sermones in Cantica*, 85.9 PL 183:1192C.
[32] This topic is discussed with insight by K. J. Wallner "Geschmack finden an der Liebe Jesu," *Cistercienser Chronik* 103 (1996) 269.

doctrine on taste-wisdom is identified with the finding of spiritual fulfillment in the person of Christ.

My view of Cistercian life then, in brief, is that it is ordered to the glory of God by offering him the best service possible: the recovery of the likeness to the Word of God through whom the whole cosmos is created. We will achieve this goal by developing the whole of our person, including the spiritual senses through adapting the same basic practices as our Fathers, lived out, day by day, in loving fidelity. For the cultivation of our spiritual senses both grace and enlightened practice accompanied by self-analysis are required so that theory is rendered effective by practice and its validity demonstrated by personal experience. This analysis of the experiences that accompany prayer, undertaken in regular sessions limited in time, contribute to the self-knowledge essential for discerning interpretation of inner experience. The more precise our knowledge of the various conflicting desires and images that arise at times of prayer the more effectively can we deal with them and bring our emotions and the desires associated with them into harmony with our search for union with God. In this way our deeper attitudes become conscious and we can bring them under the influence of grace during prayer and by our manner of living thus bring about a transformation which raises our inner life to a higher plane of perception. For this work, faith is essential for the fruitfulness of practice, but must be accompanied by earnest study of scripture and attention to its mystical sense. Further, at the same time we must undertake to mortify the operations of the physical senses and, in prayer, stretch and discipline the faculties of the soul. Do these senses represent ways of functioning of the intellect and will or are they the spiritual analogues of the corporeal senses, elevated, purified, and rendered responsive to the divine presence and activity within the spirit and in the world? In any case, let us do all we can to assure that we grow in prayer and that we lead a life harmonious with the demands of the Gospel, thus becoming increasingly conformed to the risen, glorified Christ. For when we shall have become sufficiently like him, we shall be able to share the life of God himself, rejoicing in the light of God's glory shining on the face of his beloved Son.

ENCLOSURE:
THE HEART OF THE MATTER[1]

by Gail Fitzpatrick, OCSO

INTRODUCTION

What does "monastic enclosure" mean for monks and nuns today? Is the idea of separation implied in this term something to be preserved? Do monastic women and men actually choose enclosure, or is it a vestige of an earlier period that "comes with the package"? Is enclosure a worthwhile practice for twenty-first-century monks and nuns, or for lay men and women who are drawn to monastic spirituality?

These are not idle questions. They are currently being studied in depth by our Order, Cistercians of the Strict Observance, in an effort to express in our Constitutions the purpose of monastic enclosure based on our tradition, sound monastic practice, lived experience, and post-Vatican II theology. Another purpose of the deliberations is to bring into harmony the legislation for both monks and nuns because historically the rules regarding their enclosure have been quite different. We also hope the results of our work will be relevant not only for the vowed members of the Order, but also for lay Cistercians and any person attracted by monastic spirituality.

The reflections that follow probe only a few facets of monastic enclosure: a brief look at how it evolved and three approaches

---

[1] The origins of these reflections was a talk given to Associates of the Iowa Cistercians (AIC), and later at the Second International Meeting of Lay Cistercians held at Holy Spirit Abbey, Conyers, GA, April 26, 2002. The talk was later published as "Enclosure and Solitude" in *Cistercian Studies Quarterly* 38:1, 99–104. It has been revised and expanded for this publication.

to understanding it; the interaction between enclosure, solitude, and purity of heart; a question of boundaries; St. Bernard's teaching on the three degrees of truth examined from the viewpoint of enclosure; monastic hospitality and enclosure; and an extended discussion of how we are called to live enclosure in an authentic way at the beginning of this new century—monks, nuns, and interested laypeople. Because the practice of guarding the heart is inseparable from the practice of enclosure, it permeates the entire chapter.

I chose this topic of enclosure for two reasons. First, of course, because it is a current issue in the Order, and I want to delve into the questions myself. The second reason is that several years ago the Associates of the Iowa Cistercians (AIC) asked me to speak about enclosure to help them understand this element of monastic life. During our subsequent discussion we formulated a question: Does the practice of enclosure have any relevance for lay women and men?

A year later I learned that many Associates had pondered that question, taken the monastic discipline to heart, and made significant changes in their lives. I was moved by their serious response. They describe some of their experiences in the latter part of this chapter.

Finding answers to the questions posed initially is neither quick nor easy, yet it is fascinating and challenging. There are hints that something new is happening in our Order and our world, and the concept of enclosure is part of it. My hope is that these thoughts may pique interest in a topic which holds more meaning, perhaps, than has yet been plumbed.

ENCLOSURE: ITS EVOLUTION

During the first centuries of Christianity, a period of both expansion and persecution, fervent men and women sought ways to live the Gospel message more completely and perfectly in order to find God. They usually lived alone or with a few others who had similar goals, in urban areas.

During the third century, when cities seemed less friendly to their religious lifestyle, some of these Christians fled to the deserts of Egypt or to other isolated places. There they lived as hermits or in small communities. They developed ascetical practices that helped them acquire control over their bodies and desires, grow in holiness, and pray unceasingly. Many became known for their wisdom and sanctity; some attracted disciples.

Even after persecutions ceased and Christianity became an official religion early in the fourth century, urban life was still such that the flight to the deserts continued. By this time "monasticism" was a recognizable phenomenon with a number of variations. Monasteries sprang up where like-minded individuals could work and pray and support one another as they all searched for God. The movement continued to grow and spread, gradually becoming somewhat institutionalized, and developing differently in the East and in the West.

Since one of the tried and true means of achieving their goal had been for men and women to withdraw from mainstream society to a desert, or a place apart, solitude was seen as an essential element of monastic life. Gradually rules evolved regarding places within a monastery set apart for the privacy and solitude of the monastics, and guidelines for the monks and nuns who lived there. "Enclosure" or "cloister" were terms that began to be used to refer to the monastery spaces and even to the guidelines for living.

Beginning in the sixteenth century the rules regarding enclosure began to be incorporated into the Code of Canon Law; that is, Roman Catholic Church Law. Over the centuries there have been many changes in these laws. The study being undertaken by our Order will help us determine whether more changes are needed.

Although some aspects of enclosure have changed since Benedict wrote his Rule in the sixth century, its purpose has not. This will become clear in the sections that follow.

UNDERSTANDING ENCLOSURE

During our discussion about enclosure at the AIC meeting we concluded that there are several ways of looking at enclosure in order to understand it better. Three of them are included here.

The first way is to look at the material aspects of enclosure, that is, things you can touch or see. If a sign on a fence or a door says "Enclosure," you know immediately that only those who belong to the monastic community belong inside that physical area. In this case enclosure is a particular space, clearly defined, into which only persons who belong to the monastery may enter, and from which they may leave for specific purposes. Non-monastics may enter the space only for a valid reason as determined by the abbot or abbess. Such signs, along with related rules and guidelines, preserve solitude and silence as well as the privacy of the monastic community.

A second way to understand enclosure is to look at the juridic aspects, that is, the specific rules and regulations regarding enclosure contained in the Code of Canon Law. Before a monastic group can be officially recognized by the Church they must examine these rules, choose the form of enclosure most appropriate for the community's particular way of life, and then request approval. Once that approval is given, the community and its members are responsible to live within that juridic framework.

The third and most important way of understanding enclosure is to look at the spiritual aspects and their effects. The material and juridical elements of enclosure are obvious, but do they, or can they, affect the spiritual life of the monks and nuns? The first two elements do not do so directly; instead they provide a framework so that solitude can be found. In this solitude the monks and nuns pray alone and together, enter their own deserts, and seek God with their whole hearts, for their own sake, and for that of the entire world.

Ideally, this solitude does not cause isolation from anyone or anything. Instead it gradually renders a person free, unencumbered, open to the Spirit and to the others in the community, finally embracing all people, all creation, in God. In this environment monks and nuns pursue the ultimate goal for them and for all Christians: to attain purity of heart and thus to see God.

Jesus had taught his followers in Galilee that the pure of heart would be blessed, for they would see God (cf. Mt 5:8).[2]

---

[2] All Scripture references are from the New Revised Standard Version.

Early monastic writers took Jesus' teaching to heart. By the early fifth century John Cassian († 435), following the lead of Evagrius (345–399), stated that purity of heart was the goal of monastic life and the perfection of apostolic love.[3]

For St. Benedict, purity of heart describes a life cleansed of vices and sin with the help of the Holy Spirit;[4] a life characterized by virtuous living motivated by love;[5] and "a life that, even now, exhibits that love of God and neighbor which will come to full fruition in the kingdom of heaven."[6]

As Christians and monastics we try each day to live the Gospel imperative: love God, love your neighbor. Whatever dilutes, falsifies, or blocks this love is foreign matter: it is not pure, and does not belong in our heart. This purity of heart is not esoteric or a pie-in-the-sky state of being. It is within the realm of possibility for all people, but it does require a discipline of life, and prayer that is so humble and constant that it penetrates the depths of God's mercy. Columba Stewart observes: "Fidelity to prayer defines the pure of heart."[7]

The *Encyclopedia of Catholicism* points out another facet of purity of heart: "[It] is gained, according to the Desert Fathers, by ascetic practices and *attainment of tranquility*."[8]

The tranquility which leads to purity of heart is not just a warm feeling of goodwill towards all on a quiet summer evening. It is a deep unconditional oneness with God's will that holds us firm in any adversity. It is a presence to persons and events that

---

[3] Cf. Institute 4.43 and Conference 1.6, edited by Columba Stewart, osb, "Introduction." *Purity of Heart in Early Ascetic and Monastic Literature: Essays in Honor of Juana Raasch, osb,* Harriet Luckman and Linda Kulzer (ed.), (Collegeville: Liturgical Press, 1999) 9. Hereafter: *Purity of Heart.* Evagrius used the word *apatheia,* the Greek word for passionlessness or tranquility. Cassian preferred the biblical term, purity of heart, to express this concept.

[4] Cf. RB 7.70. Timothy Fry, osb (ed.), *RB 1980: The Rule of Saint Benedict* (Collegeville: Liturgical Press, 1982). Hereafter: RB.

[5] Cf. RB 7.68.

[6] Cf. RB Prol. 50; RB 4.72. Benedict M. Guenin, osb, "The Beginning and End of Purity of Heart: From Cassian to the Master and Benedict." *Purity of Heart,* 214.

[7] Stewart in *Purity of Heart,* 12.

[8] Richard P. McBrien (ed.), *The Harpercollins Encyclopedia of Catholicism* (San Francisco: HarperSanFrancisco, 1995) 1071. Italics are mine.

is free and not clouded or blocked by wayward emotions. It is
the steady gaze of one who has embraced inner stillness and
finally sacrificed ambition and egoism on the altar of love and
service to others. Such a sacrifice cannot be forced. It is a gift.
Only in union with Jesus Christ and in communion with his Spirit
can one freely choose to give one's self for the sake of others.

Solitude and love now become inseparable partners. A
monastic community and each member therein chooses solitude
for the sake of entering into the self-emptying love of Jesus. I can
only let go of pleasant distractions and ego-building involvements when I permit Christ's love to draw me: "Come, follow
me (Mt 19:21); Love as I have loved (John 15:12); Count nothing
more important than knowing Christ . . . desire to know Christ
and the power of his resurrection and to share his suffering in
growing conformity with his death" (Phil 3:7–10). Solitude then
becomes a solitude of encounter, sometimes in darkness, sometimes in light, but always in freedom. This freedom to love
emerges as we focus our hearts and strive to "set our love in
order."[9] This is the monastic's reason for being, as it is for every
person.

The practice and discipline of enclosure is a way of guarding
one's heart so as to set one's love in order and work toward becoming pure of heart. To guard one's heart is to recognize that
many things may be good in themselves, but they may not be
conducive to growth in one's heart of love, compassion, centered-
ness on Jesus Christ, and the ability to give oneself in daily and
hourly prayer for the kingdom. Guarding one's heart means
continually discerning God's call to love so one can choose the
good and exclude from one's innermost heart the trivial, mere
curiosities, and those animosities that destroy tranquility and the
reign of God's peace within. I find the term, the guarding of one's
heart, a good description of this process.

---

[9] Cf. CS 50.8; *Bernard of Clairvaux on the Song of Songs IV,* Kiliam Walsh and
Irene Edmonds, trans., CF 31 (Kalamazoo: Cistercian Publications, 1979) 37. "The
theme of *ordinatio caritatis* is never far from the forefront of Bernard's awareness,"
writes Michael Casey, ocso, in *Athirst for God: Spiritual Desire in Bernard of
Clairvaux's Sermons on the Song of Songs,* CS 77 (Kalamazoo: Cistercian Publications, 1976) 197.

In a recent document on enclosure a Cistercian nun wrote:

> The heart of the monastic purified by asceticism becomes the space where all creation enters into the silence of God and the solitude of adoration. The real cloister or enclosure is the heart of one dedicated to undivided love of God, not the enclosed space of the cloister.[10]

Truly there are many ways enclosure fosters solitude and the attainment of purity of heart, but for me the practice of guarding one's heart is the *raison d'etre* of enclosure.

A QUESTION OF BOUNDARIES

As noted in the discussion of material enclosure, signs are often used to designate enclosure. A sign is like a door that can both allow or prevent entrance and allow or prevent exit. The door has a dual function. So we might want to ask: what is it that enclosure excludes from the monastery?

Saint Bernard, in the twelfth century, made a list that still rings true. He wrote:

> You enjoy the solitude [which enclosure makes possible] if you refuse to share in the common gossip, if you shun involvement in the problems of the hour and set no store by the fancies that attract the masses; if you reject what everybody covets, avoid disputes, make light of losses, and pay no heed to injuries.[11]

We could add to Bernard's list a few of the twenty-first-century beasts which we would like to bar from entering: the cultural "isms," that is, consumerism, materialism, and secularism; the idols of the world of entertainment and sports; the glut of information. With regard to the information glut, however, there is always a fine line between what we need to know in

---

[10] "Enclosure in the General Context of our Cistercian Monastic Vocation": Working Paper for General Chapter of 2002:3.

[11] SC 40.5; *Bernard of Clairvaux on the Song of Songs II*, trans. Kiliam Walsh and Irene Edmonds, CF 7 (Kalamazoo: Cistercian Publications, 1976) 202–03.

order to carry the burdens and sufferings of our world in prayer, and what is too much, what is idle curiosity. This distinction must be continually discerned. A question to consider when deciding how to use one's leisure time might be: What is needed and legitimate for enjoyment and relaxation?

Everyone can surely extend the list of things to bar or to embrace, as well as questions that assist discernment. The whole point of the discernment is to ask: What feeds the spirit? What fosters purity of heart?

Since the enclosure door enables both entrance and exit, it acts as a boundary. Based on my own experience of living on the inside, this boundary is not necessarily a barrier. I entered Cistercian life in 1956. During all these years I have seen the monastic side of the door and enclosure signs frequently, every day. I have never experienced them as barriers or something imprisoning. Instead I have felt a deep union with people outside the enclosure, especially those who are suffering.

Other monastics have a similar experience. Some have felt called to deep union in Christ with people suffering in various ways. A nun I know prays with tears and great compassion for women who bear the burden of violence. As encounters and involvements are curtailed, one can go deeper into communion with others, and with God.

Such communion is not only a monastic phenomenon. It can be the experience of anyone who chooses to find and live some measure of solitude, and consciously guard the heart. A certain distance is necessary in order to bear the light of God's presence and the darkness of one's own and the other's shadow or evil, and then to respond in depth. The distance may be physical, as it is for most monks and nuns. For non-monastics, finding such distance may be more difficult, but the challenge for both is to make use of whatever is available in order to find God.

CONVERSION, COMPASSION, CONTEMPLATION

St. Bernard's description of the path one takes to attain purity of heart is relevant to our understanding of the meaning of enclosure and the guarding of one's heart. In his treatise on *The Steps of Humility and Pride* Bernard explains his idea of truth:

"There are three degrees in the perception of truth. We must look for truth in ourselves; in our neighbor; and in itself."[12]

The first degree of truth, self-knowledge, is that radical knowing of oneself that is without subterfuge. I recognize in myself the image of God. I know I am a beloved and graced child of God. But I also recognize in myself the defacement of that image through my own forgetfulness, selfishness, or in whatever other way I place myself above God and others.

In the process of "coming to oneself" or gaining self-knowledge, monastic enclosure acts like a protective boundary around the sacred place where one carries on the necessary tasks of finding God and discovering one's true self. These tasks require both solitude and the company of like-minded seekers. Pursued honestly, they cause a vulnerability that can be quite frightening, especially in the beginning. Inevitably we encounter periods when not knowing oneself would be much more comfortable than continuing the quest for self-knowledge.

The boundary of an enclosure, physical or virtual, creates a "safe zone," safe from the distractions of persons and things that draw one away from the spiritual journey, and safe for the opening of one's heart to the good and the stripping away of the false self. Enclosure can then become a visible sign of commitment to continue the encounter within oneself in the heart of community.

The relationship between monastic solitude and self-knowledge can also be illustrated in terms of the traditional concept of *eremum* or desert. A recent document on monastic solitude observes:

> It is the very nature of the desert to introduce the monk to its elements of the wild. Those who seek its peace find instead a raw encounter with all that is untamed and unregenerate in their hearts, and they come to realize that there is no other path to the elusive goal of purity of heart. For we do not come to the monastery simply to be quiet in the most material sense, but through the ministry of that quiet, to enter the redemptive depths of Christ's healing mission. It is in the whole experience of one's radical need of redemption . . . that we enter the mystery of the desert and find a

[12] See *The Steps of Humility and Pride*, trans. M. Ambrose Conway, CF 13A (Kalamazoo: Cistercian Publications, 1989) 34. Hereafter: *Steps*.

more profound form of interior quiet-contentment with the Father's salvific will.[13]

This inner turbulence, under the pressure of the desert, at first may seem more disturbing than the kind we left outside the monastery, "but the only way into what we have come for is a wilderness path that can often seem to be going in the opposite direction."[14]

For all Christians, monastic and lay, this coming to terms with one's truth is the beginning of conversion, the movement beyond oneself into the mystery of Christ—the first degree of truth.

As this grace of conversion continues to do its work of transformation, one discovers Bernard's second degree of truth—compassion—coming to know and understand our neighbor through the experience and acceptance of one's own weakness.

One does not learn compassion through one's strength. We learn compassion through experiencing our common humanity with others. Through this knowledge we find the deepest levels of union with those who make this desert journey with us, and thus we join a communal search for God.[15] St. Bernard observes:

> The merciful quickly grasp the truth in their neighbors when their heart goes out to them with a love that unites them so closely that they feel the neighbors' good and ill as if it were their own. "They rejoice with those who rejoice and weep with those who weep" (Rom 12:15). Their hearts are made more clear-sighted by love. It is fellow sufferers that readily feel compassion for the sick and the hungry.[16]

This purification of love is subtle. It happens almost imperceptibly as one slowly accepts the inner light of one's own sin and the forgiveness that flows over one from the merciful Lord Jesus.

Accepting our own weaknesses and vulnerability and those of our neighbor, purifies our hearts. Then God reveals himself in

---

[13] Cf. "Monastic Solitude According to our Cistercian Tradition . . .": Working Paper Requested by the Central Commissions, Scourmont 2004, 32.

[14] Ibid.

[15] Cf. ibid.

[16] *Steps*, 34.

various ways, and we see God. This seeing is contemplation, Bernard's third degree of truth. He writes, ". . . pure truth is seen only by the pure of heart."[17] The deeper the grounding in self-knowledge, and the more one has opened to God in humility and love of neighbor, "the clearer will be the eyes of the heart which 'see God.'"[18]

Penetrating the haze of our self-centered universe is the fruit of long labor. It is also the gift of our merciful God. The practices of inner solitude, guarding our hearts, and quieting our minds in spite of innumerable clamors for our attention, lead to growth in loving compassion for the struggles and sorrows of others. All of these prepare our hearts for the simple "ah" of vision.

Michael Casey summarizes the long journey "to see God" in a few words: "Contemplation is the fruit of radical self-honesty and of kindness to others."[19]

This monastic work of perceiving the truth in ourselves, our neighbor, and in God, is ongoing. We never have it all together; we are never finished. St. Benedict writes: "The workshop where we are to toil faithfully at all these tasks is the enclosure of the monastery and stability in the community" (RB 4.78).

Contemplation, the loving gaze that perceives Truth, is well worth the patient waiting and labor. St. Benedict places the monk or nun within the enclosure, surrounded by brothers or sisters, simply to allow the person to focus, to set roots deep in Christ, and to open one's heart more and more to the love of God. The heart, so expanded, delights in the enjoyment of God. Thus the guarding of one's heart bears fruit.

MONASTIC SOLITUDE AND HOSPITALITY

While monastic enclosure sets up a kind of separation, a "filtering out," for the sake of solitude, it must also be concerned with those who come to the monastery. In his commentary on St. Benedict's Rule, Mayeul de Dreuille explains why this is so:

[17] Ibid.
[18] Cf. Stewart, *Purity of Heart,* 12.
[19] *Fully Human, Fully Divine: An Interactive Christology* (Ligouri/Triumph, 2004) 207.

> By its hospitality and its enclosure, the monastery is, so to
> speak, on the margins of the world, separated but not cut
> off from it. Solitude and communion in the monastery wit-
> ness to the fact that human life is communion with God and
> with others.[20] That is the reason guests can and should be
> received by the monastery. When practiced together, en-
> closure and hospitality can integrate the guest into the mo-
> nastic community, enabling the guest to share in the common
> search for God.[21]

Hospitality is one of the most sacred ministries within a
monastery. No matter how remote the monastery may be, guests
come. Most often, their coming is a search for something. The
liturgy may be the first attraction, or perhaps the church as a
work of art. The kindness and friendliness of the monks and nuns
may also attract them, but all of these are only surface reasons.
The real drawing card is the Presence of God in this place of
prayer. The only reason for the church structure to exist at all,
and for the monastic community to live out their lives there, is
God.

St. Benedict regards the reception of guests as a sacramental
act. "All guests who present themselves are to be welcomed as
Christ, for he himself will say: 'I was a stranger and you welcomed me'" (Mt 25:35; RB 53.1). The needs of the guests are
placed by Benedict on the same level as those of the sick in the
community. The guests, too, are to be served as Christ who said:
"I was sick and you visited me" (Mt 25:36), and "What you did
for one of the least brothers you did for me" (Mt 25:40; RB 36).

How does a monastery open its doors to all who come and
at the same time maintain the solitude, silence, and exterior and
interior peace to which it is committed?

The monks and nuns, each and every one, must remain
mindful of their reason for coming to the monastery. Purity of
life and serving Christ in every person—the guests, the sick, the
hungry, and the poor—this is the liturgy of monastic hospitality.
It is also its ascesis.

---

[20] *The Rule of Saint Benedict: A Commentary in Light of World Ascetic Traditions*
(Westminster: Newman Press, 2002) 335. Further: *Commentary*.
    [21] Ibid., 337.

When the monastic community does this well—reverences the guest and remains deeply faithful to its own life of prayer and singleness of purpose—the guests are drawn into an actual experience of Christ's peace. Usually guests who are thus served respond by entering into the silence and prayerfulness themselves. They pick it up in the atmosphere. They learn to listen to the Word, which in turn leads them to God. The monastic enclosure, providing both distance and participation, is one of the best means of allowing this to happen.[22]

Short-term visitors also come to the monastery, often in groups. A busload of fifth graders touring the local holy places may not add to the peace and tranquility of the monastery. On the other hand, when young people are well prepared for the visit, their open curiosity and transparency are a welcome joy. One never knows how one of these young guests may be drawn closer to God in his/her own life after such a visit.

A boundary can become a place of meeting. Nowhere is this more true than in the monastery guesthouse. The necessary solitude of the community can nourish the meeting between the monastics and the guests. Where there is authentic solitude, the words that are spoken come from and return to a place of communion with God. Not all the words spoken are about God, yet the Spirit of God impregnates all the words with simplicity and truth. The monastics then carry back into solitude the concerns, hopes, and needs of the people with whom they spoke, and the guests return to their own lives, changed by the encounter with the monastic peace and solitude.

The more deeply the monastic lives solitude of heart, the more he/she will be a real brother or sister, one who has discovered and experienced in the depths of one's being the stuff common to all—fear, doubt, violence, and love. The monk or nun returns to solitude of heart richer for having encountered Christ in the other, whether a needy brother or sister, a sincere seeker for spiritual truth, or a friend simply sharing life's journey.

Challenges abound for the monastics who perform this ministry of hospitality. St. Benedict recommends prayer as soon as a guest arrives, to place all in the presence of Christ (RB 53:4-5).

---

[22] Cf. *Commentary*, 335.

He even calls on the abbot to perform the most Christ-like act of humble service: to wash the feet of the guests (RB 53:12-14). This is no light matter. To kneel before another to wash his or her feet is to wash away in one's own heart any prideful or self-serving inclination. The person whose feet are washed becomes a humble receiver of Christ's uttermost love.

Today this act of hospitality is not performed when guests are welcomed, for our culture has changed. Instead they are received with a simple, unaffected reverence. An attentive and respectful greeting, an absence of over-familiarity, and a genuine care for the person's needs, go a long way toward conveying a prayerful and sincere welcome.

St. Benedict not only recommends prayer and ritual to recognize Christ's presence in the guests, but he also insists that only those who are deputed to this ministry of receiving guests should be involved (RB 53:23-24). The monastery strives to achieve a balance between, and a healthy integration of, the two contrasting values of solitude and hospitality. The monastic is to be ready to offer a warm welcome to guests, and also ready to withdraw to the solitude of the enclosure.

This is the work of guarding one's heart. Discernment and discipline are both necessary to achieve the desired balance. Where either is missing, imbalance arises and both solitude and hospitality suffer.

In many monasteries today a new way of showing hospitality is evolving: that of receiving guests who stay for six weeks, three months, or even longer. They come from all walks of life; they are of varied ages. They ask to live with the community as closely as possible so they can profit from the rhythm of monastic life, and deepen their own spiritual lives. They are not necessarily pursuing monastic life for themselves.

In our community we call such women "Long Term Guests." They live inside the monastery and share the community life in all its aspects: prayer, work, *lectio* and study, and meals. The enclosure of the monastery is opened freely, but not blindly, to these women. Those who come into the heart of the community so completely need to be interviewed to determine whether their goals and expectations correspond to the reality of the community's life as well as to its possibilities. Termination of a stay is always possible from either side if it does not seem to be beneficial to the person or to the community.

Our experience of accepting women who desire to share our monastic solitude and prayer has been very positive. We ourselves are not only encouraged in our vocation by the presence of people who love it, but, by their example, these women often lead us more deeply into the mystery of selfless service and commitment to prayer. This movement, I believe, will grow stronger in the coming years.

There is a sense in which we can say that hospitality plumbs the depths of the meaning of enclosure in a monastic community. If love for solitude and the active guarding of the heart are alive and well within a monk or nun, then the reception of guests, whether in the guesthouse or within the community itself, can be a graced Christ-event for all.

By being on the margins of society, a monastery takes on a beacon-like quality of the Presence of God which invites people to "come away and rest awhile" (Mk 6:30). This is a word that our world longs to hear.

ENCLOSURE AND SOLITUDE— FOR NON-MONASTICS[23]

To what extent can non-monastics integrate elements of monastic enclosure and solitude into their lives? Is it worthwhile for them to try this? If the guarding of one's heart is a necessary practice in the monastic's ongoing pursuit of purity of heart, and if many men and women find themselves drawn to some sort of monastic spirituality in their own lives, then what is actually possible and helpful for them in this practice of guarding the heart?

I am not qualified to hazard an answer to these questions myself, but I have listened and observed, and it seems there is a creative, spirit-led movement in this direction. As one Cistercian Associate observes:

---

[23] I want to thank the many associates who contributed ideas as well as material for this article, especially for this section.

Bringing the value of enclosure into non-monastic life seems
to be a reversal of the usual phenomenon: instead of religious folks spiritualizing a physical aspect of lay life (e.g.,
the spiritualization of human sexuality in Bernard's interpretation of the Song of Songs), lay folks are "spiritualizing"
a physical aspect of religious life.

The call to solitude, inner quiet, and contemplative prayer
is not unique to monks and nuns. It is universal. The monastic
life uses special means, honed by centuries of experience, to foster
growth toward purity of heart and union with God in Jesus Christ.
By its fidelity to the monastic way, a monastic community can
become a visible sign of hope and encouragement even for those
whose lives do not or cannot have such obvious structures.

Reflection on this monastic solitude and its supportive enclosure has led some Cistercian associates to make changes in
their lifestyle. Their comments, insights, and practical applica-
tions can be roughly grouped under three headings: a sacred
place, the use of media, and a reverence for persons. Much of
what follows comes from these women and men.

Some associates have created a "place apart" for silence and
prayer in their homes (see Mk 6:31). Such a place does not separate them from family or friends; it is just a place for focus, for
prayer, for being centered on God. For one married couple their
place of prayer is their car as they drive to work together. Morning praise and quiet prayer set the tone for their day. A fourth-
floor office has become an enclosure for another associate, simply
because not many people want to climb all those stairs.

A place apart is not always possible, but a time apart is often
available. It may be the pristine moments of the early morning
before the daily activity demands attention. For some the evening
hours are conducive to reading and prayer. Large city parishes
often offer the Eucharist at noontime which can be a profound
moment of renewing one's heart contact with the Lord in the
midst of God's people. Solitude of heart is possible even in a
crowd.

Reflecting on solitude sometimes enables one to discover
the solitude that is already present. A person who lives by herself
told me that our discussion on enclosure at the AIC meeting

helped her recognize the value of her own "unplanned enclo-sure." She said, "It had no meaning before I came to think of it as a naturally monastic aspect of my life."

For all of us, it seems, there are such unplanned, unsought times and places of what we might call inevitable or "necessary" solitude. Sickness, prolonged unemployment, forced retirement, the limitations of age or disabilities—all of these impose a certain separation from the mainstream of activity. To recognize, accept, and value these as "necessary solitude" rather than a disagreeable happenstance, requires a leap of faith, but the positive effect is well worth the effort.

The area where most associates feel a clear need for defining boundaries is in the use of media: television, movies, newspapers, e-mail, the Web. Some couples have either completely eliminated television from their homes or drastically reduced their use of it. As one put it, "Now I am more watchful of what comes into my environment." Another noticed the effects on her inner life that could be traced to the messages and perspectives promoted by television. She is not as fearful of picking up those values or lack of values as she is of becoming depressed or angry about the perspectives of our culture and world that are reflected in the media. To me, all these comments express an active and dedicated guarding of the heart.

Reverence for persons and prayerful, concrete openness to the needs of others is clearly a priority for many associates. A sense of balance and the ability to set boundaries is as necessary in lay life as it is in monastic life. Discernment is also needed in order to recognize when an interruption may be Christ in disguise, and when it might be a challenge from which one would do better to retreat.

As we have seen, discernment can be described as a filtering process that takes place as one asks of every stimulus, activity, or relationship: "How does this help me achieve my goal of living a spiritual life, of seeking God in everyone and everything?" Filtering thus helps cope with sensory overload and our culture's fascination with what is "different."

Keeping people or things out is only one aspect of this filter-ing process. Inviting people or things into one's inner space—whether heart or home—is another. The "boundaries" of enclosure can widen to include a group of people, a community, who share the same goal of consciously living in God's presence. These fellow travelers have the ability, through their shared life experiences, to encourage and even challenge one another to hang on even when one becomes weary of the struggle. We all need this simple support of "cheering on," and we all are called to do this for each other. "Bear one another's burdens and so you will fulfill the Law of Christ" (Gal 6:2).

St. Benedict makes a clear connection for monastics between "enclosure in the monastery and stability in the community" (RB 4). This same connection may hold true for all Christians who desire to grow in their life of communion with Jesus Christ in solitary prayer, and of communion with others in the service of love.

One of the greatest gifts a monastic can give to his or her community is perseverance. Staying the course to the end has none of the glamour of feats of asceticism or fame of acclaimed holiness, but holding steadfastly to one's commitment through good times and hard times is heroic. It is proof of the power of God's grace hidden within even the poorest and least spectacular of God's creatures. It is a sign of hope for all who seek to follow Jesus by lives of unsung fidelity.

Such fidelity and perseverance of one member of a community, whether in a monastery or a home, strengthens the whole community. Ultimately God alone is our strength, but often monastic brothers or sisters, husbands or wives, relatives and friends, are vehicles of grace for us and enable us to weather the storms. Abusive situations or relationships, however, ordinarily call for severance, not perseverance. Here, too, God's help and support from community, family, and friends are needed to make the change.

One view of solitude and reverence for the sacredness of the other is unique to those who are married. Here is the testimony of a married woman:

> I am trying to pay more attention to the sacramental nature of my marriage and the way it functions as a source of grace in my life. Part of being married means working hard to be totally open and accessible to one another—to hold nothing

back, to have no secrets, to be willing to be vulnerable. But it also means not to make unreasonable demands, not to desire more than the other is able to give. In this sense enclosure is an important issue in my marriage and it involves trying to honor and respect those parts of each other we have no right to intrude upon.

Stability in relationships, which derives from the spirit of monastic enclosure, may also have relevance for married persons, that is, the determination to do nothing that would endanger the relationship to which one has made a commitment. As one associate remarks: "Life is full of opportunities to enter into relationships that are dangerous to one's marriage; part of the commitment of marriage is to avoid . . . places, people, and situations that offer such inappropriate relationships."

The above reflections illustrate how the interaction between the monastic and associate communities can offer both groups insight, challenge, and refreshing ideas about the search for God. Although enclosure, solitude, and guarding the heart are practices that are centuries old, they acquire freshness when examined from a non-monastic perspective, and we see how they can still enrich our lives. Probing their meaning together uncovers riches of value to all of us.

CONCLUSION

Enclosure, the heart of the matter. As we bring these reflections to a conclusion we can say that the heart of the matter—the heart of the practice of enclosure—is the guarding of one's heart in the communal pursuit of purity of heart and ultimately, of the vision of God. How monastic communities incarnate this practice will evolve, with discretion as their guide.

The monastic ambiance of solitude, silence, and tranquility bear fruit not only in the monks and nuns themselves, but also in the guests who come to the monastery. Where there are signs of radical self-honesty, kindness to others, love for prayer, and great compassion for the suffering of others, one can say: "Truly, God is in this place" (Gn 28:16); ". . . it is good for us to be here" (Lk 9:33).

The law and external structure of enclosure are an essential part of monastic life. But enclosure is lived primarily from the inside out; it is an interior disposition that holds one's heart in loving attention, and one's whole being in a singleness of purpose, a focused existence. This guarding of one's heart is a discipline of love, the ordering of love according to St. Bernard.

Monasticism, a God-centered way of life lived in Christ in the midst of one's brothers and sisters, is a precious gift in the Church. More and more that gift is being expanded and multiplied through the men and women who integrate the values and some of the practices of monastic life, including that of enclosure, into their own lives. This can only be a source of new life and great fruitfulness for the kingdom of God.

"May God bring us all together to everlasting life" (RB 72).

TO WHAT HOLINESS?
MONASTICISM AND THE
CHURCH TODAY

by Francis Kline, OCSO

INTRODUCTION

Monasticism is seen in some quarters today as a panacea for what ails our culture. Many have unlocked the treasures of the monastic tradition and brought out meditation practices, concepts, and attitudes that have helped the people of our time cope with the myriad brutal aspects of present-day existence. My concern in this essay, however, is how to set in order the treasure house itself, as it relates to the Church. Many of the valuable items inside have become devalued or have gone out of taste in the changing climate of today's Church. I speak of authentic separation from the world, radical silence, and effective control of the appetites. We have been the beneficiaries of magnificent scholarship which has made us aware of the challenge of updating our monastic thinking. Perhaps we need to introduce some new treasure into our house to make better sense of the old.

In particular, we need to address what is spiritually distinctive, or theologically cogent, in a church of persons that removes itself to a "deserted" place in order to pray, when all of the Church is concerned about the youth, vocations to ministry and religious life, re-evangelization, etc. We are no longer talked about or admired, or even known in many parishes, expect by caricature and/or hearsay. The Church, while caring for us, does not promote us in a way in which it once did, when priests and religious brothers and sisters talked fervently about the contemplative monks and nuns. The universal call to holiness, beautifully enunciated in the document, *Lumen Gentium,* of Vatican II, puts religious all the way back at Chapter Six, and insists, quite rightly, that they enjoy ". . . a special gift of grace in the life of the Church and may contribute, each in his own way, to the saving mission of the Church" (*Lumen Gentium* c. 6, n. 43). Yet, the Council document, and other further legislative documents in its wake, seem intent on placing religious, without bothering to speak directly or particularly to contemplative monasteries, in a broad category of those professing the evangelical counsels of poverty, chastity, and obedience. These are not the ancient monastic vows of obedience, stability, and conversion of life. Nor do these documents explain what is unique about the contemplative, monastic tradition, source of so much of the prayer spirituality of the Church. Neither do they posit a clear place for this tradition in the new structure of the Church seen as the Pilgrim People of God.

The task of redefining our place in the Church must come from us and from our lived experience before it can pass into ecclesiastical documents and legislation. The Council, by its call for the renewal of religious life, invited us to do this work. Monastics have responded generously by reflecting on their lives in the light of the monastic scholarship mentioned above. Our new OCSO Constitutions (1990) represent a thoroughgoing elaboration of our Cistercian tradition as we are called to live it in our time. Yet, what is still lacking in such a successful document is a clear indication of our place in the Church in the light of the universal call to holiness. Our tradition, as part of its renewal and thrust into the future, needs to reflect on and articulate its own ecclesiology.

The foundations for our place in the Church are going to have to be (re?)discovered from our own lived experience, which may then feed academic and theological reflection. In this essay, our own practice of *Lectio Divina,* that is, prayer with the Scriptures, will be the *locus* for new ways of holiness, which then flow into a proposed new ecclesiology. But while we are making our way there, we see immediately that any monastic holiness is really a universal holiness that is valid everywhere because it comes from the Gospel. Monastics may use unusual ways to get there, such as withdrawal from the world, celibacy, etc., yet the only possible difference between a monastic holiness and a universal holiness is that we take the same holiness to the very heart of the Scriptures, which is where every holiness is ordered and where every holiness finds its source. From the heart of the Scriptures, therefore, the monastic church offers to the universal church an eternally and refreshingly new insight into the Christian mystery. Monks and nuns do this in response to a direct gift from the Holy Spirit. Thus the unity of the holiness of the Church will be revealed in all its manifestations, high and low, far and wide, as well as the real, true, and eternally valid place of the monastic tradition or its equivalent in the Church.

This essay is elaborated from a thorough reading of the Scriptures in *Lectio Divina*. It makes no pretense at theological sophistication. It comes from one monk's prayer experience with the Word of God.

As a beginning, I propose four ways of holiness: 1) the courteous and prophetic living out of the oneness of the Church according to the baptismal grace, which, as a font, overrides all other differences, hierarchies, or vocations; 2) conversion of life as the preeminent model for the Pilgrim People of God; 3) suffering, or the Cross of Christ, as the inevitable but faith-based yoke of the Lord, which he makes to be easy and light through love of him; and 4) the vision of the eternal value of all things in a renewed creation made possible by Christ's ministry of reconciliation which he shares with us. Each of these ways is particularly addressed by the monastic tradition. Each way depends on the other three, and, altogether, continue the reflection and introductory work of the Council when it called the whole People of God to holiness.

In this essay, only the second mark will be included, the call to conversion of life. The others will be written up in future essays. We must first make clear the concept for the baptized faithful, and then show how the monastic tradition may illuminate it. Then we can delve further into the Gospel roots of the concept and there discover the foundational aspects of conversion of life for the spiritual structure of the Church. We are then in a position to suggest the ever ancient and ever new place of the monastic Church in the universal Church.

THE CONCEPT OF CONVERSION

We work out our salvation in fear and trembling (Phil 2:12). In other words, we work out our baptismal grace in a continuous way. Baptism starts a dynamic process in the individual that ends, or, one should say, is consummated, in death. All through one's life, daily we hear the call of the Lord to follow him further up and into his own journey to the Father in the Spirit.

Great and sudden conversions play a part in this process of the baptismal grace, but they are no substitute for it. They must be seen as turning points, pivotal events, perhaps, that lead us to more subtle conversions as we continue to work out our salvation until the end. Dramatic conversions, tumultuous changes, even ideological ones, where we want to turn our backs on former positions we have held so dear, still must be seen in function of one grace, one offered salvation, guided by God's merciful hand.

Newman's quote rings as a clarion call for this idea of conversion. "Growth is the only evidence of life" (*"Apologia pro Vita Sua"* [1864]). We work out our salvation in time, in salvation history in which as individuals we seem to play such a small and anonymous part. Yet the long line of individuals and God's way with them is what constitutes salvation history. God wants a relationship with me personally. He is not accessed by old pieties in new circumstances. He had already explained the danger of putting fidelity to him, a living, breathing presence in our lives, into old practices where he may have been in the past, but is no longer (see Mt 9:16-17). We cannot access him by cultural freezing, as if rigidity and mere conformism to the past can substitute for the inspiration of his live-giving Spirit here and now. Of course, like scribes, we bring forth from the Church's treasure-house, things both new and old, but we do this from the storeroom of the myriad traditions of the Church, with the guidance of the Holy Spirit (see Mt 13:52). Blessed by God, the old things we bring out or retain, carefully and with discretion, reinforce and illumine the one tradition of the Church to be discerned all through salvation history even in so many and varied guises and appearances.

Ideas, practices, self-identities, however, are not easily abandoned, nor should they be. Yet, the Christian life, and its baptismal grace unique to each life, calls us to follow on the road after the

Savior in his intimate company where the Kingdom of God breaks out like so many wildflowers along the roadside in spring. We travel light, in the sense that our ideas of ourselves are apt to be challenged and cleansed of their delusions rather frequently. And a readiness to follow the law of love and selflessness, especially when it comes to dealing with abusive and abrasive people (enemies) is demanded. Jesus put it succinctly: "Repent (or change), and believe in the good news" (Mk 1:15). And this conversion will be called out of us, not just once, but repeatedly, until it finds the fertile soil deep within our hearts. Conversion is not a happening, so much as a way of life.

The concept of salvation history can help us here. Some may think that it is the narrative history of God's holy people of Israel and fulfilled in the Church, the People of God. But the far truer understanding of the concept is the way of God with his People. The form of narrative history gives way, in the eyes of faith, to a description, no matter how poor or inadequate in our human language, of God's thoughts, directions, and saving power in his ultimate care for his people. The Bible always takes God's perspective, never Israel's, so that the sacred writer can lament Israel's stubbornness and stiff-necked attitude, yet never defend Israel's behavior over against God. As salvation history moves out of the Old Covenant and into the Christ event, the Church is seen as the definitive move of God toward us in Christ Jesus under the ever-present aegis of the Holy Spirit. Here, all wrongdoing, sin, and guilt melt away under the overwhelming and purifying light of God's mercy on us in the Paschal Mystery of Jesus. Narratives of infidelity, punishment, and lamentation over the loss of God's presence in the Old Testament, are superseded by God's continuing presence in the New Testament when Jesus goes to his Father and sends the Spirit among us.

Our personal salvation history follows the course of our baptismal grace as it directs us through our development of learning right from wrong, suffering the consequences of our wrongdoing, to the acceptance, sometimes soon, sometimes not, of Christ as a living, intimate presence in our lives, and our vigilant and repentant response to him throughout our lives. The baptismal grace can be seen most clearly when it leads us to reinterpret constantly our sinful, and/or confused, or abused lives in the light of God's mercy and forgiveness. Even and especially the misfortunes we have lived through may become revelatory of God's constant providential care in this temporal and woeful world. The baptismal grace always leads to a deeper understanding of God in our lives, and this by means of our constant turning to him in moments of grace. Instead of considering our lives as righteous or not before God, we can turn and consider his ways with us, and celebrate him in his goodness.

SOME CHARACTERISTICS

The Christian people have discerned certain guideposts or roadmaps in the process of living out our baptismal grace that are valid for all times. We begin to notice a certain pliancy toward our neighbor. The imperiousness of a strong ego-intellect, so often a characteristic of youth, gives way to a tolerance and even deference to the opinions and judgments of others. Far from relinquishing our own ideas, we learn from others to modify our positions wisely for the sake of a richer attitude and a more universal stance.

There are no shortcuts through or detours around the process of the baptismal grace. No matter what our station in the Church, no matter how many gifts of the Spirit we may seem to enjoy, we cannot depend on these to arrive at an automatic holiness. They provide us with a way and a means to holiness. The grace bestowed, however, presupposes a "disponibility" to receive it at depth so that within our vocation or state of life one may continually turn toward God in whatever journey the Spirit suggests in an ever-deeper purification of one's life.

Continual conversion implies also a growing capacity to "understand" and accept, according to the will of God, all the events of life, especially those which go contrary to personal ambitions, desires, or perceived destinies. Glibly we pray in the Our Father, "Thy will be done." But only the grace of holiness can begin to lead us through the temptation of personal delusion and self-glory, past the great trials of life, to a full acceptance of God's will for us throughout our lives.

Our personal history is the place where the baptismal grace is located. Chronic or terminal illness, the death of loved ones, opportunities almost grasped, then lost, may sour us and leave us discouraged. God uses these means not as punishments, but as opportunities for us to rethink our program in the light of God's Word, and in the light of the passing nature of this world. If our misfortunes were punishments, how do we account for reversals in the lives of those we believe to be good? Or should we ascribe our calamities to God, who wills to punish us? How would our relationship with God proceed beyond fear of a malevolent and implacable authority? The answer to these questions lies in the passing away of all temporal things, in the angst, pain, and revulsion toward it, which the Scriptures tell us is the product of sin and moral corruption which we see and experience in the world. This is not God's doing, but ours, insofar as we share in the collective human sin. Only with time and repeated conversions of our point of view, can we own our part in this tragedy.

THE MONASTIC RESPONSE

Having briefly examined the process of conversion in anyone's life, we must now consider the monastic response to the same holiness. The Cistercian contemplative tradition identifies stages in the life of conversion. With the basic monastic ascesis in place, that is separation from the world, silence, control of the appetites, etc., we begin to notice the peeling back of accumulated layers of a false identity, a *persona,* which we show to the world, but which hides from ourselves the unpleasant aspects of who we really are. And there stands revealed, especially to ourselves, a vulnerable, often frightened person prone to sin. In the strength of God's grace, that new-skinned person is more free to love the Gospel, to follow along the road after the Master, and to be more pliant to the promptings of the Holy Spirit. According to St. Bernard, in his first published treatise, "The Steps of Humility and Pride," the immediate effect of a serious dose of self-knowledge is a compassion and understanding of our neighbors in all their foibles and imperfections. Self-knowledge levels off our own false high self-esteem to the point where we see ourselves equal to our neighbor. St. Paul would recommend seeing ourselves lower than our neighbor and counting others better than ourselves (Phil 2:3). This Pauline doctrine bases itself not on a poor self-image produced by a wounded personality, but on the touch of God, who, as he approaches the human person, burns away pride and ambition. The purified one automatically sees others in a noble light, perhaps even as God sees them, as his precious children.

Obviously, one undergoes many such conversions before arriving at a humility in the continual presence of God. Cleansed from sin and vice, and loving, as if naturally, Christ and his Body, the Church, the penitent approaches the source of all Truth, God himself, by the power of the Holy Spirit.

With God in sight at all times, one faces the reversals and misfortunes of life with new eyes. Nothing can separate us from the love of God in Jesus Christ, neither cancers, nor death, nor hurricanes, nor earthquakes, nor betrayals in the community. In fact, these "bad" things can become good things, or, if not good, then blessings, if they lead us to plumb further the depths of God's love. This new vision defines more clearly what it is to be a contingent being in the palm of God's hand, and it qualifies life in this temporal world, by letting us see that it is no longer an end in itself, but the gateway, and the only one at that, to God and his heavenly Kingdom.

As a conclusion to this presentation of the concept of conversion, both along its general lines and with monastic precision, we may say the reconstruction of the human person in the Risen Christ constitutes the very essence of the Christian life when viewed in its ultimate and eschatological perspective. The constant call of the Savior's voice, through the faithful celebration of the sacraments and adherence to the Gospel teaching, awakens a faith in the human person which goes deep enough into the will to rehabilitate it and allow it to follow the Savior through every suffering, every trial, even unto death. This conversion is to begin to live eternal life even in the here and now of this world. It invites the human person to become "spiritual," in the Pauline sense of the word, to put on Christ, to be mature in him, to leave behind childish ways of the flesh, that is, an understanding of Christ according to a human point of view (see 2 Cor 5:16), and to "press on toward the goal for the prize of the heavenly call of God in Christ Jesus" (see Phil 3:14).

Given Jesus' call to conversion, growth in the spiritual life, and how the monastic tradition views both, we must ask the question, which way from here? Is conversion better to be seen as a means to the Kingdom of God, along which we discover other ways, such as continual prayer, acceptance of suffering, control of the appetites? Or does it describe something more fundamental about the human person before God? Is it perhaps a structure of being which we all adopt as God approaches us and we approach God in the Paschal Mystery of Jesus? And if this is so, shall we not find evidence for it in the Scriptures themselves, and especially Jesus' teaching and experience in the Gospels? And if we shall adopt it, shall it not appear in the Church, and in the Church's self-understanding? It remains for us to examine the Gospels and to trace the lines of conversion in the lives of those who interacted with Jesus, heard his preaching, and "vowed" to be with him to the end. As we do so, we shall discover, as if never before, where the particular emphasis of conversion in the life of a monk came from and why monastic life can be understood fully only in the light of this particular holiness. From here, we can also see how conversion to Christ, with monasticism close by, lies at the heart of the Church.

THE MODELS OF CONVERSION

The encounter between Jesus and the penitent woman in the Gospel of Luke (Lk 7:37-50) serves as a model for repentance in the Christian Church. It shines as a grand and sudden conversion such as we see in the life of St. Paul and many others in the history of the Church. But though it is sudden, it was perhaps prepared for a long time. In such greathearted souls, where there may have been a strong and longstanding refusal to a call from God, we see the anatomy of grace. God eventually topples their refusal, and once freed from their blindness, their love for God proves stronger than their former iron resistance. What seems to be a dramatic and immediate turnaround could have hidden a bitter struggle between the person and God.

In her great act of repentance, the sinful woman behaves nobly and courageously by boldly coming to Jesus and disregarding the religious laws and social customs surrounding that encounter. Her love, based on God's forgiveness, overcame all obstacles and won for her the object of her spiritual desire. Henceforward, in the Christian church, the heroic conversion of the great sinner become the great saint serves a paradigm for repentance and a reminder that with God, all things are possible.

An even more probing example, and one that introduces us into the very Paschal Mystery of Jesus, is the behavior of the Apostles in the Synoptic Gospels, but especially in the Gospel of Mark.

In the first written Gospel, the Apostles exhibit a slowness to understand Jesus' mission and person. Time and again, Jesus finds them incredulous, self-absorbed, or cowardly. In the end, they abandon him. The other Synoptic accounts, that of Matthew and Luke, soften the failure of the Apostles, and in the Gospel of John, Jesus himself excuses them. But in the Gospel of Mark, and, indeed, in all of the Gospels, nothing except the death and Resurrection of Jesus alters the pattern of the Apostles' behavior.

Signs and wonders do not soften the hearts of the Apostles to believe that Jesus is God. Having multiplied the loaves and fishes for the five thousand, Jesus dismissed the crowd, and bade his disciples to get into a boat and go ahead of him to the other side. An adverse wind had them straining at the oars. He came to them walking on the sea. They took him to be an apparition and cried out in terror. He spoke to them to comfort them and got into the boat with them and the wind ceased. The Gospel text tells us at this point that "they were utterly astounded, for they did not understand about the loaves, but their hearts were hardened" (Mk 6:51-52).

Jesus' power over the elements, a sure sign of his divinity, terrifies the Apostles but leaves them perplexed. They recognize the power just demonstrated before them, but their hearts are too thick with materialism and tradition for them to confess Jesus as Lord. They cannot yet believe that this teacher in front of them, who looks like them and befriends them as a fellow human being, is also the God of heaven and earth. After all, the Scriptures are full of the majesty and power that surround God, either in his theophanies at Sinai, for example, or in the sanctity and ritual that surrounds his presence in the Temple at Jerusalem. The God of heavenly glory they would recognize, the humble teacher in front of them belongs to this world. He is one of them, even though he performs signs. The Holy Spirit cannot yet break through their hardness and coarseness of heart. Their tradition blinds their eyes to the truth of what they are seeing. They do not yet understand that God's omnipotence allows him to come among us, to hide his divinity, and, from time to time, to break forth in glory by exercising his authority. Nor do they allow that God in all his majesty, surrounded by celestial powers "with cloud and darkness as his raiment" (Ps 97:2), would ever be interested in them and in their petty concerns on the lake of Galilee.

The Kingdom of Heaven as the intimate presence and action of God offered by the Teacher in the here and now seems to be Jesus' point as he tries to convince the Apostles after the second multiplication of the loaves. Knowing that they had only one loaf of bread with them in the boat, that is, not enough for a meal, Jesus cautions them against "the yeast of the Pharisees and the yeast of Herod." But they confuse his image of the yeast with concern for their supper. Jesus then becomes explicit. "Why are you talking about having no bread? Do you still not perceive and understand? Are your hearts hardened? Do you have eyes, and fail to see? Do you have ears, and fail to hear? And do you not remember? When I broke the five loaves for the five thousand, how many baskets full of broken pieces did you collect? Do you not yet understand" (Mk 8:14-21)?

The Apostles do not yet understand, presumably, because they still are permeated with the yeast of the Pharisees, that is, a trust in religious observances and ritual instead of trust in God. The yeast of Herod, too, that is, a materialism which blocks religious faith, keeps them from believing in the Kingdom of Heaven present and acting in Jesus. In his company, they need not worry about their lack of bread. They need attend only to one thing, his presence among them. Everything else, including their daily bread, will be seen to by God. The trust in God's intimate and providential care in one's daily life is what is offered by Jesus in his signs and in his presence. Yet, the Apostles keep lapsing back into a religious safety net, the yeast of the Pharisees, where God is distant and accessed only by ritual deeds. In this vacuum, a materialism based on what I can get for myself, the yeast of Herod, substitutes for God's saving presence in the physical and temporal world.

The lessons imparted to the "wicked and perverse generation" of the Apostles continue when he comes upon them in the embarrassing act of their argument about who was the greater. He calls them aside and teaches them the unforgettable doctrine: "Whoever wants to be first must be the last of all and the servant of all" (Mk 9:35).

To demonstrate his teaching, Jesus calls to himself a little child whom he takes up in his arms as the least and the most vulnerable. To be last must mean to go with the last, to be with them and minister to them. Likewise, any who are ill, possessed, or thought to be unacceptable, are the objects of the ministry of Christ's disciples. For as he did, so must we. While others may argue about who is the greater, or may spend their time and energy looking to be acceptable and "appointable" by powers of the age, the Christian minister must be fervently seeking the last place where Christ is to be found with his friends, the poor and the outcast.

The most confounding failure of the Apostles in the Gospel of Mark occurs when, having just celebrated the Passover meal, they go out with Jesus to the Mount of Olives and abandon him there as he is arrested by the crowd sent by the chief priests, the scribes, and the elders. This desertion comes after and on top of their protests that they would never abandon him. Peter, himself, asserts that though every one else may desert him, he will not. Jesus replies with the terrible prediction that Peter will deny him three times before the cock crows twice on that very night (see Mk 14:30-31).

This enervating and deplorable action by the Apostles is couched in the starkest terms by the evangelist to highlight the extreme contrast between the paucity of human merit and the abundance of divine mystery. That we are dealing with the will of God, even in the failure of the Apostles, becomes evident when Jesus quotes the Prophet Zechariah, "I will strike the shepherd and the sheep will be scattered" (Mk 14:27 [Zech 13:7]). God wills that divine power should be made most manifest in human weakness, and not in human strength, which when puffed up in the human heart over against God, is an abomination to him.

This prediction of the Apostles' failure by the prophet lies in direct continuity with God's way with his people. He leads the Israelites on a circuitous route so as to allow the Egyptians to catch up to them. Thus, when God acts at the Red Sea, the people could never conclude that it was their speed, their strength, or their cleverness that saved them from the Egyptians, but God alone (See Ex 13:17-22). At the failure and the death of Saul and the crushing defeat of the Israelites by the Philistines (1 Sam 31:1-13), it is the bravery of David, an insignificant youth but inspired by the Holy Spirit, that turns the tide of victory for the Israelites against their enemies. Not Saul's stature, nor his anointing as king, could make his heart right with God. Only the coming of the Holy Spirit upon David could change the military situation of Israel (2 Sam 5:17-22). God's power is made obvious and glorious in human weakness and failure.

The evangelist dramatizes the failure of the Apostles by underscoring in sublime detail the denials of Jesus by Peter, the appointed head of their circle. Peter it was who led the protest against Jesus' assertion that they would all become "deserters." Peter said, "Even though all become deserters, I will not." And when Jesus retorts that on that very night before the cock crows twice, Peter will have denied him three times, Peter vehemently insists that, "Even though I must die with you, I will not deny you. And all the Apostles said the same thing" (Mk 14:27-31).

The scene is set for the Evangelist's careful and effective intertwining of the narrative of Jesus' prayer at Gethsemani, his arrest and "trial" by the high priest and the chief priests, with Peter's denial of Jesus, the last and lowest of the long list of sad behaviors of Jesus' intimate circle. When a servant girl of the high priest spotted Peter in the Courtyard warming himself as Jesus' trial proceeds, she stared at him and said, "You also were with Jesus, the man from Nazareth." Peter denied it and went on to deny again that he was one of Jesus' followers, until, a third time, "He began to curse, and he swore an oath, I do not know this man you are talking about" (Mk 14:71).

Peter curses and swears not just against Jesus, but against himself, and all the Apostles whose leader he is. In the anatomy of his relationship with Jesus, i.e., his vehement and impetuous declaration of love for Jesus (". . . I will never deny you" [Mk 14:31]), contrasted with this loud cursing and swearing that he did not even know him, we see to the bottom of the human heart, not just of Peter's, not only of the Apostles', but of everyone's. We see our utter inability to do what we want to do, because of a previous commitment made to Satan, shrouded in the mists of time and dismissed by the mind as untrue or unfair. Yet, our world, broken by war, violence, and greed bespeaks the bitter truth. The mess we see is our doing. It is Satan's miserable victory over us, stretching from the Garden until now. Yet his victory is not final. And this is where we need to keep reading in the Passion Narratives to see what happens to the Apostles once Jesus rises from the dead.

As the Apostles scatter in fear, Jesus tells them that he will rise from the dead and go before them into Galilee (Mk 16:7). His saving victory over sin and death will reconstruct their broken loyalty and their intimate circle and absolutely nothing else will. The striking of the Shepherd and his resurrection alone will reunite the scattered sheep, so that it may be made clear that no human virtue or strength remained loyal to Christ. Only God's power and mercy constitutes the new community of the Apostles around his risen body.

CONVERSION AT THE
HEART OF THE SCRIPTURES

What we see in the Synoptic tradition and the Acts, but especially highlighted in the Gospel of Mark, is a model of repentance as the response to God's mercy in the Christ Event. We see individuals fall and come to repentance, such as Peter, but we see them living out their forgiveness in a community who holds them in God's forgiveness. The early Church's experience of human weakness in the face of persecution and memory of the failure of the Apostles, guaranteed that the Good News of Jesus Christ would be preached only around the saving power of his Resurrection. Thus, the Christian community would be based not on human merit but on absolute faith in that Resurrection in a continual move toward greater and deeper repentance.

THE POST-RESURRECTION PERSPECTIVE

The Apostles were gathered in prayer "with certain women, including Mary, the mother of Jesus, as well as his brothers" (Acts

1:14). What was their thought as they prayed in that space between the Ascension and Pentecost? Surely, they reflected on the miracle that the risen Jesus had reconstituted them as his circle. He had appeared to them through forty days, interrupting their attempts to return to a normal life, that is, a life without him. But he would not let them alone. And now, they were gathered at his bidding, waiting to be clothed with power from on high. Before the event of Pentecost, or, perhaps because of it, their conviction about the risen Christ was cemented. But part of that foundation had to be an eternal memory of their weakness. After all, they had abandoned him, and they had experienced the nothingness of their own power. They were now ready to sing with the psalmist, "Not to us, Lord, not to us, but to your name give the glory" (Ps 113 [115:1]:9).

One cannot help but notice the juxtaposition of Mary and the gathering of the Apostles. A broken community, reconstituted by the power of Christ, is prayed for by one who never abandoned the grace of the angel, but bore her mysterious son and saw him through his awful fate, all by the power of the Holy Spirit. What she had learned about openness to God, and the concomitant humility that goes with it ("He looked on the lowliness of his handmaid," Lk 1:48), she now prays may be the Apostles' joy as well. As she had given birth to Christ and presented him to the world at the meeting of Simeon and Anna in the Temple (see Lk 2:25-38), so now the Apostles would give birth to Christ in their hearts in a new configuration of their own persons. Open to his Spirit, they would present him to the world in all its languages.

THE MONASTIC CONNECTION

The early monks, separated from this event of prayer in the Acts by several hundred years, nevertheless, intuited that they were in direct imitation of the Apostolic circle (see John Caman, "Conferences," 12, 16, 18). Not that they were the Church. Not that their way of life was the only way to be a Christian. But, rather, in the conviction that what the Spirit was calling them to do by renunciation, was in direct communion with the Apostles' experience of the risen Christ, that is, the passage from considering Christ from a human point of view, to a life permeated by his Spirit.

When the monastic tradition applies the Apostles' experience to itself, it does so in learning steps. Whereas the cataclysmic event of Jesus' suffering, death, and resurrection was stamped forever on the Apostles' minds and hearts, nevertheless, they learned from his intermittent appearance and the corroborating testimony of others, to fashion fully in their beings the conviction of his saving power and merciful forgiveness. The monks, in imitation of the fifty days in the Lucan story of waiting for the Spirit (see Acts 1:12-14), adopted a similar mode of construction. Step by step, and grace by grace, they learned to admit the saving word, a two-edged sword into their flesh (see Heb 4:12), so that it could work its purifying task. For the monks, the Apostles' fifty days might be fifty years, but lived in the same enthusiasm and urgency. For with the Spirit, there is no wasting of time or vagueness of purpose. We see, therefore, a lifetime spent in the formation of the Risen Christ in the heart of a monk. The Paschal Mystery of Christ becomes the monk's own journey. The monk suffers and dies with Christ so as to be raised with him in the full power of the Holy Spirit. Only the Spirit knows, and only the Spirit can direct those actions and experiences which lead a person through the great trial in imitation of the Lord Jesus. One passes from interpreting one's life more and more according to a Christ perspective as conversion occurs, to turning the corner in one's life in a definitive move by the Holy Spirit. Then, one considers Christ no longer from a human point of view. Rather, one can say with St. Paul, "forgetting what lies behind, and straining forward to what lies ahead, I press on toward the goal for the prize of the heavenly call of God in Christ Jesus" (Phil 3:13-14).

Steps of humility, stages of conversion, levels of self-knowledge, all conspire as so many graces to invite the Spirit to confer on the monk the crowning grace of passage to life in Christ Jesus.

THE MONASTIC CHURCH

The monastic ecclesia lives in the hope that each of its members will make this passage to live in Christ Jesus. Not all the members are granted it, not all are ultimately called to it. Not all answer when it is given, "for many are called, but few are chosen" (Mt 22:14). Nevertheless, at the center of the monastic Church, because of the gift of the Spirit which calls that ecclesia together, lies the memory of sin and repentance, that is, the desire and zeal to return to God and to keep turning toward him in the countless ways he asks us to follow. The memory begins with Jesus himself who stands before the throne of God as the Lamb once slain, or with the marks of slaughter still on him (Rev 5:6). From that eternal memory of what he suffered for us, and what he achieved for us by his passion and death, there flows another memory into those who repent of the rebellion that sent Jesus to his death. The memory of his suffering illuminates and activates our memory of sin and repentance, so that, as we are drawn closer to him in his heavenly glory, our repentance and our continuing conversion grow brighter and warmer. Like one magnet to another we race along this journey, now not out of our own volition or energy, though that is active, but by a spiritual attraction to the Truth, overwhelming in its purpose and passion.

This is what makes the monastery the place of holy challenge that it is. Not because of the holiness of the monks who live there, not because the ground is made more sacred by the footsteps of their holy persons. For many of them may not be very holy. But because of the hope that lies in the heart of the community, in that hope, the action of the Holy Spirit causes gifts of conversion, self-knowledge, humility, and so many more, to flow back and forth until, and, if only, a single person lights up with the memory of the wounds of Christ in his heart and the consequent stance of repentance. This hope is what gives the monastery the élan and the spiritual peace it enjoys in the minds and experiences of visitors. With no means to explain what they sense, they nevertheless intuit that God is active here. After all, it is God alone who is holy. We but share in his holiness.

The monastic ecclesia holds up this hope of bringing people to the memory of Christ as if it were a single ray of light, warming and illuminating the whole Church from within. As St. Benedict was given the vision of the whole world caught up in a single ray of light, so the monastic Church, governed by his Rule, holds aloft the grace of the Holy Spirit for the whole Church. Every other gift looks back to it as if to its source, for it is the source, insofar as it is the Apostles' testimony to the Risen Lord. Every inspiration in the Church breathes from this one maternal breath, this primordial grace which went to the heart of Peter at Jesus' three questions of love, or to the heart of Paul, when, knocked to the ground and blinded by the light of the risen Christ, was forever converted. The monastic Church is called apart from all other gifts and missions of the Church, so that this light of Christ which it guards, proclaims, and lives by, may guide the Church on its way of return through all its manifold activities.

THE CHURCH:
ONE BODY, MANY MEMBERS, GIFTS AND MISSIONS

The baptismal grace at the heart of believers calls them to many different positions in the Church: to preach, to teach, to heal, to serve, to govern, to prophecy. Yet each of these missions is not an end in itself. Each is an avenue for the individuals to find the way of return in ever deeper levels of their being. The Spirit will accomplish through them what it wills to do for the Church. The Spirit will not fail, however, to offer the workers in the vineyard their own contemplative rest which is based on constant repentance and conversion. What is offered every baptized person is the call to follow after the Lord to the point of gratitude for the gift of life, self-knowledge, and repentance for sins and for the greatest sin, that of crucifying Christ. We all share in that greatest sin.

Yet, in the great demands made by the missions of the Church, the narrow way of living the Gospel, as if in the intimate circle around Our Lord, gets lost. The Church has become endlessly complex in keeping with her mandate to go to all the world and preach the Gospel (see Mt 28:19; Mk 16:15; Lk 24:27). We should never think that, in her missions, the Church grows thin, extended, or attenuated. The same baptismal grace is as full of the seed of hope in the African infant as it is in the Deacon in Rome, or the monk in his cell. But each is called to repentance in many different ways. What the Church keeps forgetting, inevitably because of its weakness, is that holiness of life must follow the way of constant conversion leading to a humble repentance.

THE MYSTERY OF THE CHURCH

The monastic ecclesia supports the wide net of the Church to which many are called. It throbs with the missionary heart of the Church in all its varied works. It commiserates with Bishops as they carry the weight of pastoral anxiety. But with all of this outward activity, in which there is always the call to holiness due to the baptismal grace, the monastic Church keeps a light of memory on the way of return to the heavenly glory. It keeps alive the structure of the Church as both the wide net and the narrow way. It does so by taking the same holiness to which all are called, to the heart of the Scriptures from which the holiness emanated. If there was no monastic Church, the Spirit would have to go and get one (and, indeed, that is the reason behind the capacity of the monastic ecclesia to reform itself after the example of the early monks). Only in such a way could the Church be completely itself—a mystery in this world but not of it. Broad and welcoming in its preaching and pastoral zeal, yet not flinching from the deep truth about our sinfulness and the narrow way of return by repentance and obedience, the Church can never be one or the other, but both as it proclaims a universal holiness wherever the Spirit is at work.

A UNIVERSAL YET MONASTIC HOLINESS

The Church was born into this human reality as Christ lay dying on the cross. The monastic church keeps alive the memory of that day, and its glorious counterpart, the Resurrection. At the foot of the Cross, and in the heart of the monastic church, the confines, rules, and safety of this world begin to give way to a raw contingency, a radical dependence on God where the kingdom of heaven begins to break through to this temporal world. Hidden to all but spiritual observers, the monastic church appears to make no sense, to be a collection of weaklings and losers, who have thrown away their lives in a useless round of monotonous and unrewarding prayers. But to God, and to those who see with the eyes of God, it is where his light begins to shine on this temporal darkness, where his strength shoulders human weakness, where human weakness is so known, tasted, and accepted, that his power can be admitted where human pride had previously shut it out.

The Church makes no spiritual sense without this hidden gift of total surrender to Christ and constant conversion to him. It is the Church's wedding garment which it only partially wears when it forgets the monastic way. The Church is not its complete spiritual self without this total abandon to the love of God, this total joy of the freedom of the children of God, this total sacrifice which is held up as a single ray of light, made up of all the other rays of light, which is the mystery of the Church.

Thankless, rootless, without a home here, unknown or derided, thought foolish and meaningless, the monks and nuns look out on the eastern horizon for Christ the Bridegroom of the Church, in a world still too busy with itself, still too taken up with its own seriousness. The monks and nuns keep the Church on its toes in vigilant waiting for the Savior. The monks and nuns hold aloft the light of the mystery of the Church, still in this world, but well on its way to full communion with the mysterious God. The light shines on, but in a fog where only the intently gazing can see it.

THE FRUITS OF MONASTICISM: A VIEW FROM WASHINGTON

by Daniel P. Coughlin

The Cardinal had said in his phone call that he simply wanted to know if I was available to come to his house the next morning. "I do not want to appear mysterious about this. I will get back to you and explain everything before your meeting is over. Now I have other details to attend to about this."

I was so fully engaged in conversation with one of the Archdiocesan lawyers, now that the meeting had ended the Cardinal's call had escaped my mind.

When he made his second call, Cardinal Francis George said: "When you come to my house tomorrow morning, come to the back door. Sister will let you in and take you upstairs by the back stairway. I will be meeting with the auxiliary bishops and others in the front room.

"You may have heard that Speaker J. Dennis Hastert, Speaker of the U.S. House of Representatives, has gotten himself into a bind. He is looking for a chaplain. He asked me for a short list of names of priests. I put your name on the list. I think you could do the job. If you agree to do this, you will be in the history books!"

Then he laughed.

I had not heard of Mr. Hastert's dilemma. I am not sure if at that time I even knew that Congress had a chaplain.

"Don't talk to anyone about this. The Speaker wants this to be kept quiet," the Cardinal said. "There will be two men from the Speaker's office here tomorrow to interview you."

When I got off the phone I simply wanted to go home. What did this mean? I needed to pray. How was I to prepare for this meeting? The two men were probably from the FBI, I thought. I guessed they already knew a lot about me.

When I arrived back at St. Clement rectory, I reached for my breviary ready to pray Evening Prayer. Upon my desk was the prayer of Thomas Merton. "My Lord God, I have no idea where I am going . . . and the fact that I think that I am following your will does not mean that I am actually doing so . . ."

I had come across this prayer some weeks before on one of my visits with my spiritual director. I had been seeing this Jesuit for some years. In recent months he was helping me with an impending transition in my ministry. My present position as Vicar for Priests was coming to an end July 1st. It was now March 13, 2000.

That evening I prayed the Merton prayer slowly and deliberately. ". . . And I know that if I do this you will lead me by the right road though I may know nothing about it."

It was then I decided to call a good and prudent priest friend, Rich Hynes. When I described the Cardinal's phone call to him, he laughed. Then, he asked, "What do you think you will do?"

I told him I planned to reach my Jesuit spiritual director and see him in the morning before the interview.

When I told Ted Tracy, s.j. about the Cardinal's phone call the next morning, he laughed.

Ted had guided me in the past months through a series of "right questions." When I first told him my term as Vicar for Priests was coming to an end, he asked why I seemed upset. I told him I had no idea what I wanted to do next. At first, that might mean I should continue on in the important work Larry and I were doing with priests in the Archdiocese.

But leaving that work seemed inevitable once the process for selection of my replacement was announced. Then he asked how I was discerning the future. Was I looking for a job description? What could I do to help the Cardinal? How to serve the Archdiocese? Why was I hesitant to become a pastor at this time?

When it became clear I was not just looking for another job, he asked: "What is the deeper question of your heart?" Perhaps it was: "What do you want to do for Christ?"

Some weeks later I came back to him and said the question was not "What do I want to do for Christ?" But: "What does Christ want to do with me?"

As we laughed together on March 14, 2000, tears came to my eyes. He smiled and said: "See, once you hand it over to the Lord, you can expect anything."

I went to the interview knowing that this was not my doing. So I was not nervous, anxious, or desirous. During all those weeks while I was working through Ted's guiding questions of spiritual direction I had taken upon myself what I called "fasting of the heart." I denied myself any wondering about the future or any daydreaming about a future assignment. No "what if" games or "if only" meanderings as I stood before the mirror shaving. Also I would not bring up the topic in conversation with other priests, family, or friends. If they brought it up, I simply asked for their prayers and said that if something more definite came up I would let them know.

I carried Thomas Merton's prayer in my pocket to the interview. I carried it every day after that. I prayed it at least once or twice a day until I was on a plane ten days later flying to Washington, DC. It was in my pocket when I was sworn in as the first Catholic priest to be Chaplain of the U.S. House of Representatives on March 23, 2000. To this day, I keep copies of the Merton prayer in my desk drawer at the Capitol and frequently find it opportune to give a copy to others.

The summer before I entered the major seminary I read Thomas Merton's *Seven Storey Mountain*. At the time I did not appreciate his writing about Communism and his experiences at Columbia, but I was thrilled by his conversion story and baptism as a Catholic. His additional adventure of entering a Trappist monastery was a simple encouragement to me as I left home to prepare for the priesthood. Little did I realize how much affinity there was at the time.

The major seminary with its horarium, its formal liturgies, multiple rules, simplicity of lifestyle, and observance of "the great silence" was a better formation school for a monastic vocation than for diocesan priesthood in those days. We spent many hours alone in our individual rooms when not in class. There was no talking in the corridors of the residence, no TV, no radios, newspapers, or magazines, except for a couple Catholic periodicals. Unlike the monastery there was little manual labor. Free time was filled with sports and friendship.

At the seminary I met other young men who had been taught by monks in high school or in prep schools. During evening walks I would learn from them more about their liturgical and monastic routine. I would love any stories about monasteries.

During my first year at St. Mary of the Lake Seminary I was encouraged to keep a journal to develop better skills in writing. I was delighted to learn that Thomas Merton kept a journal. When I heard that some of his monastic experiences had been published in a book, I was anxious to read *The Sign of Jonas*. Once I laid hands on a paperback copy I would have loved to have devoured the whole book. But to keep focused on my studies, I disciplined myself like it were chocolates. Only after I had done my homework, would I allow myself to read *The Sign of Jonas* for a half hour. To this day I remember distinctly the evening I came to "The Fire Watch." I remember leaning on the doorjamb between the bathroom and the bedroom overwhelmed by the growing drama built by choice of words and imagery. I thought those pages to be the most insightful and beautiful rhetoric I had ever read.

It was then I began to wrestle with the impulse to write poetry, the desire to be a monk, the hope of experiencing true contemplative prayer, and someday the joy of loving Christ with 100% of my heart and soul. Even before I ever visited the Abbey of Our Lady of Gethsemani the place had become a part of my life.

After fifty years of retreats, a five-month sabbatical there, and many visits, the Abbey of Our Lady of Gethsemani and its community have led me to amass a library of my own, built around Thomas Merton, contemplative prayer, Eastern religions, and monastic writings. It is there that I first became acquainted with Trappist sign language and Cistercian "manners." Over time I have witnessed recent monastic reforms take shape there. Anyone who knows me knows Gethsemani's influence upon me cannot be measured.

The Cistercians have affirmed my vocation as a priest time and time again. They have helped me through major transitions in my life. They have provided me with an atmosphere in which I could learn to deal with my own solitude. When needed, they have offered me a place to seek lasting truth amid passing concerns with quiet friendship. They have always been open to listening to my story. Without knowing it, they have conditioned my choices and purified my intentions. Although I remain a priest of the Archdiocese of Chicago and have family there, Gethsemani has become a second home for me.

Amid all the wonderful memories, anecdotal stories, and wisdom sayings this and other Trappist monasteries have given me, here I will narrow my witness to just three lessons I have learned from the Cistercians. I name them: "The Darkness of a New Day," "The Balance of Attachments and Detachment," and "The Power of Prayer."

THE DARKNESS OF A NEW DAY

When I first visited the Trappists, I found rising for Vigils a great challenge. Often when on retreat, the first morning I would sleep in. During the ensuing week I would struggle to stay awake during the Night Office. Most often I would succumb to the temptation and go back to bed as the monks disappeared into the darkness at the end of the community's prayer. As time went on and as years of aging moved me to become a morning person, I found the Night Office more and more stimulating. The silent darkness called for slow and deliberate moves.

During my sabbatical stay at Gethsemani I came to find the earliest hours at the monastery the most beneficial ones. In the end, they proved the greatest revelation of true monastic living.

When the chant of the Night Office ended I would find a place on the floor of the chapel and stay there. I would simply reflect on the passages of Scripture I had just heard and sometimes I would just listen for other inspirations. As I became more comfortable with the lack of stimulation in mind and imagination, I found my heart more open to simply be there. I found delight just in being present to the Lord of darkness, waiting patiently for some light. At last comfortable in my own silence, free from performance and anxiety, I was ready to respond to the Word when spoken. This became the only word that I wanted to hear, the only word that would make sense. Now, what I recall most was—leaning. I found myself content to be leaning on the wood of a choir stall. Leaning into the emptiness of the room and the night, I waited for an inner stir. Later on, I became indifferent to that expectation as well. Soon I simply spent the time leaning and waiting. Then almost automatically, on a cue from some inner time clock of tiredness or a familiar sound, I would leave the chapel and go for a walk.

Out in the darkness I moved forward to address all my fears and hesitations about the approaching day and the rest of my life. It was during these walks before sunrise that I learned a new form of contemplative listening. There came a time when I could shut myself off and only be attentive to "the Otherness" outside myself. Sometimes, but only rarely, did I hear anything profound. During the last part of my walk or over a cup of coffee, I would search for a "tessera" (a small memorable piece) of that dark time. I would recall this over the course of the day so the joy, and the peace of the darkness, would return.

I came to love those early dark hours of the monastic day most of all. They gave meaning to the rest, to the wholeness of everything else. But I could never describe how or why. Perhaps this became a new and different way of praying or meditating for me. I have never been sure. All I know is that ever since then I can no longer live my life of ministry without some long quiet hours at the beginning of the day. On work days I usually wake at 5:00 AM so I have a number of hours before I begin public ministry. When I have a free day, that morning time is easily extended. When on retreat, back with the Trappists, I love stretching those hours backwards into the darkness.

THE BALANCE OF ATTACHMENTS
AND DETACHMENT

During a sabbatical year in 1985 I planned to spend Lent and Easter at Gethsemani to ready myself for study in Eastern religions and prepare myself for a three-month stay with Mother Teresa's community in Calcutta. As winter approached, I would return to the Abbey as a fitting summary.

I was there about a month, when on a Sunday, Father Raymond came up to me after the community Mass and said: "I was watching you during Mass today, Dan. Something is bothering you."

I said, "Not really, Raymond. I have been here about a month. I think I am fitting in. I think all is going well."

"No," he said. "Tell me, Dan. What it is that's bothering you."

I questioned him, "During Mass? When during the Mass did it look like something was bothering me?"

He said, "When you sat down during the Offertory Rites."

I thought back and then I asked, "After the homily?"

"Yes," he said. "Right after the homily, when you sat down."

I smiled as I thought back to my sentiments at that time. I said to him, "I was thinking of all the drivel I had preached during the years."

He reacted boldly. "Enough of that! You always tried to do your best. Enough of that kind of thought! Move on."

Then he walked away.

The instance made me realize that even in the silent world of the monastery you cannot run away from yourself, your past, or your problems. And most often, you cannot help but communicate all of this in one way or another to others. No matter how hard one tries not to show what is going on inside, it usually shows. No wonder we need to be our very best—for the good of others.

That day I began to realize how intensely I had been observing the monks. But they were also watching me. In such silence a person can come to know a great deal about others as well as oneself. Some monks were by nature or disposition distant. Some were beautifully happy. Others were naturally kind and thoughtful. Some I could choose as friends. With others I could find comfortable space. Only with a few did I have any conversation. But after a month I knew almost all of their names and I had observed something very identifying about each of them.

One of the monks whom I had never met on previous visits became very dear to me. I met him when I was encouraged by the Prior to visit the monks who were in the infirmary. I took his advice not only as permission to move around the cloister but almost as an exhortation to practice a corporal work of mercy or even some kind of ministry.

In the infirmary I met Brother Octavius who had been the monastic tailor for years. Now he had difficulty walking and his hands were arthritic and his sight was failing him. In his little room he used a magnifying glass to look at postcards and pictures he had collected throughout the years. During our brief visits we would talk about foreign places I had been to or he would listen to my plans to visit India. I loved to hear of his pride in being born in Cologne, and the beauty of Germany. He also loved to talk about his early days as a Cistercian in their house in Rome. As I left on my sabbatical journey to India I promised to add to his collection of postcards. When I returned, together we thumbed through the postcards and relived the stories connected to each of them. I was so pleased I could share this joy with this wise and dedicated religious.

How happy and honored I was when the abbot invited me to narrate my adventures with the Missionaries of Charity to the whole community in the chapter room. I felt it was something I could give to all of them in exchange for all they had given me. With my photos I could throw some light on the larger world beyond the walls of the cloister and ask the community's prayer for simple yet happy people I had casually met on the other side of the earth.

One of the younger monks approached me a few days after my chapter talk. He asked me to walk with him in the woods one afternoon. My story of the poverty in India had disturbed him. He said that as monks they had taken a vow to be poor. Then he gestured to the landscape of the rolling hills and woods around us and said: "You have seen real poverty. This is not poverty. How can you reconcile this?" I thought for a long moment.

He was a very good monk. I had known him for some years. I visited him more than once when he was a young student studying theology. Now I knew him as a respected member of the community, deeply committed to the Cistercian life and not easily impressed by things of the world.

Finally, I said to him, "I do not think that you came to this place to be poor. I believe you came here to live a life of contemplative prayer. Here in this out-of-the-way place with its Kentucky knobs and its acres of forests you have come upon a silence they hold. Thank God all this helps you to pray. The poor have no such silence. Real poverty is surrounded mostly by noise. There is no aloneness and no silence for the poor of the world. Living with the MCs and their ministry to the poorest of the poor,

I found it very difficult to pray and give a retreat to them. It was always difficult to find any silence for contemplative prayer that would separate one from the din of unending work and hopelessness."

The longer I lived with the monks the more I came to know them and the more I came to admire them. I saw them as truly "the free children of God." They were freer than most people I knew. They had their personal issues, their common concerns, their needs. But on the whole, they seemed freer than I would ever be. I had a need to travel. I had a need to preach. I needed to tell my story. I had a great desire to celebrate public prayer and minister to others. By contrast these monks would hear many stories, know the world's problems, anguish with grieving masses, and simply take it all in. As contemplatives they were willing to be transformed by others and yet remain free enough to do nothing to change their situation. They were capable of suffering the ultimate truth of humanity and simply keep on praying. They could deny themselves any ego satisfaction of changing the world and at the same time expose themselves to all its pain and problems. They were in the very process of becoming more and more vulnerable through compassion without hardening their hearts.

The sabbatical allowed me to see that Gethsemani was often what I wanted out of life; but not what the Lord wanted for my entire life. I had always idealized the monastic life but now I was seeing it really for the first time. I found out that I could live by their rules with little effort. What really surprised me, was the day I discovered that I truly loved the members of the community as brothers. I learned that the Lord does not only lead us by our hopes and ideals. The Lord accepts us and loves us and even directs each of us by accepting us along with our limitations, shortcomings, and attachments. Once we are humble enough to admit our own vulnerabilities and needs, we are more apt to accept others as they really are. Once this reality dawns, the Lord can reveal even more to us and free us enough to follow where He would like to take us.

At the end of my sabbatical, I could honestly say to the Abbot, I arrived there loving the place but when it came time to leave, it was the community that I loved. Because I could finally accept some profound truths about myself, I could also understand my relationship to the Abbey and so many other relationships in a much more healthy way. It was my attachments that grounded my being. Detachment for me was often an illusion. The contemplative life of Gethsemani was not all of my life but it definitely was an important part of my life.

THE POWER OF PRAYER

As the Chaplain of the U.S. House of Representatives my chief responsibility is to keep prayer alive in the House. Each formal session in the chamber begins with prayer. The history of this chaplaincy and this tradition of prayer in the government of the United States of America is traced back to the Continental Congress of 1774. Even before America had its cherished independence or a constitution, the founders gathered and they asked themselves, "How shall we begin?" In the face of differing churches and the uncertain issues of the day which they wished to address they decided to begin with prayer. They sent for an Episcopal priest, Father Duche, who led them in prayer. So as they set the course for this great experiment called America, they offered a great example to the people who would form this new nation: begin every work, especially when creative decisions are to be made, with prayer and trust in Divine Providence.

To lead the House Members in prayer is a great honor and privilege. It is also a great challenge. As Catholics we have a tradition of having great books of prayers. But as the Chaplain I now compose a prayer and submit that prayer to the Congressional Record every day there is a session of Congress. (Unless we are honored to have a guest chaplain recommended by one of the Members. Hosting the guest chaplain is not only a joy for me personally. It is a living witness to the freedom of religious expression we enjoy as a nation.)

Having prayer as the center of my work in Congress has kept me focused. Prayer has also substantiated my Cistercian commitments. It is truly an awesome responsibility to bring a bit of the sacred to secular government, an element of sacrament to the world of politics.

I have come to realize that prayer is where deepest dialogue begins. Often born out of the darkness of honest search, light gives wording to confident belief. At times, the painful anguish of composing prayer requires digging away at the human depths of a situation until compassion finds a common ground on a new and deeper level. Only then does true prayer have a chance to cry out with echoes that vibrate far beyond human imagining and reach for the heavens. To stand in prayer before others is to reveal oneself as vulnerable. At times it seems like turning oneself inside out.

Heartfelt prayer brought to the public needs to crack through all personal judgments and blow off any agenda. Otherwise it reveals only the broken soul howling out to other aliens and is not deserving of the Holy One. Prayer always seeks to unite people with the Source of all power, otherwise its poor imitation will only increase the great divide which can easily erupt right in our midst. Of its very nature true prayer unites, gives birth to love, sparks imagination, removes fear. Free contemplative prayer can magnify the most ordinary things to have inner meaning and wrap the most tragic events with tangible mystery.

To pray in public therefore is a very dangerous thing to do. All of us have been warned about this by great masters of prayer, including the Lord Himself. Yet that is my job, my responsibility. I, however, feel free in this undertaking because this role was not of my own making. And I will persevere in my conviction to keep prayer alive in Congress the more I am assured that the Cistercian community is silently standing behind me.

Before I was sworn in as Chaplain, I did not follow politics even as an indoor sport. However I always thought I lived in a large world because of my Catholic context and the universal mission the Church embraced. Since the Second Vatican Council I became more aware of the necessity for Catholic faith to be in dialogue with the modern world. "Gaudium et Spes" has become the foundation of many prayers in Congress.

Now life itself on Capitol Hill invites me into an ever-expanding world filled not only with hopeful ideals and ideas but all the painful problems that absorb the time and tax the talents of the Members of Congress. Many of them are very idealistic, committed to public service and desirous of making a difference in this globalized world. As their chaplain, I am offered the opportunity to see more of them than what meets the eye or is printed in The Record. In truth they are representative of the people they serve from across the nation in this "the People's House." They have many of the same concerns, ambitions, and frustrations as their fellow Americans. The media, political analysts, professional think tanks, and intellectual institutes may have distinct opinions about these individuals or the whole lot of them together. But I see them as very human persons struggling to shape public policy and often world opinion in the daily workshop of American legislation. Their constituents have the responsibility to pass judgment on them. The public may know something about them. But as the Lord's minister for them, I am called simply to love them. By praying with them and for them each day my care for them has grown with time—no matter their faith, their attitude, or their behavior.

Each morning my habit is to page through a picture book of the Members of the 109th Congress. I drill some basic information into my memory as I repeat a litany over and over again. I pray for those closest to them, their family members, and the staff who work with them in their offices and on committees. This daily perspective provides me with a fresh approach to the day. As I have come to know more and more of them personally, my prayer for them penetrates outward appearances. I see their effort to shape an informed and good conscience. I recognize the pressures they are under. I know of their high aspirations, hopes for the nation and the world. I have also felt their anguish expressed over problems and situations they cannot solve and the compromises they are required to make.

These frustrating contradictions as well as the present climate of politics have drawn me closer to my Cistercian brothers in contemplative prayer. Impossible situations, global concerns, inhuman atrocities, and indeliberate human obstacles demand a detachment in prayer that I have always respected in the contemplative heart. But now I see the same pain in the heart of the nation. This American culture always wants immediate results. With many Americans I believe strongly in Divine Providence guiding all aspects of life. But it is God's timing I often find difficult to accept.

A truly contemplative prayer is powerful in its sheer abandonment to God's mercy. The one who prays such a pure prayer is bound only to faithfulness in praying. There are no strings or conditions attached to such a prayer. Once uttered the prayer is lost in the freedom of praise. True dependency is acknowledged and expectations are laid to rest.

Prayer in Congress yearns for such freedom. In the midst of conflict, where politics reign, everyone, citizen and congressman alike, longs for more collaboration, mutual respect, and greater civility. Common prayer can begin this process. But experience has taught me to be a bit more cautious in my expectations. On occasion, immediately after the Opening Prayer and the Pledge of Allegiance to the Flag, remarks have sprung up from the floor which might seem to contradict any sensitivity to prayer or civic pride just voiced. It is then I realize more than ever that the prayer has been offered not for the listeners gathered; but as an appeal to the Almighty who is faithful even when we are unfaithful; who is present when we are confounded by our limited faith; and who is attentive when we are simply incapable of acknowledging any dependency upon God or others.

To pray aloud is to express an innate and often frustrating desire to touch another human soul deeply. To lead others in prayer is to take others where they sometimes do not want to go. To stand before others in prayer is not to stand above them, feebly struggling to lift them out of space and time; rather it is to stand beneath them and humbly name the common ground which already holds them together.

I was in Congress only a few days laboring to compose a prayer by scraping my own soul before I turned to the sacred Scriptures to find inspired language. Now I readily mine the Bible for treasured words and phrases which are the foundation of all Judeo-Christian prayer. Gradually I have learned more of this language which God has used from time immemorial to express His faithful love for His people. In my first weeks I turned to the words Peter used in his letters. I felt they carried a true pastoral concern for a new community.

Often I turn to the psalms because they are so powerful in expressing deep feelings of human experience. The psalms lift up the most ordinary day. When times are troublesome and it is most difficult to turn to God in honest prayer, I often scan the book of Psalms for a proper sentiment or choice of words.

A most memorable, nightlong wrestle with prayer took place on the night of September 11, 2001. A prayer was expected the next morning. After many attempts to sort out all the feelings of violation and outrage and innumerable drafts to express all the confusion and fear, I finally laid aside the book of Psalms. Then out of the frustrating, empty silence came the words: "O God, come to our assistance. O Lord, make haste to help us!" Instantly I knew a bond of oneness with my Cistercian brothers as they began their prayer. A definitive power was released and the rest of the prayer flowed with the freedom of abandonment.

Within days of being sworn in as Chaplain of the United States House of Representatives, I received an invitation from the Thomas Merton Society to attend a workshop. It would take place at Gethsemani Abbey during the Memorial Day break from Congress. I was surprised and delighted to accept.

The conference was designed to foster a continuing conversation by persons involved in government or public policy and religious leaders. Taking place in an atmosphere of monastic prayer the sessions were led by people well-trained in "contemplative listening." Born out of Merton's interest to bring a religious perspective to politics, the Thomas Merton Society was interested in honest dialogue between religion and politics. Not expected to formulate a statement or build a consensus, the persons involved were simply to witness to the benefit such a dialogue could produce. The ongoing conversation led to descriptions of personal suffering and tragic scenes in foreign countries. We shared laughter and tears which only deepened the prayer and the listening.

I saw the workshop as a well-designed bridge from all former ministry to my new work of pastoral care and listening to people in a much more secular setting. Nothing could have served as greater confirmation of the Lord's will for me than to bring me to Gethsemani where the brothers would surround me and my new life with their prayers. What a blessing!

NORTH WOODS ABBEY: ON LAKE GOGEBIC

by Mary Margaret Funk, OSB

INTRODUCTION

The date is 2030 C.E. Abbess Bridget is a lifelong Abbess from the Abbey of Saint Patrick in Sneem, Ireland. Abbess Gertrude is in her second and final six-year term as Abbess at the North Woods Abbey of Lake Gogebic, which is located in the Upper Peninsula of Michigan. We find them at the Iron Mountain airport, where Abbess Gertrude has gone to welcome Abbess Bridget on her first visit to North Woods Abbey.

* * *

Abbess Gertrude: Greetings and welcome to Iron Mountain!

Abbess Bridget: Thank you! Sorry you had to wait so long.

Abbess Gertrude: It gave me time to plan these next two weeks of your visit.

Abbess Bridget: You know, I just want to experience your community's work and prayer. I look on this as a time of sharing rather than a formal visitation.

Abbess Gertrude: Don't worry, you will have time for just living with us, but there are a few special people to meet and places I want you to see.

They get on the local express people mover . . .

Abbess Bridget: If you were still located in Iron Mountain we'd be at your monastery by now. Why did you move out of the city?

199

Abbess Gertrude: That was twenty years ago, when I was still a young nun—we had been in Iron Mountain since the 1950s. We needed to start over rather than just make incremental adjustments to life in this millennium. We were below critical mass in the number of members, and the buildings were a burden rather than an asset. We needed to reconsider our obligations of ministry, and how to maintain a sustainable livelihood. We were also in crisis about our mission.

Abbess Bridget: What is your "mission"? In Ireland we never talk this way . . . "mission," sounds so . . . outside of yourself. Is this your obligations to Church and society?

Abbess Gertrude: The crisis facing us was that we could no longer respond to the ever changing needs of the times. We twisted this way and that with each passing concern, issue, or cause. We needed to look deeper into the tradition and into our own hearts. The monastic way of life is our mission. If one small group can live in radical Christ consciousness then we believe that this benefits the entire planet, the cosmos! And yes, mission-talk is obsolete. Remember how we did all those planning meetings where we constructed those phantom "go-for" mission statements? (They laugh!)

Abbess Bridget: So, has the move from the city been helpful? Is your monastery thriving?

Abbess Gertrude: You'll soon see for yourself. We need to change people movers here.

On a second transporter at the town of Marenisco . . .

Abbess Gertrude continues: . . . Our biggest insight was that when we were an urban monastery we were socially engaged, but had little time or energy for *lectio*. We moved deeper up the North Words by Lake Gogebic and inverted our priorities: *lectio divina* became our primary concern, and all else was secondary.

Abbess Bridget: Did you sell your property in Iron Mountain?

Abbess Gertrude: No, we still own the property. We use the property for health care and assisted living for the elderly poor. We use the proceeds to finance our capital budget for our abbey on Lake Gogebic. But the biggest advantage of being in the woods rather than the city is that this keeps us free to follow our monastic calling in greater solitude.

Abbess Bridget: Is this Iron Mountain property economically self-sustaining?

Abbess Gertrude: Yes, we also care for elderly priests and religious, including our own when that need occurs.

Abbess Bridget: When you moved to North Woods Abbey did you lose members?

Abbess Gertrude: No, vocations are attracted to solitude; our membership has grown from 25 to 40 since we moved.

Abbess Bridget: And how do you make it financially? Your address is Stage Coach Road and you are nine miles from the town of Marenisco. Remote! Even by Irish standards.

Abbess Gertrude: With these rapid people movers we are only five minutes from town, 20 minutes from Iron Wood city airport. That's a close enough connection. Remote might be what people call it from the outside, but we see enclosure as collective guard of our hearts. Our vocation depends on our actually living the monastic way of life, not some virtual reality that could be similar to a theme park!

Abbess Bridget: But again, how do you make a living financially? How do you heat your buildings with such long snowy winters?

Abbess Gertrude: We have a three-pronged approach to our economic well-being. We live within our means, we work to secure the means to live our life, and we live in such a way that we can help the poor. We've used that new solid fuel system that is produced from corn. The old coal bins now have corn and the converter breaks down the protein and the energy burns clean and without toxins in the air. It was an amazing discovery about 60 years ago by some farmer in Indiana.

Abbess Bridget: Sounds tidy, but how do you live within your means, give to the poor, and be a self-sustaining autonomous monastery?

Abbess Gertrude: You'll see.

At North Woods Abbey by Lake Gogebic in the Upper Peninsula of Michigan . . .

Abbess Gertrude: Sister Karina, meet Abbess Bridget from Ireland. I know you've got a room ready for her. Take her on a short tour . . . and give her a cup of tea. I'll look in on you after Vespers, Bridget, but meanwhile, do get some rest after your journey.

Sister Karina: We've been looking forward to your visit, Abbess Bridget. I'll show you your room and take you on a short tour so you'll be able to find your own way around later. First, let's go to the guest dining room for some tea and homemade cookies.

Over tea and cookies:

Abbess Bridget: Where is everyone? If there's a resident community of 40. . . . Plus, what, 25 guests? All I can see are the woods, a large lake, a boathouse, some cabins, and two nuns working out in the herb garden. It's so quiet!

Sister Karina: It's meridian time. Most people are in their cells either doing *lectio* or resting. We rise at 4:00 a.m., and a nap feels grand about this time of day. Some sisters don't actually need the sleep, but we all take a time of solitude.

Abbess Bridget: Such beauty: original paintings, hand-carved wood furniture, wood inlaid floors, windows everywhere. Natural light. I still wonder how you finance this place?

Sister Karina: Through our monastic practice of obedience, the forty of us who live here pool our talents within this contemplative setting. Some are musicians, artists, writers, gardeners, or wood workers. We have no farm animals, but try to protect the wild animals around us. We have separated our need for income from our contemplative arts, and try to offer hospitality with some built-in boundaries. Most of our income comes from the guesthouse.

Abbess Bridget: Don't you make money by selling your art and craft work?

Sister Karina: We do sell our products, but this only ensures that this work is self-sustaining. Our biggest profit center is these little handmade crosses that you put over doorways. The hand-painted one goes over the front entrance where one can touch and bless oneself upon coming in and going out.

Abbess Bridget: If your products only cover the cost of the materials, but don't pay for your labor, I still don't see how you pay for forty nuns to live in this beautiful setting.

Sister Karina: The handmade threshold crosses pay also for all the utilities of the complex and cover our health care costs, too. We just don't take from this income any labor costs. Most of our income is generated by the retreat center. We specialize in the art of discernment. We are open ten months out of every year for people to check in for weeklong stays. We provide this environment conducive to prayer and solitude. We also meet with each person, should they request it, and we try to teach them spiritual practices and skills in discernment and dialogue.

Abbess Bridget: Most monasteries have guesthouses and retreat centers, but none that I know are self-sustaining.

Sister Karina: Each person pays only the cost of room and board when they are here for their stay, but we ask them to make a donation at Christmastime toward this monastery. These donations are steady and generous. In turn, we keep them in our prayer, and they know they are welcome back according to space available. Many return when they are facing transitions in their life and feel the need for discernment. And the other secret is that we live within our means. We have no debts. It took us ten years to set up this facility and pay all start-up costs before we moved here from Iron Mountain.

Abbess Bridget: And the built-in boundaries? How did you set up the ministry of hospitality and maintain the atmosphere of solitude?

Sister Karina: The guesthouse is only open for retreatants ten months of the year. The nuns take a time for solitude during the months of December and January. We each take individual "hermit" time to do the necessary inner work to sustain our zeal. We have a community retreat the first and last week of this period. Even Christmas is solo time, although we gather in silence to celebrate the liturgies together. As you know shared silence is beyond powerful. The other boundaries are that the retreatants share our solitude the whole time they are here. They are each assigned a nun to meet briefly every day, but there's no group gathering of retreatants with themselves or the community. Many other places offer group exercises; we try to offer a space for the inner work for each individual. We specialize in discernment.

　　Oblates use the retreat house during the month of December, but they minister to each other, and only join us for prayer. In January any major repairs required are made to the guesthouse by outside contractors. All the nuns spend the winter months of December and January in community solitude. When you get stilled, really quiet on those long winter nights and early crisp dark mornings you go as deep as the winter itself!

Abbess Bridget: Do all the nuns work with retreatants?

Sister Karina: Yes, but according to their individual talents and gifts. You'll meet many of them and can ask them directly how they see themselves doing this hospitality outreach. We have a waiting list of people wanting to book a time in the retreat house. It seems that sincere seekers need support as their lives take many turns: marriages, divorces, job and location changes, children, discerning spiritual practices and paths, retirement necessities, hospice workers, care providers, business transitions, bankruptcies, chronic illnesses. You know the inevitable list these days.

Abbess Bridget: I'm getting the picture that the monastery is centered on the retreatants. You are here for them and to help them discern God's way for them.

Sister Karina: Yes, in a way. We have no other program than to live our monastic life and to listen to the stories of their lives with the ear of our heart.

Abbess Bridget: So, you live within your means, and live your life in such a way that you can help the poor. . . .

Sister Karina: Being able to give to the poor is one of our motivations for living simply. Once a year we bring our suggestions to Chapter for how these funds should be allocated, and we have a major dialogue about how we are living, and how we can contribute to others. If we live simply others can simply live.

After Vespers there's an hour for lectio, *for strolling in the grounds, or for other activities done in silence before a supper of hearty soup and homemade bread and jelly.*

Abbess Gertrude: I thought I'd find you here in this meditation garden by the trout stream. Did you rest this afternoon?

Abbess Bridget: Yes, I nearly stayed in my cell for the rest of the day, but I really wanted to join you for Vespers. The chant was beautifully pure and clear—are most of the nuns professional musicians?

Abbess Gertrude: No, we have only three "real" musicians; the rest of us are musical. We do, however, provide a little training for our guests to help them chant softly with the choir. As nuns we have both a *schola* and choir practice as needed. It's part of our common life to keep our minds in harmony with our voices.

Abbess Bridget: Your monastery is all female. In Ireland we've returned to our early Celtic tradition of double monasteries of men and women monastics seeking God alongside each other.

Abbess Gertrude: Is it working out for you?

Abbess Bridget: It's too soon to tell. We've only had these double communities for 40 years now. To our surprise it isn't the celibacy issues that are proving difficult, but power and control. Gender factors are much more complex than sexual attraction! It seems to depend on the patterns in the members' families of origin. Some of us come from families with the traditional dominant male parent, and they tend unconsciously to want to put a male in charge even if a female has been elected leader . . . it's often women who tend to insist that the leader must be male. We spend most of our house meetings on this problem. But we still think it's worth the problems to tap into the wonderful energy of complementarity. Why didn't you open your membership to men? And notice, we are not a mixed community, but double. Male and female alongside with one or the other Abbot or Abbess the chosen Archabbot or Archabbess.

Abbess Gertrude: In theory we had no difficulty with the concept of complementarity, but we felt that we had issues of evolutionary development to negotiate first.

Abbess Bridget: Like what? Evolutionary development? Sounds like a scientific experiment.

Abbess Gertrude: (laughing) Three factors were giving us pause. We did not feel solid enough for us to open our membership to males. First we thought that celibacy would be easier to maintain in a same-sex environment. There are other institutions for encounters between the sexes, called friendship, marriage, and family. Many of us are still beginners in celibacy practicing the interior disciplines that govern not only individual afflictions, but also group afflictions.

Abbess Bridget: I get the celibacy issues and even the questions of gender roles, but what on earth are individual and group afflictions?

Abbess Gertrude: You know how in the last century there was much research into the way groups "form, norm, storm, and reform again." We realized that this happens because the individual members are unconscious. The group can in fact be stable and thriving from early stages of being together if each person is aware of her own patterns that get in the way of community harmony, such as anger, depression, acedia, vainglory, and pride. We also are deeply conscious that groups take on a corporate personality that can also manifest collective afflictions, such as greed, pride, and anger. Our Benedictine Rule provides the teachings to be fully conscious of being human and strive toward ongoing conversion.

Abbess Bridget: I know the eight thoughts well. I have of course personally experienced afflictions. So, you are saying that if everyone is interiorly conscious of her afflictions and moving out of them individually, then this reduces the ups and downs within the group? And you also speak of group affliction—is this the same as social sin?

Abbess Gertrude: I'm not sure one can eliminate all the highs and lows, and certainly we would never claim to be beyond the human condition but at least we can strive to keep the community in equanimity. You see, this interior life is the "work" of the monastery. If we have too many other agendas we can't do the essential work of the monastery, which is fostering silence, humility, and obedience. We take literally the challenge of the *converstatio morum* vow. In practice this means that we prefer nothing to Christ.

Abbess Bridget: I'm glad I am staying two weeks; I'd like to discuss this further. But I can see that gender issues, economic ventures, and social outreach are all secondary to the service of staying focused on this plot of land, with these people and the particular needs of the guests that come. It feels very wholesome to me.

Abbess Gertrude: We've not mentioned yet our way of being cenobitic.

Abbess Bridget: I was going to ask about that. You seem to have more of a propensity to solitude than community? Is that so?

Abbess Gertrude: Alone together, or together alone? Life in common or common life together! We like to think of ourselves as cenobitic: We live in community, sharing common space under one designated with the Christ role, the Abbess.

Deeper than any of these words is that felt-shared-silence punctuated by community dialogue and life together in the daily *horarium*. As a requirement of cenobitic living we share leisure and ceaseless repentance. We anticipate our human mistakes and devote time every day to reconcile differences and affirm one another. This is our little chapter time before Compline, which tries to anticipate needs rather than doing damage repair. Ongoing communication is the practice of our vow of conversation, as Thomas Merton taught so well!

There's the bell for supper. We have a community gathering after supper and then Compline. Would you come to the Community room so I can introduce you?

Abbess Bridget: Would love to, then I'll retire early and join you after prayers tomorrow morning, maybe for Mass at 9:00 a.m.

After Mass, next day

Sister Karina: Did you sleep well, Abbess Bridget?

Abbess Bridget: Yes, I awoke early, but stayed in my cell. The silence here is so profound.

Sister Karina: It's not been easy to foster this silence. Sister Anna has had to insist that machinery is quiet; vehicles and air handlers are the whisper-only variety. It cost a little more, but silence is an essential part of our quality of life.

Abbess Bridget: Yes, I notice. Tell me about the "silence spoken here," as you have on your signs.

Sister Karina: When we moved here from Iron Mountain we had the opportunity to start over in all sorts of ways. It wasn't just buildings and property. We consciously shifted our group culture from one in which social outreach dominated to one dominated by *lectio divina*. We focused our efforts on creating a setup that would nurture, protect, and promote our contemplative way of life. As you know, many contemplatives live an outwardly "ordinary" life in the world, but a monastic community provides forms that foster our contemplative way of life in community.

Abbess Bridget: Yes, a life of renunciation for the sake of a conscious abiding awareness of God is making explicit the purpose of the monastic way of life. Christ Consciousness, you say is the reason for cenobitic life. All the structures are designed and maintained for the sake of Christ consciousness . . . common meals, common prayers, common things keeps the heart true, the energies pure. There's actually a felt vibration that is sustained through these practices.

Sister Karina: Our discernment centers on identifying what contributes or takes away from our Christ Consciousness. What contributes to it is the practice of silence, contemplative arts, manual labor, healthy eating and drinking, moderate exercise, and sleep. The things that get in the way of Christ Consciousness are being too busy, interpersonal strife, personal afflictions, and heedless use of things, secular entertainment, intrusive fads, or superficial teachers.

Abbess Bridget: I'd add that even too much scholarship and research destabilizes the mind, as does absence from the monastery; preoccupation with personal projects, animals as personal pets, attachment to private collections, or relationships can be addictive, too!

Sister Karina: We spend most of our chapters finding creative ways to prevent negativity. Our silence is poisoned if there is murmuring.

Abbess Bridget: So, does talking it out help?

Sister Karina: For chronic negativity that comes out in murmuring we have imposed exclaustration for acedia. The person in question is asked to take a leave of absence and take treatment for depression if necessary. But this is after we've tried to do face-to-face dialogue and listening to the differing points of view. We are not talking about honest dissent, but that corrosive negative drag that manifests itself in sarcasm, critical remarks, and harshness of judgment. We have found that these behaviors break down community so subtly and pervasively that we can't afford to keep that person in our midst. Also, if it is simply depression we ask them to take treatment and accompany them every step along the way.

Abbess Bridget: Negativity is the cancer of a group. It's wonderful when we can speak from the heart, honestly and humbly.

Sister Karina: From our first day in the novitiate we learn that obedience is intended to enable us to cultivate an abiding Christ Consciousness.

Abbess Bridget: I notice you keep using the term "Christ Consciousness." Do you mean that in the broad sense of Christ of the cosmos? There are so many manifestations of Christ in this vast planet of ours.

Sister Karina: You'd better ask Abbess Gertrude about this, but I think that although we are very respectful of the fact that there are many manifestations of Christ in the different faith traditions, for us here at North Woods Abbey our Christ is the Jesus of our Christian Scriptures, and our way includes Baptism and communion within the Catholic Church.

Abbess Bridget: Can you insist on that? Isn't it up to each person to pray as they can?

Abbess Gertrude puts her head round the half-open door. . . .

Abbess Gertrude: I'm on my way to take Sister Anna to see the doctor. Are you doing ok here?

Sister Karina: Do you have a minute? We were just discussing Jesus as our way to Christ Consciousness. Can you take a moment to help explain? I'll go with Sister Anna to the doctor, if you'd like.

Abbess Gertrude: That would be fine with me. She's only going to town for the dentist. (She hands Sister Anna's documents to St. Karina.) So, Bridget, what's the question here?

Abbess Bridget: I was asking Sister Karina if you could insist that everyone here have a Jesus-centered "Christ Consciousness." We consider that how God comes to each person is a very personal matter.

Abbess Gertrude: It is personal, of course, but cultivating a love for Jesus is not just optional here. Perhaps I should tell you about how we discern vocations and our formation program. We've discovered that to awaken and sustain the spiritual energy of the community, the spiritual senses of each of us have to be rooted in Christ Jesus. This is a tangible reality, not just some speculative idea.

Abbess Bridget: I am not sure I understand this. We have many at St. Patrick's Monastery who enter via a dual practice. They believe in Jesus, but practice Buddhism. Or they may believe in the Christ of Mystery, but practice Christ Consciousness from the Hindu tradition. Or they are both Sufi and Christian. Can anyone insist today on being "purely" Christian in the traditional sense? We wouldn't dream of quizzing our newcomers about such an intimate matter—or even our vowed members, for that matter.

Abbess Gertrude: In discerning a vocation we enter into a deep dialogue with the candidate. If their psychic imprint is Muslim, Buddhist, or Hindu we steer them towards a more appropriate form of living their given faith. If they are formed in Christ Jesus, then we encourage them to take the next step with us. It seems that many try other paths, but sometimes the "hole" in the candidate's heart means that it "fits" with our life here. For our way of life we must all be convinced that Jesus Christ is our center, our way, our truth, and our life. In fact some of our candidates have come to us via Hindu or Buddhist communities, where their guides helped them to see that their "heart," their deepest level as it were, carried the imprint of Christ. Just as the Buddhist takes refuge in the Buddha, we take refuge in Christ Jesus. This is our baptismal initiation. This life quickened in us is real, not just an empty ritual.

Abbess Bridget: Isn't this too narrow a definition of belief in Jesus Christ?

Abbess Gertrude: We don't experience this as narrowness, but actually liberating. Everyone here believes in Jesus Christ with her whole mind, heart, and soul. We feel a palpable bond of Christ Consciousness through Jesus. Once this psychic imprint has been discovered, it becomes a source of strength. We receive our vocation rather than choosing our own way. We receive Christ Jesus as our deepest calling. He is our burning bush, as it were.

Abbess Bridget: What happens if this manifestation changes? Would the sister have to leave if her faith in Jesus grows cold or becomes invisible? Or if she experiences another calling?

Abbess Gertrude: This brings us to our formation program. Have you been to our novitiate yet?

Abbess Bridget: No. I would love to see it.

Abbess Gertrude: I'd like you to meet some of our newcomers. I'll set up a gathering before Vespers if that's ok.

In the novitiate . . . nine young nuns gather in a semicircle round the two Abbesses.

Abbess Gertrude: This is Abbess Bridget, as you know she is with us for a few days. She would like to know more about our formation program. Novice Teresa, can you begin?

Novice Teresa: Certainly, I'm originally from Arizona and came here to discern my vocation. I had just finished nursing school, and had three options for employment, but wanted to clarify my deeper questions before I started my job. Nursing school had been demanding, since I had to pay my tuition by working my way through school. I thought I was just coming here to rest up, and then return to Arizona, but I loved it here so much that I entered 16 months ago. So far, I've recommitted myself to my baptismal promises and to living closer to the Gospel. I also found that my deepest desire is to know and love Jesus by direct experience—not like in my former way of life where I had an intellectual belief system, but not my own felt commitment.

Abbess Bridget: Direct experience? Isn't that a grace that comes to some, but not to all, and even to those chosen ones, perhaps only for brief periods in life?

Novice Teresa: That's why I'm here, to have my own experience of Jesus Christ. If He's real, and if I'm real, then it seems to me I can become aware of the presence of Christ Jesus.

Abbess Gertrude: If I can chip in here, I'd like to try and explain how this North Woods Abbey brings each and all of us to this abiding consciousness of Jesus Christ. It's our tradition, but is so little known outside these walls, and since no one sees it we often lose our contemplative vocations to the monastic traditions of the East. The Orthodox Church has kept this life more central than we Catholics have done in the West.

Abbess Bridget: In Ireland we don't have that Catholic versus Orthodox question, as we have gone back to our earlier pre-Roman roots when the Church was mercifully both East and West and less institutionalized. But let me return to the topic of Christ Consciousness. . . . I'm not following. Is developing this Christ Consciousness part of your formation program?

Abbess Gertrude: Here's the curriculum that we provide. The newcomer is eager to find ways of living a contemplative life. We provide "above the river" structures (that everyone can see, as in the exterior life) for solitude, for living in common (how we relate to eating, to things, to prayer). We provide meaningful work: working with our hands, art, music, the skills of farming, and gardening. We provide training for our mind. (This goes on below the river . . . where no one else can see, the interior life.) Each newcomer undergoes an intense period of discernment to help them understand how, when, and why the various thoughts rise. Each is given spiritual direction intended to teach them to discern for themselves which ascetical and prayer practice is most suitable for their temperament and particular personality. Each is given time to practice interior work. Much attention is given to skillfully and consistently treating the afflictions . . . whatever they may be: food or drink, sex, things, anger, depression, acedia, vainglory, or pride. These afflictions are taken very seriously. We do our utmost as a community to provide the individual with the tools they need to do this interior work. We also take great care during our collective practices to guard our hearts. We've taken care to set up a climate where each of us can change and grow. I'm certainly not the same stubborn woman I was a few years ago.

All our chapter meetings, individual conferences, friendships, and confessors are dedicated toward this interior work. We have no input from academics or others who do not have an inner praxis themselves. *Conversatio morum* is our way of life, and everything is orientated towards this work. This is really the work of the monastery *conversatio morum* through silence, humility, and obedience!

We also do our positive praxis with attention of our minds to the present moment guarding our hearts and watching our thoughts not only to prevent afflictions from taking root, but also to purify our motivations and intentions. We all have some sort of a ceaseless prayer practice. Let me not get carried away here. Have I said too much?

Abbess Bridget: You seem to be so serious about this. Doesn't it just happen with many years of living the monastic life? It seems that your effort is all about self-sanctification. Might this be too self-centered?

Abbess Gertrude: I can't identify with self-sanctification. What I can say is that our monastic culture is about Jesus Christ becoming our innermost consciousness. We work diligently to remove obstacles to our living toward, in, and with Christ. We also prevent conditions that negate our monastic culture. It's really not us doing the work, but the Holy Spirit at work in us. Jesus promised the Holy Spirit to accomplish his Word.

Abbess Bridget: So, this is a monastery for mystics. I thought a monastery was meant to be for ordinary people, living a basically ordinary life. Life is good in itself, and there is not a "higher" or additional level to reach. To be fully human and fully alive is the goal at St. Patrick's.

Abbess Gertrude: Abbess Bridget is raising such important questions, anyone have a response?

Sister Sarah: May I try? I'm from California and we have all the mystical tangos dancing there. (Laughter)

Abbess Gertrude: Certainly, Abbess Bridget, this is Sister Sarah. She lived in a Buddhist nunnery for a few years in Seattle. . . . Wasn't it?

Sister Sarah: I was in Vancouver as a Buddhist nun. But I was born and raised in California. Here's the way I describe it to my family and to myself: I have a Christ imprint in my soul that makes me feel at home when I experience the manifestation of Jesus Christ. I was dead to Christ before I came. I had taken refuge in the Buddha, but after the first flush of zeal I didn't find that this was a source of life for me. For others in that sangha they had found a home. I had a thin faith formation, and had a great affliction of anger, mostly directed against the Catholic Church for squandering the youth of my generation . . . but that's another story. When I came here for discernment I felt the solitude, the peace, and the deeply human satisfaction of being close to myself and to other like-minded souls. Through the program here I got some relief from my affliction of anger and replaced it with ceaseless prayer. After about a year of being faithful to the monastic practices, I had experienced a major new awareness of feeling the Presence of Christ. It was an awakening. This presence is amazing.

Abbess Bridget: Did you have to become a nun to feel Christ's Presence? Do you think you would have found that someplace else? And you know that this feeling goes away over the years, don't you?

Sister Sarah: So, I'm told. I understand that that felt presence is replaced with felt-faith. What attracts me and makes me willing to embark on this monastic way of life is that I'll be helped to prevent and remove afflictions that obscure my consciousness. I'll also get continuous training to keep my mind pure and alert. Some people could do this in the world, but I know I need all the help I can get, and it seems that a monastery is where I fit best. In a way it is my "natural" grace-given home. Living here is deeply satisfying, even when it is hard.

Abbess Bridget: So, do you consider yourself a mystic?

Sister Sarah: Yes, why not? A mystic is just a person who lives in conscious awareness of God. It is the most fully human calling for a Creature of God!

Abbess Bridget: Tell me more about the ongoing training. We all have zealous novices; it's sustaining that zeal, remaining awake year after year that is so difficult.

Sister Natasha: I'd like to give that question a try. May I?

Abbess Bridget: Certainly, are you from California, too?

Sister Natasha: No, I'm from Maine near Canada. I came for discernment, too. I'm a musician and wanted to give my gift the time and attention it deserved. I felt empty after performances, and also didn't feel fitted to be a teacher or a composer. When I came I found that music itself wasn't my gift, but it was my door into the spiritual senses that wanted to be liberated.

Abbess Bridget: Spiritual senses? We Celts are famous for living in "thin" places; is that what you mean? Iona Abbey is known for mystical experiences.

Abbess Gertrude: It's nearly time for Vespers and that is such an important topic that I think we should stop for now and resume this conversation tomorrow afternoon. Same place, same time?

Abbess Bridget: Yes, of course, but Sister Natasha, I hope we will hear how music led you to the spiritual senses. I'm a musician, too.

(The young nuns file out. Turning to Abbess Gertrude, Bridget continues . . .)

Isn't this all too inward-looking? This still sounds to me like self-sanctification. Don't we all have an obligation to try to improve the world around us?

Next day before Vespers . . . semicircle of 9 sisters in the Novitiate sitting around Abbesses Gertrude and Bridget.

Abbess Gertrude: a short reading:

> "You are my friends if you do what I command you. I no longer call you slaves, because a slave does not know what his master is doing. I have called you friends, because I have told you everything I have heard from my Father" (Jn 15:14-15).

Abbess Gertrude: We were beginning to talk about the spiritual senses yesterday. How is the formation program here training our spiritual senses?

Sister Natasha: For me, the practice of silence was my way into the vast world of the spiritual senses. Here at North Woods Abbey we enjoy the silence of these woods, these sacred trees, the artistic beauty around us, and the stillness of our own individual cell. In this solitude our Formation Director, Sister Carolyn, is teaching me the practice of inner silence. I am learning how to discipline my thoughts, desires, and passions. I have entered into the interior world of knowing myself. Equipped with tools to remove the obstacles of prayer and practicing ceaseless prayer, I am gradually being stilled, totally stilled. First I got my body stilled, and now my mind and eventually my heart is in peace.

Abbess Bridget: Back up here—you had to learn what to do in silence? Doesn't that come naturally to anyone with a vocation?

Sister Natasha: It wasn't natural for me. As I said I'm a musician and my mind was going free-fall all the time from this to that. I've a quick mind, and I enjoy learning new things. It was a new territory to learn to watch my thoughts and guard my heart.

Abbess Bridget: Did I miss something? How does this open the spiritual senses?

Abbess Gertrude: Sister Natasha, rarely do we disclose such personal matters, but do continue with your story—how did solitude, silence, and stillness open your spiritual senses?

Sister Natasha: I honestly don't know. Perhaps I could tell the story in music, but not in words? I'm not sure I even know . . . there's no storyline to tell.

Sister Teresa: Perhaps I can speak here. I've been doing some writing about this. I'd like to see if this makes sense out loud.

Abbess Gertrude: Novice Teresa, do tell us more. The spiritual senses open and then. . . .

Novice Teresa: As you know I came from a nursing background. From a scientific point of view I saw the wisdom of getting stilled in body, mind, and soul so that I could be present to the Presence. I had been so busy with life issues and projects before I came that it took me months to let those memories fade away. Then, I consciously dropped attachments to those memories whenever I noticed them rising with ever new costumes and voices. Not too many weeks had passed before I learned to pray ceaselessly. I found my home in the Jesus Prayer. It now rises unbidden.

Abbess Gertrude: Let me understand this, you learned to practice stillness of body, mind, and soul through the Jesus Prayer?

Novice Teresa: Yes, it went hand-in-hand with watching my thoughts, guarding my heart. It was risky to let go of the familiar old stories in my head and to simply be attentive to the present moment. The Jesus Prayer simply went deeper and deeper, and soon it seemed to rise up from beneath everything else. I not only practiced the Jesus Prayer with my mind, but through this practice I am learning to still my mind and body. I use an icon to hold me in the present moment when I sit in my cell.

Abbess Bridget: I know this is the Orthodox tradition, but Roman Catholics don't often teach the Jesus Prayer. Tell me more.

Novice Teresa: I needed a practice to stay focused, disciplined, and to lead me to deeper levels of consciousness. I know there are other methods, but this seemed to be my path.

Abbess Bridget: Don't stop. Continue . . . then what?

Novice Teresa: After about a year the Presence rose in a powerfully felt way. I was taken out of my ordinary patterns. I continued the Jesus Prayer while still following the *horarium* of the monastery, and it seemed to take on a life of its own.

Abbess Bridget: A life of its own . . . not sure I understand.

Novice Teresa: As you know I've only been here two years, but let me say that since I came the Presence has been everywhere and my own awareness became quite keen. This is what I understand about the spiritual senses. . . . I could see, hear, taste, feel, smell, and intuit a whole new dimension beyond my ordinary way of sensing in my former way of life. Water was amazing, sunsets were spellbinding, sounds in the woods were sweet, and my senses were starting to overlap. I experienced a sort of spiritual synesthesia—I saw flowers dancing and smelled trees swaying in the wind. It's hard to describe, but my scientific training burst out of its limitations. All was new, wonderful, real, and alive. Light was brilliantly luminous, music welled up from below my soul, and matter was radiant with glory. Words fail! I guess they are meant to—our spiritual senses lead us into mystery.

Abbess Gertrude: Our ongoing formation is intended to sustain this level of consciousness, and to make this awareness an abiding reality, rather than some episodic interlude between developmental periods of one's life. What we have not discussed is the fact that the whole of our life with daily Eucharist, praying the divine office, the common meals with reading, the evening recreation gathering, our manual labor, our individual *lectio divina*, our collective discernment chapters keep us with our feet on the ground and rooted in our everydayness.

It's time for Vespers . . . tomorrow I want to take you for an excursion on Lake Gogebic. . . .

Next afternoon . . . standing together at the steering wheel of a
12-passenger motorboat under the canopy. . . .

Abbess Bridget: I enjoyed our conversation of yesterday. Can we
   continue?

Abbess Gertrude: Of course. I've some questions for you, too.

Abbess Bridget: How is this level of spiritual senses connected
   with Christ Consciousness? Isn't this just natural altered
   state of consciousness?

Abbess Gertrude: Not really. The spiritual senses are ways of
   describing the capacity of the soul that is lifted up by God's
   grace. Altered states of consciousness are mechanically and
   chemically induced technologies that raise awareness with
   the ego at the center for the sake of pleasure and self-
   satisfaction. Christ Consciousness has Christ as our center
   whereas altered states of consciousness have self as the
   center. Spiritual senses are the human portals to experience
   the divine Presence.

Abbess Bridget: This makes sense and I also have another topic
   I want to hear about . . . how do you practice *lectio divina*?
   And again, you have the primary practice of *lectio divina*
   and is there any time for social ministry? Our world so badly
   needs to change. There is so much violence on our planet.

Abbess Gertrude: Let's talk about social ministry first. Notice the
   full-bodied trees on the Canadian side of the lake. We did
   a major campaign to root out emissions from the midwest
   power plants that caused acid rain up here a 1,000 miles
   away.

Abbess Bridget: What kind of a major campaign did you do from
   here?

Abbess Gertrude: We put together a documentary that took us
   three years to produce. We followed the tree life through
   all four seasons of the year and showed how so many were
   dying and not from natural cycles of growth and decline.

Steering the boat through a narrow but rushing stream, Abbess Gertrude continues. . . .

I'm glad you are staying another week! Our main way of helping this turbulent world is by simply being monastic. We believe that if we live our monastic life to the full, then we are changing the world. Monks have intuited this from the desert fathers, to Saint Thérèse to the wonderful Seraphim of Sarov. It demands great authenticity—there is clearly scope for a lot of self-aggrandizement, pride, and delusion here . . . of seeing oneself as a "special person." History is littered with such would-be "perfect" communities! Yet surely this is part of our monastic charism. The universal must be particular, but equally our particular, personal, and community quest must be that of "everyone." We must pray—call it what you will—in and for our world. As Christians, we are called to be Christ in our time.

Abbess Bridget: You remind me of those monks of Tibhirine who seemed to impact the whole of Algeria and even all Christian-Muslim dialogue by simply being monks at their place called Atlas.

Abbess Gertrude: The power of symbol, if blessed by Christ, is beyond understanding. The particular monastic way is compelling, isn't it?

Abbess Bridget: In our monastery everyone is encouraged to have an anamcara, soul friend. Is that an expectation here? I owe my perseverance of my vocation to my dear soul-friend.

Abbess Gertrude: You've read that twelfth-century monk, St. Aelred. In his treatise *On Spiritual Friendship* he writes: ". . . your friend is the comrade of your soul, with whose spirit you . . . so share your spirit that you become one instead of two; . . . you entrust yourself to your friend as if he or she were another you, from whom you keep nothing secret (and) from whom you fear nothing (3.6). Although Aelred is speaking in that passage about friends here on earth, he is insistent that our best friend is Christ Jesus himself. As he writes elsewhere in the same work, "The ascent (of friendship) does not seem too steep—the ascent from Christ, who inspires the love by which we love our friends, to Christ, who offers himself to us as a friend to love" (2.20). Not only does Aelred thereby affirm Christ's leading us to friendship with him, he also asks the somewhat daring question, "Should I say of friendship what St. John, the friend of Jesus, says of true love? Should I say that God is friendship (just as John writes that God is love)?" And Aelred answers in the affirmative, even though he grants that this might sound unusual. He writes: "What is true of love I do not really doubt can be said also of friendship, since those who abide in friendship abide in God and God in them" (1.70).[1]

Abbess Bridget: So, you encourage human friendships?

Abbess Gertrude: Yes, but toward Christ Jesus as our intimate spouse, then all other friendships are right ordered, as St. Bernard would say.

Abbess Bridget: Do I detect a fear of being simply human who love one another as human?

Abbess Gertrude: What you detect is that Christ Consciousness provides us to see human love the way it really is!

Abbess Bridget: So, I take it, you encourage soulfriends?

Abbess Gertrude: It's a gift to be received, but can't be obtained by effort. Christ is our focus. From Christ Jesus flows our way of loving each other. I actually think marriage is the same dynamic, don't you?

Abbess Bridget: Not sure. Isn't marriage a vocation that by loving each other you love God?

---

[1] This section on friendship is taken from a homily written and given by James Wiseman, osb, of Saint Anselm's Abbey in Washington, DC. The twenty-second Sunday of Ordinary Time.

Abbess Gertrude: Yes, and the way to learn to love is through direct intimacy with Christ Jesus.

Abbess Bridget: So, there's no effort for friendship and all is grace given. Is our intimacy with Christ Jesus also a grace given that no effort can achieve?

Abbess Gertrude: Yes, relationships are grace and our effort is to be awake and receive like Mary did when the Angel Gabriel came to her. If we start our return to the Abbey now we'll be in time for *statio* before Sunday Vespers. . . .

On the way to Ironwood Mountain airport . . .

Abbess Bridget: So, when will you be coming to Ireland?

Abbess Gertrude: There's a meeting in Calcutta next fall for all monastic superiors. Maybe I could visit you at St. Patrick's Abbey the week before, and then we could fly on to India together.

Abbess Bridget: Wouldn't that be wonderful! I can't tell you how many things this visit has made me think about. We never did get to the topic of *lectio divina*. You said you had some questions for me?. . . .

Abbess Gertrude: I've a nagging question that I'll entrust to your confidence. . . .

When do you know that it's time for a monastery to start a new foundation? We have as many nuns as our facilities can house, but as you know that could shift in a month's time. I'll write you my thoughts on this matter. We are almost at the gate now.

Abbess Bridget: Do write me about what you are thinking. And yes, I'll hold your confidence sacred. You know that I'll be sharing my impressions with the community at St. Patrick's of course—above all the courage with which this Community of the North Woods Abbey on Lake Gogebic is focusing on being Christ Conscious. Please God, your example will help us renew our own practice. Do you have any word that you particularly want me to share with the monks and nuns at St. Patrick's Abbey in Sneem?

Abbess Gertrude: In our silence we know the Lord.

The friends part company, but souls not.

EPILOGUE: *LECTIO* ON THE EASTER PROCLAMATION

by Miriam Pollard, OCSO

Tonight we gather for the Mother of Vigils.
The Church is playing with symbols tonight.

Let's step out of a world regulated by our minds and reasonings,
Into a world in which the words have become
Water and light and darkness.
Let's take time to converse with images.

Here we are on the brink of the most important night of the year.

Do we have in our minds the proper kind of attention we should
 be giving to this heart of the liturgical year?

What is it? What does it look like, this expectation?

Are we going to disappoint ourselves? Are we going to court
 endurance rather than inspiration? Will we be walking interiorly in a desert or on a lush and inviting river valley?

Wait a minute.

Most of us know that putting in a good performance is not exactly
 what is being asked.
We don't come there to do well, to be good at it.
Maybe we won't be able to set aside our inferior, worldly cares
and pay undistracted attention to a God of perfection,
a God who is the only thing worth thinking about.

Really we won't be there
to bring back a sack of worthy thoughts and holy resolutions.

225

Maybe we won't be able to set aside our jumpy nerves and our
  overtired and overstressed daily person.

This is a big thing, sure, the Mother of Vigils,
but this is not the time to become someone else,
someone worthier and nicer and deserving of the attention of
  God.

That kind of God,
the God whose attention we have to deserve
is really not worth cultivating.

> We start where we are; why not?
> There is nowhere else to start.
> This is where God wants us to start.

This is where he is waiting.
> But where is that? Where are we?

Let's close our eyes
Take gentle, deep breaths.
What is the last thing that bothered you?
Or the thing that bothers you most right now?
The thing that is most likely to "damage your prayer,"
Your receptivity to the Paschal Blessing?

Let be whatever irritation bites
Whatever anger is smoldering,
Whatever fear is threatening.

Just set it down right there in front of you,
Or within you,
And let it be.

Whatever project is beckoning.
Whatever list cries to be checked off, item by item,
Whatever task needs doing and will not leave your mind in peace
  until it is done,

Whatever task you wish you had done better,
Whatever argument you wish you had had a better answer to.

Whatever in yourself you would most like to get rid of or improve or pretend isn't there,

Whatever relationship has gone bad
Or might go bad if you don't keep digging at it and worrying
     about it
Or trying to make it over.
Whichever person in your life you have to change or you will go
     nuts.

Whatever you are ashamed of in yourself and wish you weren't,
Whatever you wish you hadn't done,
Whatever you wish you could do over
Whatever you are desperately trying to improve,
Or have given up on.

Let be whatever is in you right now.

Right now you don't have to be nicer, or more charitable
Or smarter or better organized.
You don't have to scratch the itch of all those letters you haven't
     written
Or inner improvements you haven't had the courage to make.

Let be whatever you are right now.
Be quietly with the discouragement, the satisfaction,
The joy, the goodness you see in yourself,
The physical disabilities and the physical strengths.

BE.
BE what God knows you are right now and embraces in his silent
     heart.

NOW,
Now when it's a little late to make yourself and your world over.

Then,
Imagine a soft darkness moving slowly over all these qualities
     and concerns, these emotions,
every part of your body.

The darkness slips in like the tide,
Enveloping one by one the personal being you are offering to it,
The now of you.

Slowly, give to the dark one feeling, one part of you, one by one,
There is no light at all. It is pure darkness. Seamless, quiet,

without change or action.
There is nothing you can do with it
Or about it.
It is simply dark.

How do you feel in the dark?
Protected?
Afraid?
Diminished?
Guilty?

Comforted? Bored?

Are you alone, or
do you feel called to reach out to all your fellows who are lost in
    the dark?

Do you remember Jesus caught up into darkness as he approaches
    the culminating moment of his mission? Or as he lies in the
    rocky tomb,
Yesterday gone and tomorrow not yet?

No light. You are covered.
You can't see.
You breathe in and out, slowly, quietly.
You are pillowed in darkness. You let the darkness embrace you.
Taste the dark. Feel it with your hands.

THEN
Imagine a tiny seed of light before your face.
The tiniest seed imaginable.

Stay with it. Sit with it, there in the dark.

Then let it grow
Slowly, a little at a time.

One by one, the pieces of you that the darkness has covered emerge
    into the light.
The light penetrates each piece,
One by one.
Warmly, gently.
It touches each with its affirming, sweet presence.

Until all of you is exposed and peacefully cradled in the light,
Happy in the light,
Saved and loved and valued by the light.

Light is disclosing the inward beauty of all that you are.
It is turning everything you regretted or felt as a burden
into the mighty victory of Jesus.
Light is not impersonal.
It is not something over there, outside of you.

It is your now,
It is a person.
It is your being lifted into the life and offering of Christ.
Everything in you,
The me who is now and here and
Ragged and faded and eaten by discontent
Or anticipation
Or contentment.

Let the light be.
Don't resist it. Let it rest on your bruised heart and your memories
     and your failures,
On your small successes,
On what you most genuinely are.

Let the light be beauty in you.

Then let the mighty words of the Paschal Blessing sweep over
     you.

Forget how you are supposed to respond or listen or pray.

Be who you are in darkness that has turned to light.

Let the Paschal Blessing seep in little by little.

As you are yourself, let the Blessing be itself.
Christ is risen.

NOTES ON CONTRIBUTORS

John Eudes Bamberger, ocso, entered Gethsemani Abbey in 1950, having earned an M.D. from the University of Cincinnati the previous year and done his internship at Georgetown University Hospital. A student of Thomas Merton from 1952–1955, he worked with Merton, after his ordination in 1956, in screening applicants to the abbey. He served as abbot of the Abbey of the Genesee, in New York state, from 1971 until 2001. Since returning from a term as superior in the Philippines, he lives in a hermitage at Genesee. He recently published *Thomas Merton: Prophet of Renewal,* in the new Monastic Wisdom Series of Cistercian Publications.

Michael Casey, ocso, is a Cistercian monk of Tarrawarra Abbey in Australia. He is a frequent retreat master and lecturer on monastic spirituality all over the world. Casey is the author of many books, including *Towards God: The Ancient Wisdom of Western Prayer; A Guide to Living in the Truth: Saint Benedict's Teaching on Humility; Fully Human, Fully Divine: An Interactive Christology; Strangers to the City: Reflections on the Beliefs and Values of the Rule of Saint Bendict,* and most recently *The Uninteresting Life: Benedictine Spirituality.*

Joan Chittister, osb, a Benedictine Sister of Erie, Pennsylvania, is an award-winning author and well-known international lecturer on behalf of peace, human rights, women's issues, and contemporary religious life and spirituality. She served as president of the Conference of American Benedictine Prioresses for 16 years and was prioress of the Benedictine Sisters of Erie for 12 years. Sister Joan is the founder and executive director of Benetvision, a resource and research

231

center for contemporary spirituality located in Erie. Currently she serves as co-chair of the Global Peace Initiative of Women, a partner organization of the UN, facilitating a worldwide network of women peace builders, particularly in Israel and Palestine. She is also a founding member of the Inter-religious International Committee for the Peace Council. Her 1990 book on monastic spiritualilty, *Wisdom Distilled from the Daily* (Harper-Collins) is considered a classic in contemporary spirituality. Sister Joan writes a weekly web column for the *National Catholic Reporter,* "From Where I Stand."

Daniel P. Coughlin, born and raised in Chicago, Illinois, attended Catholic schools and the Archdiocesan seminary before being ordained a priest on May 3, 1960, at St. Mary of the Lake University. He lived and served in parishes while taking on work as Director of the Office of Divine Worship and later as Director of a retreat center. During a sabbatical he lived at Gethsemani for five months, studied East/West religions and worked with the Missionaries of Charity in Calcutta. He was serving as Vicar for Priests in Chicago when he was recommended by Cardinal Francis George to Speaker J. Dennis Hastert to be sworn in as Chaplain of the House of Representatives on March 23, 2000. He has written articles for liturgical periodicals on prayer and spirituality, and was a contributor to the study and publication of the NCCB document *The Spiritual Renewal of the American Priesthood.* Since ordination he received a Master's Degree in Pastoral Studies from Loyola University of Chicago and an honorary Doctorate Degree from Lewis University, Romeoville, Illinois.

Lawrence S. Cunningham is professor of theology at the University of Notre Dame. He is a frequent lecturer in Benedictine and Cistercian monasteries of both men and women. He is the author or editor of sixteen books, including *Thomas Merton: Spiritual Master* and *A Search for Solitude: The Journals of Thomas Merton, 1952–1960.* He is currently translating Dom Andre Louf's book on *The Way of Humility* which will be published in the Monastic Wisdom Series for Cistercian Publications next year.

Gail Fitzpatrick, ocso, the Abbess of Our Lady of the Mississippi Abbey since 1982 is well-known and respected in monastic circles as a thoughtful teacher and sensitive spiritual leader. She was born in Fairfield, Connecticut, entered monastic life at Mount Saint Mary's Abbey, Wrentham, Massachusetts, and was later transferred to the new foundation of Our Lady of the Mississippi near Dubuque, Iowa. She has recently published *Seasons of Grace: Wisdom from the Cloister* (Chicago: Acta Press, 2000). She and her Community of the Mississippi have launched a new foundation of Tautra in Frosta, Norway.

Mary Margaret Funk, osb, grew up on a farm in Benton County in northern Indiana as one of six children to BJ and Mary Funk. She entered Our Lady of Grace Monastery after graduating from the Academy in 1961. She taught four years at St. Barnabas School, Indianapolis. She holds Master's degrees from Catholic University and Indiana University. She served 14 years teaching catechists for the Archdiocese of Indianapolis. After two terms as Prioress from 1985–1993 in 1994 she became Executive Director of Monastic Interreligious Dialogue (MID). In that capacity she coordinated Gethsemani Encounter I and II at Gethsemani Abbey, Benedict's Dharma at Beech Grove, Conference on Hinduism at St. Procopius, and a dialogue on Christ Consciousness at Schuyler. In her role with MID she has participated in formal dialogues in India, Tibet, Europe, Turkey, and the United States with Buddhists, Hindus, and Muslims. Her books include *Thoughts Matter, Tools Matter, Humility Matters,* and *Islam Is.* Currently Sister Meg is director of the School of *Lectio Divina* at Benedict Inn.

Patrick Hart, ocso, a native of Green Bay, Wisconsin, did his undergraduate work at the University of Notre Dame as a Brother of Holy Cross. He entered the Abbey of Gethsemani in 1951, and has served as secretary to the last four abbots, as well as to Thomas Merton during the last year of his life. He has edited many books by and about Thomas Merton during the 38 years since the latter's death on December 10, 1968. He has served on the Board of Directors for Cistercian Publications for the past 30 years, and was appointed General

Editor of the new Monastic Wisdom Series following the alliance between CP and Liturgical Press at Collegeville in May of 2004. He was awarded an honorary Doctorate in Humane Letters from Bellarmine University in 2004.

Terrence G. Kardong, OSB, a monk of Assumption Abbey, Richardton, North Dakota, was born in Minneapolis (1936), and educated at Collegeville (Philosophy, 1959), Washington (M.A., Latin, 1968), and Rome (Lic. Th., 1977). Since 1977 he has worked as a writer and lecturer on monastic life. He has published forty articles and many books, including his translation and commentary on Benedict's Rule. He is currently editor of *The American Benedictine Review*.

Francis Kline, OCSO, entered the Cistercian monastery of Gethsemani in 1972, having studied music at Julliard School in New York, majoring in organ. After theological studies at the Pontifical Athenaeum Sant'Anselmo in Rome, he returned to Gethsemani and was ordained priest in 1986. He was elected Abbot of Mepkin, Gethsemani's fourth foundation in 1990, and continues to serve as abbot of Mepkin Abbey, in Moncks Corner, South Carolina. He more recently published *Lovers of the Place: Monasticism Loose in the Church* (Liturgical Press, 1997).

Robert Morneau, D.D., auxiliary Bishop of Green Bay Diocese, has lectured extensively throughout the United States and is constantly in demand for giving retreats including monasteries of men and women as well as diocesan priests. He is the author of *Spiritual Direction* and more recently *The Gift* (for children); *Gift, Mystery, Calling,* and *A Retreat with Jessica Powers*. He is currently Vicar General of the Green Bay Diocese.

Kathleen Norris is an award-winning poet and author of *Dakota: A Spiritual Geography,* as well as a number of popular works, especially *Cloister Walk* (1996). A recipient of grants from the Guggenheim and Bush foundations, she has been in residence several times at the Institute of Ecumenical Studies at St. John's Abbey, and has been for many years an oblate at Assumption Abbey in North Dakota. She is currently completing a book on sloth!

Bernardo Olivera, ocso, a native of Argentina, was born in 1943. He entered the monastery of Azul following his studies in veterinary science, and was elected Abbot of Azul in 1984, and was elected Abbot General of the Cistercians in 1990. At the General Chapter in Assisi in 2005 he announced his intention to offer his resignation as Abbot General at the General Chapter of 2008. He has published a number of books in recent years including *The Search for God* (Cistercian Publications) and *How Far to Follow: The Martyrs of Atlas.* He has also contributed an Introduction to this volume.

Miriam Pollard, ocso, entered Mount Saint Mary's Abbey, Wrentham, Massachusetts, where she made profession in 1959. As author and poet she has published a number of books including *The Laughter of God: At Ease with Prayer* (1986), *Acceptance: Passage into Hope* (1987), *Listening to God* (1989), and more recently, *The Other Face of Love: Dialogues with the Prison Experience of Albert Speer* (1996) and *Neither Be Afraid and Other Poems* (2000). She was elected prioress at Santa Rita Abbey in Sonoita, Arizona, in 2000, where she continues to serve the community.

Bonnie Thurston, a native of West Virginia, currently lives near Wheeling, West Virginia, having resigned the William F. Orr Professorship in New Testament at Pittsburgh Theological Seminary in 2002. She earned the B.A. in English from Bethany College, and the M.A. and Ph.D. degrees from the University of Virginia. The subject of her dissertation was Thomas Merton. She has done post-doctoral work in New Testament at Harvard Divinity School, Eberhard Karls University in Tuebingen, Germany, and the Ecole Biblique in Jerusalem. Bonnie has written eleven theological books and over 100 articles and taught at the university level for 28 years. Her scholarly research interests in New Testament include the gospels of Mark and John and the Deutero-Pauline canon, and more generally, the history of Christian Spirituality and prayer. Her church affiliations include the Episcopal Church and the Christian Church (Disciples of Christ). She was ordained in 1984 and has served as co-pastor, pastor, or interim of five churches and twice in overseas ministries. She is a spiritual director and retreat speaker.

Her poetry frequently appears in religious periodicals, and she has authored two volumes of verse.

CISTERCIAN PUBLICATIONS
Texts and Studies in the Monastic Tradition

TEXTS IN ENGLISH TRANSLATION:
- Monastic insights from the desert, and from christian monks and nuns East and West
- Cistercian homilies and treatises from the formative twelfth and thirteenth centuries

STUDIES OF THE MONASTIC TRADITION:
- Its history, customs, architecture, liturgy, and influence, from desert beginnings through the Middle Ages and into the present day
- Reflections on prayer and the christian vocation by contemporary contemplatives
- Audio and video resources on monasticism as well as books published abroad and not readily available in North America

All books are available singly or by series standing order. Standing order customers automatically receive new titles as they appear at a 25% discount from the list price

SERIES:
- CISTERCIAN FATHERS
- MONASTIC WISDOM
- CISTERCIAN STUDIES
- CISTERCIAN LITURGY

EDITORIAL OFFICES
Cistercian Publications • WMU Station
1903 West Michigan Avenue • Kalamazoo, MI 49008-5415   USA
tel 269 387 8920   fax 269 387 8390
e-mail cistpub@wmich.edu

CUSTOMER SERVICE—NORTH AMERICA: USA AND CANADA
Cistercian Publications at Liturgical Press
Saint John's Abbey • Collegeville, MN 56321-7500 USA
tel 800 436 8431   fax 320 363 3299
e-mail sales@litpress.org

CUSTOMER SERVICE—EUROPE: UK, IRELAND, AND EUROPE
Cistercian Publications at Columba Book Service
55A Spruce Avenue • Stillorgan Industrial Park
Blackrock, Co. Dublin, Ireland
tel 353 1 294 2560   fax 353 1 294 2564
e-mail sales@columba.ie

To explore the range of titles offered by Cistercian Publications, please request our free complete catalogue from one of the customer service offices or visit our website at **www.cistercianpublications.org**